Valuing Architecture

Robin Hood Gardens, Poplar,
London, 1972. © Sandra
Lousada/Mary Evans Picture
Library/The Smithson Family.

Installation view of Raimund
Abraham, House Without
Walls, Architecture I, 1977.
Washington DC, Archives of
American Art, Smithsonian
Institution, Leo Castelli Gallery
records, c. 1880–2000.

Editors
Ashley Paine
Susan Holden
John Macarthur

With contributions by
Daniel M. Abramson
Tom Brigden
Alex Brown
Amy Clarke
Wouter Davidts
Bart Decroos
Susan Holden
Jordan Kauffman
Hamish Lonergan
John Macarthur
Joanna Merwood-Salisbury
Ashley Paine
Anton Pereira Rodriguez
Andrea Phillips
Lara Schrijver
Ari Seligmann
Kirsty Volz
Rosemary Willink

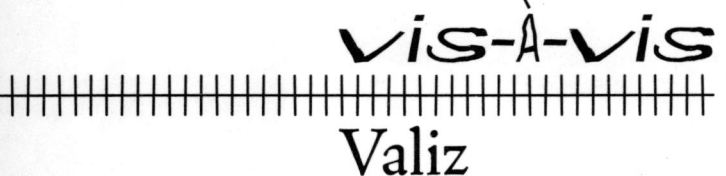

Valiz

Valuing Architecture

Heritage and the Economics of Culture

Studies in Art and Architecture

Contents

8   For What It's Worth
     The Value of Architecture as Heritage and Culture
     John Macarthur, Susan Holden and Ashley Paine

22   Values of Obsolescence
     Daniel M. Abramson

40   The Price is Wright
     Recovering Value in Frank Lloyd Wright's Architectural Fragments
     Ashley Paine

58   Model Values
     Architectural Models and the Conceptual Limits of Art Markets
     Jordan Kauffman

76   Shifting Values of Architectural Heritage at Open-Air Museums
     Amy Clarke

96 Value on Display
    Curating Robin Hood Gardens
    Susan Holden and Rosemary Willink

118 On the Architecture of the Late-Capitalist Museum
    The Museum of Modern Art and the
      Demolition of the American Folk Art
      Museum
    Joanna Merwood-Salisbury

138 Debasing The Collection
    AMO, Rem Koolhaas, and the Art and
      Architecture Heritage of the Stedelijk
      Museum Amsterdam
    Wouter Davidts and Anton Pereira Rodriguez

156 Valuing Architecture's Entanglements
    The Many Faces of KANAL-Centre
      Pompidou
    Bart Decroos and Lara Schrijver

174 The Protected Vista
    Mapping the Value of Views
    Tom Brigden

188 Antagonistic Coexistence of Values in the
      Machinations of a Metabolist Monument
    Ari Seligmann

208 Meme, Memory or Critic
    Revaluing Brutalism on Social Media
    Hamish Lonergan

226 Heritage and Housing in the Post-Political City
    Sydney's Sirius Building
    Kirsty Volz and Alex Brown

246 The Community Arts Center
    'Devaluing' Art and Architecture
       (The Case of the Albany Empire,
       London)
    Andrea Phillips

265 Index
281 Contributors

For What It's Worth
The Value of Architecture as Heritage and Culture

John Macarthur, Susan Holden and Ashley Paine

[1] Many chapters of this book were originally presented at the conference 'The Values of Architecture and the Economy of Culture', convened by John Macarthur, Susan Holden, Ashley Paine, and Elke Couchez, held in Brisbane, June 2019. The papers included here are those that addressed the themes of heritage, culture, and value. The conference was an outcome of the 'Is Architecture Art?: A history of categories, concepts and recent practices' research project of the Centre for Architecture, Theory, History and Criticism (ATCH) at the University of Queensland in partnership with the Department of Architecture & Urban Planning, Ghent University. The project is funded by The University of Queensland, Ghent University, and the Australian Research Council through a Discovery Grant (DP160101569) led by John Macarthur (UQ), with Susan Holden (UQ), Ashley Paine (UQ) and Wouter Davidts (UGent).

The conference organizers are grateful for the generous support of ATCH and the UQ School of Architecture. Macarena de la Vega de León from ATCH deserves a special mention for her expert assistance in organizing the conference. Thanks also go to Amelia Hine for her conference poster, and to guest session chairs: Cameron Bruhn, Angela Goddard, Sandra Kaji-O'Grady, Tom O'Regan, Andrea Phillips, and Roland Bleiker.

The value of architecture as a matter of cultural interest to society as a whole is a question rarely asked, perhaps because there are no certain answers, but also because of the many complex and interrelated interests at stake.[1] In any individual project the value of the architectural expertise applied is apparent, for better or worse, in a wide range of sometimes conflicting criteria. Designs can be readily weighed up and their successes decided by their owners and financiers, by the public, and by the architectural profession with its publications and awards. But where is it that we can think on the cultural value of architecture *per se*, as we do on cinema, or literature, or music? This is the question that we are stalking in this book, through the concept of heritage. Seeing buildings as repositories of cultural heritage is one of the few places where the cultural value of architecture is required to be explicit, and the more so because in heritage the values of architecture are weighed up with, or against, other reasons for the preservation of buildings, and other values of the built environment. While buildings are preserved largely for reasons of social memory, historical evidence, and as the concretization of community identity, some are preserved explicitly for their value as architecture. It is such cases that are examined in this book, alongside those where architecture's disciplinary worth is brought into conflict with numerous other values and value systems. Heritage, therefore, is not so much the topic of this book, as a lens through which to look at questions of how architecture is valued in a regularized manner, visible to the whole of society and subject to statutes. It will be no surprise that through this investigation we can offer no declarations of how we ought to think of built heritage. Instead, it is our aim to ask more questions about how the values of architecture interrelate, and about their stake within the wider economy of culture.

    Architects often assume that with the right combination of their skills—and a client with good taste, ambition, and sufficient financial means—buildings of inherent collective cultural value can be made that will be prized in the same way as a novel, painting, film, or musical composition. But this proposition of the inherent value of architectural works as culture has only cursory agreement from the public: overdetermined, as architectural value is, by wealth, social status, financial speculation, the agency of powerful clients, and the embeddedness of architecture and building in the monetary economy. While the visual and performing arts, literature and music, all rest on physical and economic infrastructure—and are all traded to some extent—we typically consider their cultural value in a separate but related set of accounts. Here, we offer some remarks on the question of architecture's cultural value, by mapping the ambiguous concept of heritage in relation to shifts in the government of culture that are at stake in the 'economy of culture.' Certainly, the concept of culture as a whole is shifting from a model of autonomous cultural value that we associate with an orchestra or a major art gallery, to models where the commercial and the cultural are mutually determining—as in popular music and architecture—as witnessed by the rise of the academic sub-discipline studying these creative or cultural 'industries.'[2] Nowhere is this more apparent than in 'heritage tourism,' which seeks a virtuous circuit between vouchsafing a nation's patrimony and filling hotel rooms and café tables. And so, we ask, what is at stake in the apparent clarity of the cultural heritage value of architecture, when the value of architecture *per se* is so occluded? Heritage buildings are a principal site at which to observe the clash, or the missed encounter, of concepts of intrinsic value and cultural value, as factors in the economy.

It is a commonplace in cities around the world that rising land values result in the demolition of old structures, that popular sentiment or active cultural policies cause some buildings to fall under statutory cultural heritage protection, and that this process limits their development potential, consequently devaluing (or making priceless) the land on which the buildings sit. In the cultural heritage protection of buildings, monetary costs borne by an individual (or commercial entity) are put up against an ineffable collective value in qualities of architecture and historical evidence that are embodied in the building. A heritage building is by definition one that is valued culturally whether for a connection to a place, person or event, and sometimes for its architecture. Although such a path to the cultural value of architecture is denied to buildings when they are new, somehow history and collective memory have the power to precipitate agreement about architectural value out of the slurry of interests in which buildings are made. While there might be strong agreement that built heritage has a public value as a tangible expression of times past—of our changing needs, ideas, technical and artistic abilities, and socio-economic conditions—we don't

---

[2] See for instance: Terry Flew, *The Creative Industries: Culture and Policy* (Los Angeles, CA: SAGE, 2012).

necessarily see present-day activities of architects as having a role in explicating the present, or easily reconcile these differing value propositions. What buildings are worth is clearly a complex space of negotiation.

Heritage as a category is also not without its own conceptual paradoxes that go beyond the interests it serves. As an idea, heritage is ambitious in its aim to be definitive, but ambiguous in its application, based as it is on concepts of memory and historical evidence: two non-commensurable forms of value. Its contradictions are further compounded by the different contexts in which the scope of the category is defined, and by the ways it is instrumentalized.[3] After all, the concept of heritage is wielded in the administrative context of protecting old buildings, just as often as it is deployed by the real estate market to sell homes with 'period features.' While the criteria for cultural heritage significance may be prescribed in powerful instruments of national legislation and international agreements, their criteria and their claims to universality are open to contest.[4] Because the built environment reflects entrenched socio-economic hierarchies, the values represented and omitted can be a process of exclusion. In Australia this is particularly the case of indigenous people and their ancient and continuing culture of land uses and place attachments. Beyond these problems of definition, application and practice, and whatever success heritage has in making a community or polity, what interests us here is the lens that heritage provides to consider architecture's value as a cultural form. Heritage is one of the few places where we might speak of the inherent value of architecture beyond individual buildings, and it is a concept that has traction both for the public and professional practice, even while its ambiguities mean that the value of particular works might be vehemently contested.[5] Understanding such contestations,

[3] There is a great range in different heritage lists which typically recognize 'historic,' 'natural' and 'indigenous' categories of heritage, and Nick Merriman's differentiation of 'impersonal' and 'personal' heritage in his study of heritage and museum visitation. See: Emma Waterton and Modesto Gayo, 'For All Australians? An Analysis of the Heritage Field,' *Continuum* 32, no. 3 (2018), 269–281; Nick Merriman, *Beyond the Glass Case: The Past, the Heritage and the Public in Britain* (Leicester: Leicester University Press, 1991).

[4] For example, in the critical engagements with preservation practices outlined by Jorge Otero-Pailos, Erik Langdalen and Thordis Arrhenius in *Experimental Preservation*. In this book, Thordis Arrhenius argues that 'preservation has become an experimental field for architecture … a way to practice architecture outside the dominant field of corporate or star architecture.' Thordis Arrhenius, 'Monumental and Non-Monumental Strategies,' in *Experimental Preservation*, ed. Jorge Otero-Pailos, Erik Langdalen, and Thordis Arrhenius (Zurich: Lars Muller, 2016), 41.

[5] For example, in the case of Brutalism, as discussed by Holden and Willink, Lonergan, and by Volz and Brown.

and their conceptual and practical ramifications when played out against the systems of value employed in the administration of culture, is the impetus for this book.

In an international context, the concept of cultural heritage has many permutations. The definition offered by UNESCO's 1972 Convention Concerning the Protection of the World Cultural and Natural Heritage (the World Heritage Convention) includes monuments and groups of buildings 'of outstanding universal value from the point of view of history, art or science'—a necessarily vague criterion for significance.[6] While the convention has been criticized for its Eurocentric focus on built works of permanence, and for the problematic notion of 'universal' values, its basic precepts continue to be echoed in heritage legislation around the globe.[7] For example, the Burra Charter that underlies the various legislative instruments in Australia defines cultural heritage significance in a similarly imprecise but inclusive way: 'Cultural significance means aesthetic, historic, scientific, social or spiritual value for past, present or future generations.'[8] Significance lies in the value of buildings or places as evidence of the importance of an individual, a community, institution, industry, and, in architecture, as an aesthetic expression of these values. Individual places and their significance to a particular group or cultural practice then contribute to a wider collective history. In other words, and like those of the World Heritage Convention, cultural heritage value is seen not to exist in the thing itself—in our case, buildings—but rather in indexical relations with an immaterial historical narrative. But it is not as if, having provided the evidence of social, technical, or spiritual history, that a building could be done away with. There is a strong logic to the arguments that buildings are historical documents preserved so that some future historian may return to the evidence to

---

[6] It also includes a third category of 'sites' that are 'of outstanding universal value from the historical, aesthetic, ethnological or anthropological point of view.' 'Convention Concerning the Protection of the World Cultural and Natural Heritage' (United Nations Educational, Scientific and Cultural Organisation [UNESCO], 16 November 1972).

[7] Laurajane Smith, *Uses of Heritage* (London: Routledge, 2006).

[8] Peter Marquis-Kyle and Meredith Walker, *The Illustrated Burra Charter: Making Good Decisions About the Care of Important Places* (Sydney, N.S.W.: Australia ICOMOS Inc. with the assistance of the Australian Heritage Commission, 1992).

correct or adjust that history. However, the social license, and the realpolitik of preservation, lies in a speculation that an experiential encounter with the heritage item will demonstrate that history. One can see for oneself the room in which a poet wrote, or experience the spaces created by a famous architect. The one criterion for significance that is not based on evidential or indexical relations, and instead supposes an affective relation to heritage, is that a place can be listed for its 'aesthetic significance.' This criterion is rarely called upon, and never in isolation: it would be very difficult, if not impossible, to evidence an affective relation to the past that we hold in common. And yet, this feeling for the past silently underlies all other criteria. What, after all, is the point in experiencing aspects of an already agreed history if this is not in some way affecting?

The idea of a value that is meaningful for past, present, and future generations is a close cousin of the idea of inherent cultural value: a qualitative concept that has historically underpinned the governance of culture, but which has lost ground in recent times as the focus has shifted to the value of culture in the economic sphere. Heritage supposes that we should appreciate things that our ancestors loved even if we do not. We preserve ghastly Victoriana for its historical evidentiary value, but also because we take a certain interest in the demonstration of difference and historical distance. It is an affective encounter with the past and its difference that are demanded in campaigns to list buildings threatened with demolition or defacement. This is an architectural relation with a building, whether the building was designed by an architect or not. In fact, one of the clearest lessons in the values of architecture is the present-day appreciation of vernacular and industrial buildings that were not thought to be of cultural value by their builders. The distance that we have from an early twentieth-century factory preserved to demonstrate socio-economic relations of the past, is also utterly in the present as a feeling, when we see in it an architecture that its designers were unconscious of. In this respect, heritage is a kind of training in liberal citizenship that occurs in two ways. First, it identifies the inevitably transitory nature of property possession in a liberal economy as a collective issue that goes beyond the present. Second, heritage assumes difference as a condition of commonality—and facilitates understanding that differences in present day taste are like historical differences, and that both are themselves cultural artefacts. In considering architectural heritage we might disagree about how, why, or whether a building ought to be valued, but the idea that there is architectural value to be argued about, is irreducible.

The logic by which heritage makes architectural value visible is implicit in heritage legislation and management, in statements of significance and conservation management plans. However, it rarely works cleanly. Usually the debates about heritage value are ones of conflicting interests between different parties who have something to gain or lose, but they exemplify the conceptual conflict between intrinsic and economic value that is increasingly at stake in cultural administration. Heritage, and built heritage in particular, opens the issues at stake in reconciling the monetary and non-monetary values of cultural artefacts, to the wider issue of whether culture can and should be valued as a distinct sphere. There has always been a private market for cultural works. While TV and cinema, music and music recording are essentially commercial, the elite and less popular sector of classical music and the performing arts is supported by private subscription as well as by subsidy. Likewise, state art galleries, despite their public mission, are symbiotic with the art market as their acquisitions and exhibitions greatly affect the primary and secondary market. This secondary market for culture is immediate and speculates on future value. As such, it has often been at odds with the transcendental values conferred by heritage classification, as if they face differing temporal directions and, thus, reinforce a conceptual distinction between markets and public institutions. This is a distinction that is the territory of the politics of culture, of the distribution of public subsidies to some cultural forms and not others, and arguments as to the importance of differing cultural forms to forming the body politic. We rarely think of architecture in this way because of its tight connection to the property market. Yet, there is a trade in architectural drawings, models, fragments, and even pavilions that follows a similar logic to that of the market for 'high' art objects.[9] Perhaps because it is so marginal compared to the wider art market, this commercial market for architecture as cultural artefacts makes a particularly acute contrast with the concept of architecture as culture through the lens of heritage. This matrix of private and public, commercial and intrinsic values still drives what culture is, but increasingly the relationship has become the object of governmental policies. While not interlocutors with the market, governments increasingly want to set the rules for the exchange of values: managing an encompassing 'cultural economy' where, for example, a publicly funded art exhibition, its effects on commercial galleries representing artists, the hotel rooms filled by visitors, and the repute of art schools are seen together and accounted for.

Such tensions in the broader governance of culture make the conversation of architecture and heritage more difficult. Culture has always been thought by government to be a way to reproduce and, for progressive administrations, to reform the norms of national and community identity and

[9] Aspects of these markets are explored in this book by Paine and Kauffman.

participation to assist in making a wider civil society.[10] Historically, cultural policy was also formulated to distribute resources for broader public benefit, and funding expended to empower this tool of cultural citizenship. But, in the late twentieth century, economists and academics in cultural studies began to argue that cultural activities ought to be put alongside the economy as a whole, allowing their costs and benefits to be measured not only as a way to inform better decision-making on spending, but also as a way to argue for their value as goods and services in the cultural and creative economy—growing sectors in the shift towards the so-called knowledge-based economy. Theorization of the relationship between culture and the economy, such as that by David Throsby, seeks to create a framework in which 'the twin concepts of economic and cultural value can be made operational.'[11] For example, the cost-benefit analysis of a heritage project can be discussed alongside the economic value of cultural goods and services, and the flow-on effects of the creative industries in urban regeneration, all to inform a broader cultural policy agenda. While there is acknowledgement that determining cultural value is 'by no means clear cut,'[12] the endgame is for some space of equivalence in which monetary returns, social benefits and 'intrinsic' cultural values can be considered together, whether by using proxy dollar values for unmonetized benefits, or through a 'dashboard' approach of putting the differing values alongside one another to be reconciled by expert cultural administrators. Such theorization, and the idea that intrinsic cultural value can be brought into a direct relation with the value of cultural activity in the economy, has had a significant and far-reaching impact on the way culture is treated as a realm to be governed. Cultural policy is now enacted in an expanded range of administrative portfolios from the arts to urban and economic development, as well

[10] Aspects of participation in heritage are explored in this book by Clarke.

[11] David Throsby, *The Economics of Cultural Policy* (Cambridge: Cambridge University Press, 2010), 18.

[12] Throsby, *The Economics of Cultural Policy*, 18.

as health and well-being, and engages distributive and regulatory policy instruments. Recently, and with little discussion, architecture has become important in culture, not because of change in opinion, any improved conceptualization, or better buildings, but because, in monetary terms as a part of the economy, it is very large.

The quantification of cultural value is part of a global wave of metrification of aspects of life previously understood qualitatively. It is characterized by aims to demonstrate value to funders and, in some cases, to argue against disproportionate funding to the old high arts that are seen as socially elitist and in favor of the value of popular inclusive forms of culture.[13] The wages of actors, the box-office returns of cinema, the ticket sales for a block-buster exhibition (and the costs of its insurance), the employment created by popular music performances and recording—all these and more can be accounted for in a table with public funding and social benefits to allow value-for-money calculations to be made. And so, we now know that in 2013 the cultural and creative economy of the world generated revenues of US$2,250 billion (larger than the whole economy of India), and employed some 29 million people.[14] In the context of the cultural economy, architecture's value is clear; it has global revenues of US$222 billion and employs 1.7 million people. As a sector of the global economy it exceeds telecommunications. Within cultural economy revenues it is roughly half the size of the visual arts and nearly twice the size of the performing arts. As a consequence, architecture is known to be of monetary value in the cultural economy as well as in the property and construction economy, but quite why it has a 'cultural' value that represents money is obscure, lost between the arcane and exclusive language of the profession on the one hand, and the transcendent values that buildings have if they are considered heritage.

[13] See, for instance John Hartley and Stuart Cunningham, 'Creative Industries: From Blue Poles to Fat Pipes,' in *National Humanities and Social Sciences Summit—2001: Position Papers*, ed. Malcolm Gillies, Mark Carroll and John Dash (Canberra: Centre for Continuing Education, University of Autralia, 2002); Flew, *The Creative Industries*. For critiques of this position see for instance: Justin O'Connor, 'Surrender to the Void: Life after Creative Industries,' *Cultural Studies Review* 18, no. 3 (2012), 388–410; Toby Miller, 'From Creative to Cultural Industries', *Cultural Studies* 23, no. 1 (2009), 88–99; David Hesmondhalgh, *The Cultural Industries*, 2nd ed. (London: Sage, 2007).

[14] EYGM (Ernest & Young Global Management), 'Cultural Times: The First Global Map of Cultural and Creative Industries,' ([Paris:] CISAC International Confederation of Authors and Composers Societies, 2015), 15.

We cannot, at present, put a monetary figure on the value of the cultural heritage of the built environment. It is not, for instance, a statistical domain for collecting data on the cultural economy by UNESCO, which treats heritage as a condition of all cultural forms—a consequence or repercussion of cultural activities, rather than one of its products.[15] The temporal direction implicit in the concept of heritage operates against understanding how it might enable cultural productivity except in tourism where the categories of cultural tourism and heritage tourism blur. Certainly, there is a growing need to better understand the interplay between intrinsic and economic value regimes now operating in cultural administration as it relates to heritage. Architecture has an important role to play in raising these questions. Not only do buildings make up a huge proportion of the tangible aspects of heritage, the issues that we raise here—and the cases analyzed in the chapters that follow—demonstrate the complexity that limits any schematization of heritage in a cultural economy, not to mention what is lost and gained in such a transactional definition of culture's value.

These developments make a double attack on cultural hierarchies. The effective trading floor of cultural and economic values raises the value of architecture relative to the high elite arts, while the ideology of inclusivity in heritage also flattens the hierarchy. At the same time as these distinctions have become blurred through metrification, architecture's appeal to a cultural audience has grown. Architecture increasingly appears in museums, galleries and exhibition spaces, while spectacular buildings are employed to drive cultural tourism and city branding. At the same time, museum de-growth and the demand for sustainable collecting are recalibrating the values of museum architecture.[16] Certainly, the strong line between commercial and creative

[15] The Australian Bureau of Statistics measures work and engagement in 'Environmental Heritage' as a part of Arts and Culture, but defines this as zoos and botanical gardens and nature reserves, excluding the built environment. ABS, 4172.0 – Arts and Culture in Australia: A Statistical Overview, 2014.

[16] Beatrix Ruf and John Slyce, eds., *Size Matters! (De)Growth of the 21st Century Art Museum*, 2017 Verbier Art Summit (London: Koenig Books, 2017).

activity that once kept architecture in the real estate pages of newspapers has become much less distinct. In this context, it might be argued that architecture has never been more valued, nor valued in such a variety of ways. Yet, there often remains a friction between cultural and economic systems of value, and how the discipline values itself.

This book is not concerned with arguments for or against the cultural value of architecture or heritage, or architecture's place in heritage regulation. Rather, it engages with the sites and occasions where such values are bestowed, exchanged, come into conflict, and are sometimes lost; and how the agency of invested parties is revealed or contested. The essays tackle concrete cases, both historical and contemporary, each attempting to make some account of the vicissitudes of value in architecture, and its stakes in the economics of culture. A number of the chapters focus on the role architecture's disciplinary values play in the built environment when the regulatory bodies of heritage attempt to manage public sentiment and economic value within systems of property rights. Others interrogate: the commercial markets for architectural fragments, drawings, and models; the authority of museums and their collections in relation to their role in the experience economy and city branding; shifting architectural fashions in social media; and the intersection of design governance and architectural heritage. All seek to understand architecture's place as a cultural form in a broader conversation about value and its cultural administration, as well as the conceptual domain of value itself. Ultimately, what emerges most cogently across this wide-ranging study of architectural value is clear. When an extant building is preserved on account of its architectural qualities—by its being listed for heritage protection or its collection by a museum— it provides a powerful demonstration of the varying, obtuse, and sometimes conflicting ways in which we value architecture. While the same might be argued in relation to the destruction of buildings, preservation is powerful because it carries the force of law, and because it implies that we ought to be able to judge architectural value in a more general sense. Still, there can be no absolute definition or framework for architectural value. Just as the law relies on both statutes and a body of precedents, the chapters of this book present cases that have the potential to create precedents for how we might think of the values of architecture in the differing regimes where such judgments are required. Arguably there is more pressing demand for such precedents today, as a means to contend with the impact of metrics and their market-driven logic in the definition of culture. And, for what it's worth, we argue that this is how the question of architectural values ought to be thought through, rather than as something totalized in a score or measured in its convergence with a norm or an ideal, like heritage.

View of Shanghai, from roof of Shanghai Municipal Council Slaughterhouse, 1933, now Old Millfun. Photo: author, 2012.

Values of Obsolescence
Daniel M. Abramson

Where does the idea come from that buildings and cities can rapidly lose their value and utility and so become expendable? How have architects and others responded to the conditions and presumptions of obsolescence? Answering these questions confronts an open issue about capitalism. Eminent historian Eric Hobsbawm asks: 'How is it, then, that humans and societies structured to resist dynamic development come to terms with a mode of production [i.e., capitalism] whose essence is endless and unpredictable dynamic development?'[1] In architecture's confrontation with obsolescence are answers to Hobsbawm's question. How might people 'come to terms' with the contradiction and competition of values between, on the one hand, capitalism's endless change, and, on the other, a deep human need for constancy?[2]

This essay constructs an historical account of the values of obsolescence. First, it details how obsolescence thinking values, or measures, architecture in functional, financial, and social terms. Second, it considers the values, or criteria, of obsolescence thinking: how it perceives the world in terms of measurable performance, competition, supersession, and

[1] Eric Hobsbawm, 'Interview: World Distemper,' *New Left Review* II/61 (January-February 2010), 150.

[2] This essay is adapted from my book *Obsolescence: An Architectural History* (Chicago and London: University of Chicago Press, 2016).

expendability. Third, it will suggest the value, or worth, of obsolescence thinking itself and its history in architecture. What might be positive in conceiving the built environment as expendable? What might be learned from an architectural history of obsolescence?

The term 'obsolescence' was first applied in English to architecture about a century ago to help explain the unsettling phenomenon of American downtown skyscrapers brought low by a process of economic devaluation, or what was first called 'financial decay.'[3] Such was the fate of the landmark Gillender Building at the corner of Wall and Nassau Streets in New York. At its birth in 1897 it had been the world's loftiest office tower. But only thirteen years later it was being torn down for a taller, more up-to-date structure. Still physically sound, the Gillender Building was considered uneconomic, valueless, and expendable, worthy only of destruction and replacement: it was, in a word, obsolete. The measurement of the financial value of architecture evolved historically out of nineteenth-century accounting principles of depreciation, which sought to measure changes in worth over time and circumstance. Experts like the New York engineer Reginald Bolton sought causes for obsolescence's sudden losses of economic value in factors of urban change, technology, and fashion. Something new and better outcompeted the old and made it disposable. Bolton tabulated obsolescence rates by building type.[4] Banks, Bolton theorized, would hold their value as economic assets longer than hotels due to different rates of change in use and taste.[5]

Further impetus for studying architectural obsolescence was given in the mid-nineteen-tens by the new US federal income tax, which allowed deductions from income for the cost of obsolescence, but without specifying exact rates of deduction. The Chicago-based National Association of

3 Reginald Pelham Bolton, *Building for Profit: Principles Governing the Economic Improvement of Real Estate* (New York: De Vinne, 1911), 73.

4 Reginald Pelham Bolton, 'Economic Existence of Buildings,' 1911. Source: Bolton, *Building for Profit*.

5 Bolton, *Building for Profit*, 23.

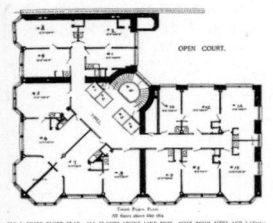

6 Holabird & Roche, Tacoma Building, Chicago, third floor plan, constructed 1889, demolished 1929. Courtesy Building Owners and Managers Association International. All rights reserved.

7 Paul E. Holcombe, 'Depreciation and Obsolescence in the Tacoma Building,' *Bulletin of the National Association of Building Owners and Managers* 137 (June 1929), 13–32; John Roberts, 'Obsolescence in the Marshall Field Wholesale Building,' *Bulletin of the National Association of Building Owners and Managers* 150 (September 1930), 41–45.

8 'Ask for More Equitable Obsolescence Allowance,' *Bulletin of the National Association of Building Owners and Managers* 153 (December 1930), 108.

9 U.S. Department of Treasury, Bureau of Internal Revenue, *Bulletin 'F' (Revised January 1931) Income Tax: Depreciation and Obsolescence: Revenue Act of 1928* (Washington, DC: U.S. Government Printing Office, 1931).

10 See, for example: Harrison Spaulding, *The Income Tax in Great Britain and the United States* (London: P. S. King, 1927).

11 Mary Ethel Jameson, 'Obsolescence in Buildings: A Selected List of References,' in *Selected Readings in Real Estate Appraisal*, ed. A. N. Lockwood et al. (Chicago: American Institute of Real Estate Appraisers, 1953 [1935]).

Building Owners and Managers then set about investigating obsolescence. So-called autopsies of demolished Chicago landmarks identified as causes of obsolescence, for example, the pioneering skyscraper Tacoma Building's inefficient, fixed interior layout of load-bearing walls.[6] The famous Marshall Field Wholesale Store was unadaptable to retail re-use: its heavy masonry base couldn't be retrofitted with large display windows.[7] Various statistics assembled from Chicago's business district supported the case for office buildings' thirty-year lifespans for tax valuation purposes, that is, a 3.3 percent deduction taken each year.[8] The building owners and managers just about got their wish when federal tax authorities set office building lifespans at forty years.[9]

The political achievement here had been to turn the extreme cases of Chicago's obsolescence rates into low building lifespan numbers for the benefit of owners nationwide. This was in effect a public tax subsidy for private capitalist reinvestment unique to the world's tax codes. In Britain, by contrast, without tax deductions for building obsolescence no similar discourse on architectural obsolescence ensued at this time.[10] This demonstrates the key role of government and public policy in how practices and perceptions of architectural value vary historically across national contexts. The cultural achievement of this discourse on obsolescence was to help establish in American public consciousness the myth of shortened building lifespans as a feature of modern life.[11] Mythic of course because buildings don't magically disappear at forty years of age. Their fates are not pre-determined. Rather, the devaluations of architecture under obsolescence, as experts knew, were based on the uncertainties of changing politics and technology, emotion, and fashion.

What the paradigm of architectural obsolescence, invented by real estate capitalists, did do was to make sense of unsettlingly changeful times. Almost by definition, obsolescence is fundamental to capitalism. In the progression of money turned into commodities for sale, turned into more money to make more commodities—the endless cycle of M-C-M—the old must be devalued, must give way to the new, or the process of accumulation seizes up. Obsolescence's worth as a concept, its ideological value, was that it helped people to 'come to terms,' to use Hobsbawm's phrase, with the chaotic process of redevelopment. It made capitalism's constant, unsettling churning seem logical, profitable, even progressive. Rapid demolition, reinvestment, and rebuilding now had a name—obsolescence—an architectural analog, in effect, to the idea of capitalism as Creative Destruction, new constantly superseding old.[12]

In the following decades of the thirties through fifties the idea of obsolescence was extended by urban planners to the scale of the city. In the United States, urban obsolescence indicated a district's sub-standard health, physical, and economic performance, quantifiable by evaluation forms, as in the case of Boston's working-class West End.[13] Explicitly denoted obsolete, the neighborhood was slated for demolition and reinvestment by real estate capitalists. Here the values of obsolescence, its principles of quantification and expendability, were applied not just to financial and physical factors, but implicitly to social ones, too. Crowded street life and multi-generational housing were devalued and deemed obsolete in comparison to standards of the single-family suburban ideal.[14]

In Europe, the term obsolescence focused more on social than economic factors, appropriate where the state rather than capitalism led redevelopment. For example, pre-World War II East Berlin tenements were deemed obsolete culturally in a developing socialist nation.[15] By the late fifties then the notion of architectural obsolescence in all its varieties—

12 Joseph Schumpeter, *Capitalism, Socialism, and Democracy*, 3rd ed. (New York: Harper & Brothers, 1950), 83–84.

13 Daniel M. Abramson, 'Boston's West End: Urban Obsolescence in Mid-Twentieth-Century America,' in *Governing by Design: Architecture, Economy, and Politics in the Twentieth Century*, ed. Aggregate Architectural History Collaborative (University of Pittsburgh Press, 2012).

14 Boston City Planning Board, 'An Obsolete Neighborhood,' 1951. Source: *General Plan for Boston: Preliminary Report, 1950.*

15 Florian Urban, *Neo-historical East Berlin: Architecture and Urban Design in the German Democratic Republic 1970-1990* (Farnham: Ashgate, 2009).

capitalist to socialist, office buildings to cities—had become a dominant paradigm worldwide for conceptualizing and managing change in the built environment: shortened building lifespans and obsolescent cities as myths of modernity. 'The annual model, the disposable container, the throwaway city have become the norms,' observed the American preservationist James Marston Fitch, who was fighting fiercely against demolitions at this time.[16]

And, obsolescence differed from past paradigms of urban change. Unlike, for example, the nineteenth-century explicitly political redevelopment of Paris under Baron Haussmann, twentieth-century urban obsolescence appeared impersonal, a matter of inevitable economic law. Moreover, obsolescence's fast, unceasing ruptures departed from architecture's traditional ideal of slow, organic development and decay, epitomized by the ruinscape, in which values and forms persisted over centuries. Obsolescence was thus a new framework for comprehending change in the built environment with which architects still had to come to terms.

How did architects respond? At first, by denial. Early in the twentieth century, traditionalists and avant-gardists alike held fast to permanence and finish as paramount values in architecture. Classicists like Edwin Lutyens in his New Delhi capitol complex designed monumental, masonry, symmetrical buildings of fixed forms and principles in permanent materials. Le Corbusier and Walter Gropius also both believed in traditional, final, formal solutions, not the endless mutability of obsolescence. The former plumped for 'a sure and permanent home.'[17] The latter decried 'transient novelties.'[18] Notwithstanding the 1914 Futurist manifesto's call in writing for 'expendability and transience,' the architect Antonio Sant'Elia's designs themselves were massive and immutable.[19]

[16] James Marston Fitch, *Historic Preservation: Curatorial Management of the Built World* (New York: McGraw Hill, 1982).

[17] Le Corbusier, *Towards a New Architecture*, trans. Frederick Etchells (New York: Dover, 1986 [1931]), 48.

[18] Walter Gropius, *The New Architecture and the Bauhaus*, trans. P. M. Shand (Cambridge, MA: MIT Press, 1965 [1936]), 54.

[19] 'Manifesto of Futurist Architecture,' trans. Reyner Banham, *Journal of the Royal Institute of British Architects* 64 (February 1957), 139.

A few outsiders did recognize opportunities in obsolescence. Buckminster Fuller's craned components for his 1928 '4D Tower' project were inspired by automobile annual model changes. In Europe, the Czech shoe manufacturer Tomáš Bat'a railed against 'obsolete houses that will strangle and suffocate the next generation.'[20] He projected mere twenty-year life spans for the factories and dwellings of his famed company town of Zlín, inaugurated in the nineteen-tens.

Designers only began to deal seriously with obsolescence in the postwar period. British critic Reyner Banham began, in the fifties, promoting 'an aesthetics of expendability' for the age's 'throwaway economy,' embracing this basic value, or principle, of obsolescence.[21] University of London researchers produced in-depth studies of hospital obsolescence so the British government could economically design new structures, fearful they would otherwise obsolesce wastefully. Their studies discovered, for example, that hospital staff and lab spaces obsolesced faster than the out-patient areas. By the sixties most every architect believed obsolescence ruled the day. 'Ours is an age of change, of dynamism, of unrest, of revolution,' proclaimed American architectural educators William Zuk and Roger H. Clark, echoing the era's dominant refrain.[22] 'Buildings which formerly took fifty years to fail, now fail in five,' declared a firm of young avant-garde architects Georges Candilis, Alexis Josic, and Shadrach Woods in 1965.[23] These are typical comments, none especially insightful. It would be in design, not words that architects engaged most deeply with obsolescence.

The prime design solution to obsolescence was the open-plan factory shed—internal adaptability versus unforeseen change in fixed structural shells—a model adapted for schools and offices, and also for labs and hospitals when the loft floors are stacked vertically with what were called

[20] Daniel M. Abramson, 'Obsolescence and the Fate of Zlín,' in *A Utopia of Modernity: Zlín*, ed. Katrin Klingan (Berlin: JOVIS, 2009), 165–167.

[21] Reyner Banham, 'Vehicles of Desire,' *Art*, September 1, 1955, 3.

[22] William Zuk and Roger H. Clark, *Kinetic Architecture* (New York: Van Nostrand Reinhold, 1970), 11.

[23] Georges Candilis, Alexis Josic, and Shadrach Woods, 'Recent Thoughts on Town Planning and Urban Design,' *Architects' Year Book* 11 (1965), 183.

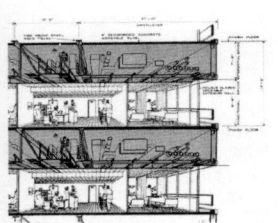

24 Charles Luckman, Veterans Administration Hospital, San Diego, 1968. Courtesy Luckman Salas O'Brien.

25 Ludwig Mies van der Rohe, New National Gallery, Berlin, 1962–1968. © Chicago Historical Society/VIEW.

26 Richard Llewelyn-Davies and John Weeks, Northwick Park Hospital, Harrow, 1961–1976. Courtesy Llewelyn-Davies.

27 John Weeks, 'Indeterminate Architecture,' *Transactions of the Bartlett Society* 2 (1963–1964), 83–106.

interstitial service levels.[24] All discussions of flexibility in architecture at this time were in effect worries about obsolescence, anxieties that functional and economic values would drastically decrease unless arrested by design.

A cultural variant of interstitialism, Paris' Pompidou Center by Renzo Piano and Richard Rogers (1970–1977) externalizes and verticalizes its service zone for obstruction-free exhibition lofts. Berlin's New National Gallery by Ludwig Mies van der Rohe (1962–1968) submerges everyday functions beneath its podium, leaving aboveground the apotheosis of the factory-shed solution to obsolescence.[25] Here change is absorbed within a fixed, monumental frame. The open-plan shed solution represented one way to come to terms architecturally with ceaseless change, to admit its freedoms internally, but contained within a fixed permanent shell.

Other architects, however, rejected the factory-shed solution to obsolescence as too fixed and monumental and thus unrepresentative of modern dynamism. Instead they promoted more fluid, open-ended design. Northwick Park Hospital by Richard Llewelyn-Davies and John Weeks (1961–1976), the largest British medical complex of its day, reflected research on hospital growth rates to get long-term value-for-money.[26] The structure featured a loose-jointed site plan of demolishable blocks and extendable ends, linked by a longer-lasting internal circulation spine.[27] Thus, permanence and impermanence exist together in an age of obsolescence, and economic and functional values hopefully are sustained long-term by design.

Permanence and impermanence harmonized was the theme, too, of the megastructure, a type associated especially with Japanese architects. Long-life, infrastructural vertical cores and frames support shorter-term, plug-in horizontal components of briefer lifecycles, replaceable as they obsolesced. One of the so-called Metabolist group, Kisho Kurokawa, designer of the Nakagin Capsule Tower (Tokyo, 1970–1972) discussed in a later chapter of this book, and the Takara Beautilion (Osaka, 1970), focused particularly upon imaging the megastructure's joints, its key detail where the two temporalities, fast and slow, conjoin.[28]

28 Kisho Kurokawa, Takara Beautilion, Osaka, 1970. Courtesy Kisho Kurokawa Architect & Associates. Photo: © Tomio Ohashi.

The inevitability but also the dark side of obsolescence was sensed in a project by Cedric Price, who was so enamored of obsolescence's value, or principle, of expendability that he officially joined the National Institute of Demolition Contractors in England. Price imagined an academic network set amidst post-industrial ruins in his unbuilt Potteries Thinkbelt projects, envisioned simultaneously under construction and being demolished, an image of continuous expendability, replacement, and obsolescence. Yet the most substantial objects in the Hanley housing site photomontage of Price's Potteries Thinkbelt are not the futuristic capsules or housing modules in the midground, but rather the stubborn remainders of the past: the background looming slag heaps, a derelict shed in the foreground.[29] Price seemed to understand that in a world governed by obsolescence, the undead waste of the past may come to haunt the promise of the future.

29 Cedric Price, Project for Potteries Thinkbelt, photomontage of Hanley housing site 7, Staffordshire, between 1963 and 1966. Courtesy Centre Canadien d'Architecture/ Canadian Centre for Architecture, Montréal, Cedric Price fonds.

30 Marc Fried and Peggy Gleicher, 'Some Sources of Residential Satisfaction in an Urban Slum,' *Journal of the American Institute of Planners* 27, no. 4 (November 1961), 305–315.

In the sixties, others besides Price were starting to question obsolescence's logic, values, and promise, its mode of comprehending and managing change based on principles of measurable performance, competition, inevitable supersession, and expendability. Social scientists disclosed people's traumas of urban obsolescence, in relation specifically to the redevelopment of Boston's West End.[30] The appraisal forms that measured urban obsolescence could not value, find a worth, quantify, or measure, what made these neighborhoods good places to live: their street life, sociability, and emotional

31 Jane Jacobs, *The Death and Life of Great American Cities* (New York: Vintage, 1992 [1961]), 187, 189.

32 Vance Packard, *The Waste Makers* (New York: David McKay, 1960), 4.

33 Bernard Rudofsky, *Architecture Without Architects: A Short Introduction to Non-Pedigreed Architecture* (Garden City: Doubleday, 1964), caption to fig. 1.

34 Bernd and Hilla Becher, Water towers, 1967–1980. © Bernd and Hilla Becher; © The Metropolitan Museum of Art/Art Resource, NY.

resonances. Likewise, the urban writer Jane Jacobs famously argued for the value, or worth, of obsolete structures. 'Cities need old buildings ... Time makes certain structures obsolete for some enterprises, and they become available for others.'[31] Culturally, obsolescence came to stand for inauthenticity and waste, not progress. The concept itself was being devalued. The journalist Vance Packard satirized the 'Cornucopia City' of the future where 'all buildings will be made of special papier-mâché ... torn down and rebuilt every spring and fall at housecleaning time.'[32] Volkswagen marketed its Beetle as immune to the superficial styling and planned obsolescence of American car makers. The values of obsolescence—that the new would always supersede the old—were being turned back upon themselves.

In architecture, too, protest arose against obsolescence's depredations. Vernacularism celebrated everyday buildings. A 1964 MoMA exhibition proclaimed that vernacular architecture 'does not go through fashion cycles' of obsolescence.[33] Artists such as Hilla and Bernd Becher of Germany revalued in their photography the obsolete remnants of industrial civilization in Europe, finding aesthetic worth in their frozen, abstract forms.[34]

Likewise, historic preservation advanced intensively in the sixties, becoming more populist and incorporating recent and vernacular structures. In numerous cities, citizens protested the demolition of civic monuments such as New York's Pennsylvania Station and London's Euston Station. Against obsolescence, preservationism revalues objects with historical and emotional meaning, reversing the rationalistic, presentist, and economistic logic of obsolescence, which conceived the passage of time as purely corrosive.

How did architects respond to these reversals of obsolescence, these resistances to its values, or principles, of measurable, competitive performance, supersession and expendability? First, they sought new images of permanence against obsolescence's transience. Inflexible, archaic concrete monoliths represent, as one commentator wrote about Paul Rudolph's designs, the 'refutation of the artificial-obsolescence theory held by planners of disposable cities'.[35] Concrete brutalism became a worldwide vernacular in the sixties and seventies versus obsolescence.[36]

In another vein, architectural Postmodernism revalued, or found new worth in, historical imagery. Italian architect Aldo Rossi sought to recreate what he called the 'primary elements' of the past: strong iconic symbols indifferent to function, already like empty ruins and therefore immune to future obsolescence.[37, 38]

Adaptive reuse also became a dominant strategy to revalue ostensibly obsolete buildings, both culturally and financially. Stripped volumes housed new fittings. Emblematic brick walls embodied soft change versus the hard traumas of obsolescence. At the urban scale, adaptive reuse largely means gentrification—the elevation of an area's social and economic markers—and a variation on urban renewal. Gentrification and adaptive reuse reverse obsolescence's logic of demolition, but not its social and political effects. The buildings may still be intact, but the prior, marginalized inhabitants are no less gone.

And, of course, environmental architecture has come to the fore, conserving existing resources, first through salvage and now with highly sophisticated technology, such as the German Federal Environment Agency in Dessau (Sauerbruch Hutton, 1997–2005), built on reclaimed land with renewable materials, featuring a high-tech system of energy efficiency under glass.[39] Indeed, what we call today sustainability might be said to encompass *all* these counter-tactics to obsolescence

35 Sibyl Moholy-Nagy, 'Introduction,' in Paul Rudolph, *The Architecture of Paul Rudolph* (New York: Praeger, 1970), 18.

36 Paul Rudolph, Temple Street Garage, New Haven, 1959–1963. Photo: author.

37 Aldo Rossi, *The Architecture of the City* (Cambridge, MA: MIT Press, 1982 [1966]).

38 Aldo Rossi, San Cataldo Cemetery, Modena, begun 1971. Courtesy Andrew Filarski.

39 Sauerbruch Hutton, Federal Environment Agency, Dessau, 1997–2005. Courtesy Sauerbruch Hutton. Photo: © Busse.

that arose in the sixties, from adaptive reuse to Postmodernism to preservationism to ecological design, which prioritized the conservation rather than expendability of resources, both natural and human-made.

The richness of nineteen-sixties architectural culture reflected the passions of a contest over obsolescence still hanging in the balance, the two sides equally creative and fervid. On the one, architectures of obsolescence accepted the values of obsolescence, the inevitability, and even the excitement of persistent change and expendability. On the other side are the counter-tactics, which revalue, or find new worth in, what had been considered obsolete, or terminally devalued and expendable, to reinstate permanence of meaning and material. By the early seventies the battle was largely over. Designing for obsolescence lost its hold over the cultural imaginary. Top-down, technocratic decision-making alienated popular feeling. Financial constraint in the wake of oil crises dried up resources for endless replacement. Urban unrest eroded public patronage for cities' renewal. Awareness of earth's fragility underscored obsolescence's wastefulness. The United Nations Educational, Scientific and Cultural Organization's World Heritage Convention, adopted in 1972, continues its global march. And preservation claimed important tax policy victories, as in 1976 when the US code began subsidizing historic rehabilitation over demolition.[40] A change in the tax valuation regime would promote developments in adaptive reuse design and perhaps, too, a renewed appreciation for the old as part of historicist Postmodernism. Today it would seem we live in the world the nineteen-seventies left us, not exuberant expendability but careful conservation—an age of sustainability.

Seeing obsolescence and sustainability in sequence points to obsolescence's part in the genealogy, the pre-history

[40] Tax Reform Act of 1976 (Public Law 94-455), Sec. 2124.

of sustainability. But we should not see obsolescence and sustainability as completely separate. The relation between the two is as much filial as agonistic. Adaptive reuse, for example, is a variation on the megastructure. In both, new components inserted into long-life frames accommodate change. Obsolescence and preservation are also mutually intertwined. Both define the past as broken off from the present, and need each other to survive. As the historian David Lowenthal writes, 'To expunge the obsolete and restore it as heritage are, like disease and its treatment, conjoint and even symbiotic.'[41] Obsolescence and ecological architecture mirror each other, too, in their dependence upon measurable performance. Today's tables of building energy use echo the data-mania of earlier obsolescence studies. In both approaches, architectural value, or worth, is reduced to experts' numbers.

Obsolescence thus endures, even if not as a dominant worldview. In design, obsolescence no longer drives innovation as it once did, when architects experimented with factory-sheds and indeterminacy, megastructures and plug-ins. Only occasionally today does contemporary architecture grant creative significance to obsolescence. Rem Koolhaas is an exception. Trained in late nineteen-sixties London, Koolhaas retains that moment's romance with obsolescence. His unrealized plan for Paris' La Défense district, for example, decreed 'that every building in this entire zone that is less than twenty-five years [old] has to be destroyed.'[42] Yet even Koolhaas has come to see the value of preservation and renovation. He characterized his adaptive reuse of old distillery structures for the Prada Foundation's new cultural complex in Milan as an 'antidote' to the 'current course of architecture forcing people to be extravagant even if they don't want or need that.'[43] Revaluing the obsolete enables Koolhaas to question the dominant value of novelty.

[41] David Lowenthal, 'The Heritage Crusade and Its Contradictions,' in *Giving Preservation a History: Histories of Historic Preservation*, ed. Max Page and Randall Mason (New York: Routledge, 2004), 33.

[42] Rem Koolhaas, 'Urban Operations,' *D: Columbia Documents of Architecture and Theory* 3 (1993), 53.

[43] Catherine Shaw, 'Rem Koolhaas on Prada, Preservation, Art and Architecture,' ArchDaily, July 31, 2015. www.archdaily.com/771156/rem-koolhaas-on-prada-preservation-art-and-architecture/, ISSN 0719-8884 (accessed June 11, 2020).

44 Jeff Byles, *Rubble: Unearthing the History of Demolition* (New York: Harmony, 2005), Chapter 8.

45 Camilo José Vergara, *American Ruins* (New York: Monacelli, 1999), 11; Andreas Huyssen, 'Nostalgia for Ruins,' *Grey Room* 23 (Spring 2006), 8.

46 Yves Marchand and Romain Meffre, with essays by Robert Polidori and Thomas J. Sugrue, *The Ruins of Detroit* (Göttingen: Steidl, 2014); Richard B. Woodward, 'What a Disaster,' *ARTNews* 112, no. 2 (February 2013), 66–73; Ben Vassar, 'Detroit's Comeback: A Sustainable City Is Not a Segregated One,' *Michigan Daily*, March 13, 2019. www.michigandaily.com/section/arts/detroits-comeback-sustainable-city-not-segregated-one (accessed February 25, 2020).

47 View of Shanghai, from roof of Shanghai Municipal Council Slaughterhouse, 1933, now Old Millfun. Photo: author, 2012.

48 Bruno Latour, *We Have Never Been Modern*, trans. Catherine Porter (Cambridge, MA: Harvard University Press, 1993).

We can see obsolescence enduring, too, in America's older suburban towns. Main Street preservation cohabits with ruthless domestic 'teardowns'—the selective obsolescence of postwar suburbia. Urban obsolescence persists, too. In Detroit, over 150,000 dwellings have been razed or abandoned in the past decades, along with much of the area's industrial infrastructure.⁴⁴ But this urban obsolescence, in selective cities, is not perceived as a general crisis as it once was. Rather there is a 'peculiar beauty' in the 'ruins of modernity,' artists and critics have observed.⁴⁵ The result has been for Detroit both what is called 'ruin porn'—lush pictures of abandonment that empty obsolescence of its menace—as well as opportunities, in this urban devaluation, for revaluation and gentrification at economic and cultural levels in the rehabilitation of downtown buildings as luxury hotels and restaurants.⁴⁶

Obsolescence endures, too, in China, where capitalist modernization today sweeps away the past, echoing the American trajectory of a century ago. And yet there are differences between Chicago and Shanghai. Unlike in mid-twentieth century America, when the centralized city form itself seemed obsolete, Chinese cities are as dense as ever, and exhibit, too, survivals from the past, as in a view from the roof of a rehabbed 1933 Shanghai slaughterhouse, looking over other adaptive reuses, surviving tenements, and postmodern additions, as well as contemporary towers.⁴⁷ In other words, our time remains, as lived experience always is, polytemporal, in sociologist Bruno Latour's term, always new and old together: obsolescence *and* sustainability.⁴⁸

In historical perspective, if obsolescence was the dominant ideology of mid-twentieth-century change, giving a name to profitable processes of wholesale expendability, then, arguably, sustainability performs the same function today, justifying profits. Eco-branding is effective marketing. And as much as sustainability promises a new, brighter future, can it ever break the current order when sustainability's abiding values, its ethics are not radical change but, rather, continuity and conservation, an ideal net-zero equilibrium?[49] Might, in fact, sustainability be merely an alibi of conservation, its practice in architecture as profligate as obsolescence? Witness super-tall skyscrapers for Jakarta, Mumbai, and Shanghai trumpeting their LEED[50] certification. In other words, sustainability no less than obsolescence is ideological, productive for design to be sure, firing architects' imaginations as obsolescence once did, but nevertheless rife with illusion and contradiction.

What then are the values of obsolescence and its architectural history? As a way of thinking about the world, obsolescence is based on values, or principles, of measurable performance, competition, supersession, and expendability. Positively, the worth of obsolescence thinking is that it acknowledges, even embraces radical change. It can reject the status quo and clear the ground for a different future. Negatively, obsolescence thinking has a harder time accounting for factors that resist quantitative valuation, or measurement—emotion, memory, and meaning—which in part led to obsolescence thinking's demise at the hands of preservationism and contextualism in architecture.

As for an architectural history of obsolescence, its value, or worth, is in part its illustration of the flexibility of capitalism, its capacity to evolve from its own contradictions. What capitalism itself obsolesced—the industrial-age built environment—it then revalued through adaptive reuse, gentrification, and historic preservation. To be profitable again, all that was solid need *not* melt into air, architectural history teaches. The architectural commodity—'C'—does not have to disappear for reinvestment to take place.

[49] Adrian Parr, *Hijacking Sustainability* (Cambridge, MA: MIT Press, 2009).

[50] LEED (Leadership in Energy and Environmental Design) is the most widely used green building rating system in the world. Available for virtually all building types, LEED provides a framework for healthy, highly efficient, and cost-saving green buildings. LEED certification is a globally recognized symbol of sustainability achievement and leadership. www.usgbc.org/help/what-leed (accessed July 31, 2020).

51 Tod Williams Billie Tsien, Asia Society Hong Kong Center, Hong Kong, 2011. Photo: author.

52 Pavel Mudřík and Pavel Míček, Building 23 rehabilitation, Zlín, 2006. Photo: author.

53 Fondazione Prada, Office for Metropolitan Architecture (OMA),' *Architect*, May 7, 2015. www.architectmagazine.com/project-gallery/fondazione-prada (accessed June 11, 2020).

54 Office of Metropolitan Architecture (Rem Koolhaas), Prada Foundation, Milan, 2015.

The architectural history of obsolescence demonstrates the value, or worth, in a vibrant architectural culture of the impulses both for accepting extreme transformation and resistance to them. This was the characteristic struggle of the nineteen-sixties. Today the impulses in architectural culture stand imbalanced. Sustainability is in the ascendant, obsolescence eclipsed. In Hong Kong, for example, at the Asia Society Hong Kong Center (Tod Williams Billie Tsien, 2011) a new steel-columned walkway runs at a respectful distance from a restored massive masonry wall.[51] The past is a precious jewel here, set off from present and future.

Less refined but more instructive, and expressive of the lessons and values, or principles, of obsolescence, is a renovated factory building in the Czech Republic. Here, in Zlín, a century ago, the shoe manufacturer Tomáš Bat'a imagined twenty-year building life spans. In 2006 the frame of Building No. 23 was refurbished as a Business Innovation Center (Pavel Mudřík and Pavel Míček).[52] The building has also been added to, on the right, with projecting bronze bays. But, more significant, something has been subtracted from the architecture, at the top. To lighten the structure, broad voids appear in the upper floors, thus shrinking the historical frame. Bat'a's intention—a limited-life architecture—is here honored unconsciously. Building No. 23 treats history flexibly, not reverentially. The past is visibly released. The present is open, as implicitly is the future. The same can be said of Koolhaas's Milan Prada Foundation, where old buildings are newly gold-leafed and juxtaposed with concrete, steel, and aluminum additions to create overall, as Koolhaas said, 'an ensemble of fragments that will not congeal into a single image'.[53, 54] This shows how to preserve memory and facilitate growth at the same time, without having one dominate the other, an answer in architecture to Hobsbawm's question: how we come to terms in architecture with these contradictory temporalities and values under capitalism, these different speeds—fast and slow together.

Perhaps the most general value, or worth, of an architectural history of obsolescence is that it teaches us that frameworks of change are themselves changeable creations. Obsolescence then sustainability—and something else may come after sustainability, yet another worldview for comprehending and managing and valuing change in the built environment. One candidate might be resiliency, defined as 'the capacity of a system to absorb disturbance.'[55] Like sustainability, resiliency perceives existential environmental threats, but without sustainability's idealization of a perfect equilibrium; there is always disturbance. Resiliency, then, like obsolescence, imagines a future of constant, unpredictable change.

In any event, the best lesson, or highest value, from a history of obsolescence may be to accept the essential *unmanageability* of change—the creative futility of so many efforts to ward off obsolescence in design. Our futures ought not be considered iron-clad but rather malleable and contingent, as unpredictable and potentially liberating as obsolescence itself. There is still then much to learn from obsolescence and all its values, its principles and its worth, in architecture and in our lives, to acknowledge both change *and* constancy, to accept and even to welcome endings.

[55] Brian Walker and David Salt, *Resilience Thinking: Sustaining Ecosystems and People in a Changing World* (Washington, DC: Island Press, 2006), 32.

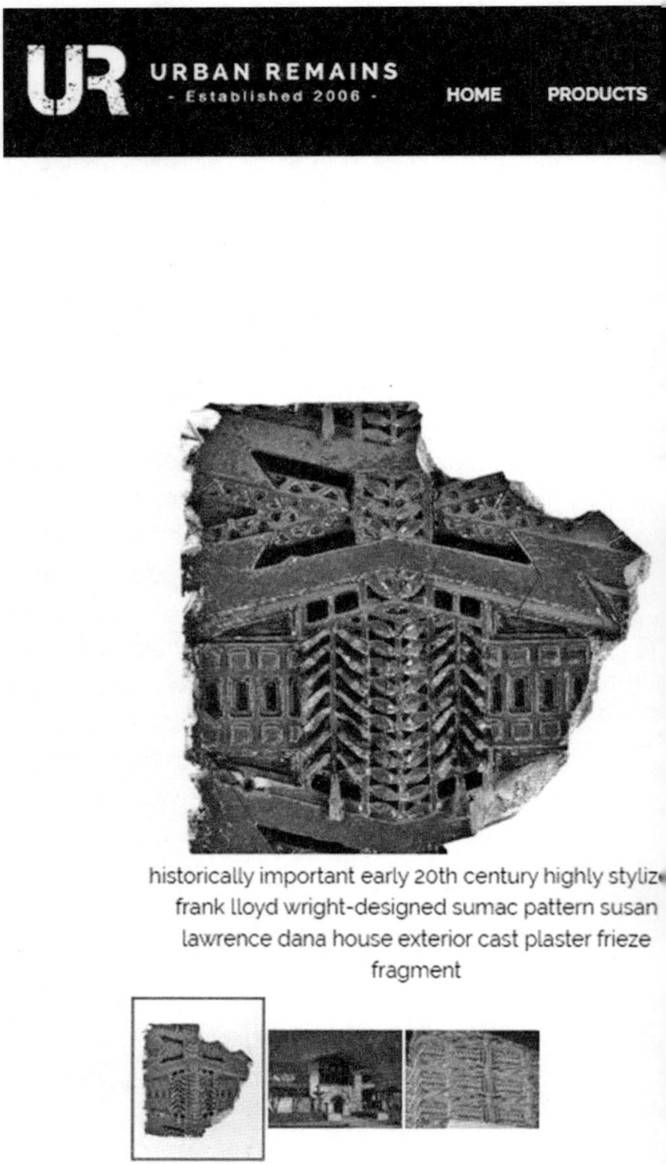

The Price is Wright

URBAN REMAINS
- Established 2006 -

HOME   PRODUCTS

historically important early 20th century highly stylized frank lloyd wright-designed sumac pattern susan lawrence dana house exterior cast plaster frieze fragment

Ashley Paine

| TS | BLDG 51 | BLOG | CONTACT | ABOUT | Search | MY CART | SETTING |

Historically Important Early 20th Century Highly Stylized Frank Lloyd Wright-Designed Sumac Pattern Susan Lawrence Dana House Exterior Cast Plaster Frieze Fragment

SOLD

SKU UR-26145-17

exact fabricator not known

Share: f ⦁ in t G+ P

Please Note: We do not appraise, nor do we disclose the prices of items sold.

Questions? Click here or call our store at 312.492.6254. Please make sure to reference the UR# when submitting an email.

Note: Shipping is not included. If required please contact an Urban Remains sales associate.

Frank Lloyd Wright, Decorative plaster fragment from the Susan Lawrence Dana (Dana-Thomas) Residence, Springfield, IL, 1902. Courtesy Eric J. Nordstrom.

The Price is Wright
Recovering Value in Frank Lloyd Wright's Architectural Fragments

Ashley Paine

1 Frank Lloyd Wright's empty grave site at Unity Chapel Cemetery, Spring Green, WI. Photo: imgur.com.

2 Ada Louise Huxtable, *Frank Lloyd Wright: A Life* (New York: Penguin, 2004), 247–248; Henry H. Kuehn, *Architects' Gravesites: A Serendipitous Guide* (Cambridge, MA: MIT Press, 2017), 117–118.

After Frank Lloyd Wright died in a Phoenix hospital in 1959, his body was returned to his hometown of Spring Green, Wisconsin, and buried in the family graveyard.[1] There he lay peacefully at rest until 1985 when, in fulfilment of the dying wishes of his third wife Olgivanna, Wright's body was hastily dug up, secretly cremated, and his ashes taken back to Arizona to be mingled with those of his late spouse. Some are reported to have been scattered in the desert, the rest were buried at Taliesin West.[2] While questions about these macabre events lie beyond the scope of this essay, the pilfering and dispersal of Wright's corporeal remains offers a fascinating parallel to the fate of a surprising number of his architectural works at the end of their useful lives: sold, broken up, and moved to museums and private collections across the globe. Even buildings that are in use and good repair have been dismembered by some opportunistic owners, harvesting pieces of furniture, windows, and other decorative fixtures and fittings for their own financial gain. Regarding this cannibalization of Wright's built works, Donald Hoffmann suggests that: 'Architecture seems the most substantial of the arts but proves one of the least enduring.' He laments that ultimately, 'a good poem or pot stands a better chance of survival.'[3]

The task of preserving Wright's architecture intact is arguably more challenging than with most other architects. As one of the most popular—and collectible—architects of the twentieth century (a status founded equally on prodigious talent and relentless self-promotion, and no doubt propelled by a hint of American exceptionalism), Wright's buildings are particularly vulnerable to being stripped and sold off in pieces.[4] Of course, the collection of Wright's works in fragments is anathema to the conventional understanding of his architecture. Wright often sought total design control over his projects, which he argued were complete works of art: interiors, furniture, and decorative designs were integral to each building; the buildings themselves unique and inextricably bound to their sites. This unity of design also underpins Wright's notion of a site-specific, or 'organic,' architecture—a powerful concept that dominates much of the rhetoric surrounding his work and its conservation today. To remove any part of a Wright building from its original context, whether it be a window, a wall sconce, or loose piece of furniture, is generally seen as an act of destruction; a willful practice of cultural vandalism that destroys that which is valuable in the building and in the fragment itself. As Hoffmann explains:

> In a Wright building, the details are conceived as minor parts or dependencies of the fabric itself.... Thus the leaded-glass shade of the Robie house lamp is a child of the great cantilevered roof. This means the idea of collecting Wright's architecture in stray fragments represents nothing so much as a contradiction in terms, a violation of the whole spirit of his art...

[3] Donald Hoffmann, 'Dismembering Frank Lloyd Wright,' *Design Quarterly* 155, no. Spring (1992), 2.

[4] There is also much material to be wrangled over: Wright's long career resulted in hundreds of built works, many of which incorporated volumes of custom-designed components, from bespoke tables and chairs, to sofas and soft furnishings, as well as light fittings, lamps, urns, and candlesticks, not to mention his highly desirable 'art-glass' windows that attract collectors from around the world.

5 Hoffmann, 'Dismembering Frank Lloyd Wright,' 4.

6 Robert McCarter, *Frank Lloyd Wright* (London: Phaidon, 1997), 335.

7 David A. Hanks suggests that one of the earliest times a house was emptied of its original furniture was in 1908 when the Littles moved out of their first house designed by Frank Lloyd Wright, taking much of their original Wright-designed furniture (and wall sconces) with them to be incorporated into their second Wright-designed house. Hanks speculates that Wright's issue would not have been with the removal of his furniture from the earlier house, but its addition to the new interiors. David A. Hanks, *Frank Lloyd Wright: Preserving an Architectural Heritage: Decorative Designs from the Domino's Pizza Collection* (London: Studio Vista, 1989), 15.

8 Alois Riegl, 'The Modern Cult of Monuments: Its Character and Its Origin,' *Oppositions* 25 (1982 [1928]).

9 David Adjaye, Nikolaus Hirsch, and Jorge Otero-Pailos, 'On Architecture and Authorship: A Conversation,' *Places Journal* October 2011, placesjournal.org/article/on-architecture-and-authorship-a-conversation/#0.

Exhibited in museums or private collections as if precious treasures of the so-called decorative arts, these pathetic fragments ought to be seen instead as evidences of greed, ostentation, and the most shallow of relationships to art. Art museums often preserve the object by killing its spirit, a Pyrrhic victory at best.[5]

Robert McCarter puts it even more bluntly: 'The complete space of inhabitation is Wright's legacy; its dismemberment is its extinction.'[6]

Hoffmann and McCarter are clearly idealistic in their insistence on the completeness and permanency of Wright's works. It is, after all, understandable that homeowners will want to periodically update their homes and décor, or to take much-loved lamps, tables, and furniture with them when they move.[7] It should also be acknowledged that it occurs in different ways: the removal of loose furniture—often complete objects and stand-alone designs in their own right—is not the same as removing a window or other building fragment once physically part of the building proper. Still, it would be impossible to deny that there is significant value in the retention of original furniture and building fabric in Wright's work: value that is bound to the idea of preserving integrity and authenticity, or what Alois Riegl would have described as 'relative art-value.'[8] Indeed, it is often through instruments of preservation that architecture is attributed value, and that value protected,[9] as the 2019 inscription of eight of Wright's works on the United Nations Educational, Scientific and Cultural Organisation's World Heritage List amply illustrates.

Issues of preservation will be returned to later. For now, what is important to note is that what McCarter and Hoffmann do not address is that architecture and heritage necessarily exist in a broader field of competing values and contradictory value systems. While such oppositions of value are a commonplace, the sheer number, variety, and intensity of examples that are triggered by Wright's built legacy make their tensions uniquely visible; their stakes exaggerated by Wright's prominence, popular appeal, and the eye-watering prices attached to those liberated fragments of his architecture. Hence, it is through a wide lens of value that this essay looks at the intersection of markets and museums with efforts to preserve Wright's built legacy. In particular, it examines what is at stake in this apparent plundering of pieces of his architecture, to rethink, and perhaps even recover, the value of Wright's disembodied fragments and those skeletons of buildings left behind.

To begin, it is useful to establish an economic understanding of value in Wright's buildings and fragments. The commercial value of Wright's extant work is, of course, governed by a web of economic and cultural forces. Land and property values, local real estate markets, the size and condition of the building, legislative protections, and the name, Frank Lloyd Wright, all have some bearing. However, the degree to which these determine sale prices—of Wright's houses in particular—is not always obvious, nor easily calculable. For one thing, and despite his popular appeal, houses by Frank Lloyd Wright are notoriously difficult to sell.[10] Many owners overestimate the commercial value of Wright's name and design, falsely equating architectural eminence with a premium dollar price.[11] While there is some research to suggest that in the special case of Oak Park—with its famed collection of more than twenty of Wright's Prairie Style houses—as much as a 41 percent price premium has been achieved, there is little evidence to support a broader price effect of Wright's name elsewhere.[12]

10 Frank Lloyd Wright, Foster House and Stable, Chicago, 1900. The house was listed in August 2017 for $205,000, and remains on the market in May 2020 with an asking price of $145,000. Photo: www.coldwellbankerhomes.com.

11 Leo Koonmen, 'Valuing and Pricing Wright Houses: General Principles,' *SaveWright: The Magazine of the Frank Lloyd Wright Building Conservancy* 1, no. 2 (2010), 17.

12 The value of those properties in the immediate vicinity of a Wright design also benefit by up to 8.5 percent. See: Gabriel Ahlfeldt and Alexandra Mastro, 'Valuing Iconic Design: Frank Lloyd Wright Architecture in Oak Park, Illinois,' *Housing Studies* 27, no. 8 (2012), 1082, 1096.

As a result, over-valued houses commonly remain on the market for years, slowly dropping advertised prices until they better reflect local market conditions. The Avery Coonley House in Riverside, Illinois,[13] for example, had been for sale on and off since 2010 when it was first listed for US$2.89 million. It finally sold in February 2019 for a mere $1.15 million.[14] As Leo Koonmen suggests, these kinds of auction results make it very difficult to demonstrate a price premium for houses designed by Wright. Rather, like all real estate, the commercial value of Wright's work is usually limited by the material attributes of the property and local market conditions.[15]

Real estate markets have other ramifications for Wright's work. In particular, many of his houses are today seen to be small and dated, but are found in highly desirable locations: a disparity that puts them at risk of demolition by developers wanting to extract greater profits from these sites. Wright's public and commercial designs face similar dangers. As recently as 2018, the Lockridge Medical Clinic in Montana[16] was successfully torn down to make way for a mixed-use development.[17] Such cases demonstrate what are familiar tensions between the cultural values of architectural heritage, in opposition to the quantifiable economic values of real estate. The demolition of the Montana clinic is therefore an all too predictable outcome of competing value systems: a trading of heritage significance for profit or, in the broader lens of value, the destruction of one value to extract another.

As collectible fragments, however, the interaction of economic and heritage values in Wright's work occurs in more interesting ways. Removed from their sites, Wright's furniture and building fragments are liberated from the constraints of property economics and the social obligation of utility. They become tradable commodities, and gain commercial

13 Frank Lloyd Wright, Avery Coonley House, Riverside, IL, 1907. Article announcing the sale for $1.15M after nine years on and off the market, February 4, 2019. Photo: chicago.curbed.com.

14 Bob Goldsborough, 'Frank Lloyd Wright mansion in Riverside sells for $1.15 million,' *Chicago Tribune*, February 4, 2019, www.chicagotribune.com/real-estate/elite-street/ct-re-elite-street-frank-lloyd-wright-riverside-mansion-20190204-story.html.

15 Koonmen, 'Valuing and Pricing Wright Houses,' 17.

16 Frank Lloyd Wright, Lockridge Medical Clinic, Whitefish, MT, 1958. Scene of the late night demolition of Wright's late project on January 10, 2018. Photo: www.arch2o.com.

17 This was despite the fact the structure was listed on the National Register of Historic Places.

value by swapping the values of architecture for those of the art market: a process that brings about a different set of challenges—and opportunities—for the preservation of Wright's legacy.[18]

The emergence of a market for Wright's fragments—his loose furniture, decorative objects and building pieces—is, however, a relatively recent phenomenon. Following his death, Wright was deeply unpopular with academic and popular audiences, and many of his interiors and custom-designed furnishings were lost through the redecorating efforts of owners. As recently as the nineteen-seventies, Wright's furniture is known to have been discarded or intentionally destroyed: the owner of the Meyer May House, for example, reportedly chopped up their Wright-designed dining table, using some of the timber to build a box for firewood.[19] It was only in the early nineteen-eighties that the market for Wright's building fragments took hold, following a series of auctions at Christie's in New York,[20] and bolstered by a broader re-evaluation of Wright's career through publications and exhibitions, including the permanent display of the living room from the Little House[21] in New York's Metropolitan Museum of Art in 1982.[22]

In just a few years, the price of Wright's decorative designs exploded. The aforementioned Robie House lamp was sold in 1988 for $704,000,[23] while a dining table with eight matching chairs went for $1.6 million in 1987—a record sum at the time, stumped up by the wealthy Wright enthusiast, Tom Monaghan, founder of the Domino's Pizza chain.[24] Collecting intensively between 1986 and 1987, Monaghan quickly amassed the world's largest collection of Wright's decorative arts, once estimated to include more than 300 items worth around $30 million.[25] As a result of this furious

18 As Jorge Otero-Pailos comments, 'the case of the Maison Tropicale makes it clear how effortlessly the system can turn architecture into art once it is transportable.' Adjaye, Hirsch, and Otero-Pailos, 'On Architecture and Authorship.'

19 Hanks, *Frank Lloyd Wright*, 16.

20 Ibid.

21 Frank Lloyd Wright, Living room from the Francis W. Little House, Wayzata, Minnesota, 1912–1914. Metropolitan Museum of Art, New York, Purchase, Emily Crane Chadbourne Bequest, 1972. © 2020 Artists Rights Society (ARS), New York.

22 Elizabeth Venant, 'The Wright Time for Household Objects: The Great Architect's Creations for Homes are now Commanding Respect—and Top Prices,' *LA Times*, December 4, 1988.
This reappraisal of Wright was also greatly assisted by the opening up of the Frank Lloyd Wright archives following the death of Olgivanna in 1985, who had previously maintained a tight control over access to its contents. Huxtable, *Frank Lloyd Wright*, 249–250.

23 Heidi L. Berry, 'The Wright Time; Outstanding Prices Mark a New Era for the Decorative Works of Frank Lloyd Wright,' *The Washington Post*, July 7, 1988.

24 *Forbes* 'Personal Affairs' supplement cover, October 23, 1989. The image features 'Pizzillionaire' Thomas Monaghan, seated on a chair designed by Wright for the Ward Willits House. Monaghan purchased the chair at auction in 1986 for $198,000. Photo: www.steinerag.com.

25 Ibid.

collecting, Monaghan was often accused of driving up prices, and putting Wright's buildings at risk.[26] In response, Monaghan tried to limit the destructive impact of his collecting. He drafted up strict guidelines for his purchases, and refused to buy artefacts offered to him by building owners, helping to protect in-situ structures. He also established a series of grants to help owners restore Wright's in-situ works, and even founded a National Center for the Study of Frank Lloyd Wright to house his collection and promote Wright's ideas to the public.[27] While the Center was closed in the nineteen-nineties, Monaghan's acquisitions need to be seen in the context of his broader philanthropic, educational, and preservation activities, complicating the idea that the collecting of Wright's artefacts is necessarily destructive.

While Monaghan ceased buying Wright artefacts and sold off much of his collection following the closure of his Center, the intense demand for Wright's fragments persists. What is surprising, however, is that the interest in, and commercial value of, Wright's houses has failed to keep pace with his decorative arts and architectural artefacts. When the Storrer House in Los Angeles was bought by movie producer Joel Silver in 1984 for $720,000—little more than what was paid for the Robie House lamp a few years later[28]—the new owner correctly pointed out that:

> There's no value placed on the homes. They're appraised at whatever the square footage of the house next door is worth. ... It's insane. There are Frank Lloyd Wright houses that are crumbling and people won't put money into them, but they'll spend $1.6 million for a dining room set.[29]

This disparity between the commercial value of Wright's fragments and that of his in-situ houses persists to this day.

---

[26] Monaghan was once quoted as saying 'I've seen prices jump 10 times just because I was interested in buying.' Abigail Foerstner, 'Wright of Wrong?: The Battle to Keep Frank Lloyd Interiors Intact,' *Chicago Tribune*, November 15, 1987, 4.

[27] Hanks, *Frank Lloyd Wright*, 15, 20.

[28] Venant, 'Wright Time for Household Objects.'

[29] Ibid.

A 2018 Sotheby's auction of some of Monaghan's collection of windows from the 1912 Coonley Playhouse, achieved as much as $200,000 apiece.[30] A month after the auction, the Playhouse itself was put up for sale, restored and complete with replica windows, for just $800,000: the equivalent price of a handful of those original windows.[31] The house was relisted in July 2019 for $750,000 and, as of May 2020, remains for sale with the reduced asking price of $650,000.[32, 33] Other buildings have struggled to find buyers at any price: in 2016, the Lindholm House in northeastern Minnesota was facing demolition when it was gifted and moved to Polymath Park in western Pennsylvania in a last-ditch effort to save it.

The massive growth in the market for Wright's decorative works since the nineteen-eighties has therefore produced the perverse situation in which his buildings are more valuable in pieces than they are whole—a situation that, perhaps surprisingly, has contributed both to their destruction and preservation. While the incredible prices paid for Wright's furniture and artefacts have encouraged some owners to strip out windows, fixtures, and furnishings for consignment with auction houses—the economic equivalent of liquidating the equity held in their properties—the newfound commercial value of Wright's decorative items also put an end to their thoughtless destruction by disinterested renovators.[34]

Importantly, the liquidity seen in the market for pieces of Wright's architecture is only possible because, liberated from a fixed place, the value systems that normally govern Wright's in-situ works are able to be traded for those values of the art world and art market—a market which characteristically involves exorbitant prices for the celebrated works of select 'genius' figures. Certainly, Wright is one of the few architects

30 Frank Lloyd Wright, Windows from the Avery Coonley Playhouse, Riverside, IL, 1912, pictured in Sotheby's catalogue for the 'Important Design' auction held in New York on May 24, 2018. Photo: www.sothebys.com.

31 Jay Koziarz, 'Unusual Frank Lloyd Wright Schoolhouse Turned Home is Back Seeking $750K,' *Curbed*, July 25, 2019, chicago.curbed.com/2019/7/25/8911480/frank-lloyd-wright-for-sale-avery-coonley-playhouse.

32 '350 Fairbank Road, Riverside, IL 60546 (MLS # 10461963),' Mike McCurry Group, last updated May 28, 2020, themccurrygroup.com/idx/mls-10461963-350_fairbank_road_riverside_il_60546.

33 Frank Lloyd Wright, Avery Coonley Playhouse, Riverside, IL, 1912. Screen capture from website of Mike McCurry Group for the house's sale. Photo: themccurrygroup.com.

34 Hanks, *Frank Lloyd Wright*, 16.

35 Museums also play a paradoxical role in architectural preservation: as Thordis Arrhenius points out, the preservation of architecture in museums necessarily requires a process of destruction. See: Thordis Arrhenius, *The Fragile Monument: On Conservation and Modernity* (London: Black Dog, 2012).

36 Hoffmann, 'Dismembering Frank Lloyd Wright,' 2.

37 Frank Lloyd Wright, Balusters from Robert W. Roloson Houses, Chicago, 1894 (below), with Adler and Sullivan, Architects, facade panel from Chicago Stock Exchange Building, 1894 (above). Installation view at the Art Institute of Chicago. Photo: author.

to achieve such a complete crossover of markets and value systems, demonstrating a rare case in which architectural value can be readily exchanged for hard currency. But what the market for Wright also shows is that the economic value of his building's fragments can be determined with some precision. What is less certain is the architectural and cultural value of such disembodied and decontextualized objects in the museum.

While the cultural and preservationist remit of the museum may seem to be at odds with the generation of economic value, such institutions are inseparable from the commercial art market.[35] The enthusiastic acquisition of Wright's furniture and fragments by museums in the nineteen-eighties, for example, did much to inflate their demand and market value. These museums were complicit with—if not directly responsible for—at least some of the 'parting out' of Wright's extant work for profit. As Hoffmann has argued: 'The forces most insidiously ruinous to Wright's architecture are a misguided museum world and its twin sister, the errant art market, both of which encourage the dismemberment of his buildings…into mere fragments.'[36] For Hoffmann, these fragments are the worthless by-products of destroyed architectural heritage—reduced to souvenirs and collectibles. And, without doubt, moving buildings and building parts into museums represents a significant compromise in heritage value, and a permanent end to their function and use value.[37] But, rather than being seen exclusively as vehicles to extract economic value from the ruined shells of Wright's architecture, these museological acts of grave-robbing can also be seen to create new kinds of value in museum collections.

Most obviously, museums bestow new value on objects through aesthetic and cultural validation—something Wright was acutely aware of, having used museums and major exhibitions of his work to gain prestige and promote his name.³⁸ Beyond this, other values can also come into play in the museum. Wright's period room in the American Wing of the Metropolitan, for example, was not only instrumental in the process of re-valuing of Wright's career in the nineteen-eighties, but was consciously used by the museum to promote an American design identity to domestic and international audiences. As such, it gained a kind of civic value and nationalist purpose. Likewise, a window from the Coonley Playhouse was donated by the American Friends of the National Gallery of Australia to the gallery in the early nineteen-nineties.³⁹ As an object of cultural exchange and international relations, the donation exposes some of the political values conferred on objects in public museums. There can even be new architectural and historical value created through the exhibition of fragmentary works. The Wright period room in the Metropolitan, for example, exhibits the furniture and décor according to the plan arrangement Wright had intended. In this respect, the interior is arguably more authentic today than it ever was when occupied by the Little family, who ignored the architect's plan.

More critically, collections themselves establish intrinsic value: they generate cultural authority and pedagogical potential by constructing new contexts for objects. They also construct order and relationships between exhibited objects with new systems of museological classification. And, while architectural fragments as cultural documents maintain an external orientation as incomplete signifiers or stand-ins for that which is lost or that lies outside the walls of the institution, the museum also gives such objects a newfound completeness through the spatial and narrative sequencing of history that could never exist in the outside world.⁴⁰ As such,

38 Wright even donated two of his own chairs to the Museum of Modern Art in 1947. Hanks, *Frank Lloyd Wright*, 17.

Donald Hoffmann, however, draws a distinction between Wright's use of the museum, and the collection of his works by museums today: 'Wright exhibited his work in museums to proclaim his cause and advance his career. His somewhat cynical use of museums as convenient instruments of publicity and prestige was nothing, of course, compared to the present-day symbiosis between museums and the art market.' Hoffmann, 'Dismembering Frank Lloyd Wright,' 5.

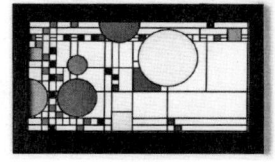

39 Frank Lloyd Wright, Window from the Avery Coonley Playhouse, Riverside, IL, 1912, Canberra, National Gallery of Australia.

40 Arrhenius, *The Fragile Monument*, 6.

museums and collections can be seen to have a restorative value, giving new function, context, and meaning to objects with little or no use value.[41]

Still, as David A. Hanks suggests, the role of the museum in the preservation of architectural fragments remains unresolved: the museum, like the market, is a space of multiple competing values.[42] What becomes clear, however, is that fragments emerge through the museum as a kind of cultural product. As such, the re-framing of Wright's fragmented work in collections must be considered as a productive process, as much as it is a destructive one.[43]

There are also good reasons to challenge the idea that the productive dimension of architecture's collection in museums necessarily comes at the expense of architectural heritage value. For one thing, there are numerous examples where the fragmentation of Wright's work has actually assisted the preservation of an original structure. Some anecdotal tales suggest that owners have tried to sell valuable art-glass windows to help fund the costly renovation of their Wright-designed houses—a case where the disparate economic value of Wright's buildings and fragments might be leveraged to help save them. There is also the documented case where some 200 fragments of glass from a light fixture in Wright's seminal Unity Temple were sold in 1969 to support restoration efforts there. Meanwhile, at Wright's best-known house, Fallingwater, now one of eight World Heritage Listed designs, it is currently possible to donate money to the Windows Legacy Fund set up to help support the renovation of the house's many windows, and to re-glaze them with new UV resistant glass to preserve its interiors.[44] While gifts of $500 or more are rewarded with a framed piece of the old window glass, it is hard to view the distribution of these fragments as acts of cultural vandalism.[45] Instead, it ought to be

---

[41] Alexandra Stara, *The Museum of French Monuments 1795–1816* (Abingdon: Routledge, 2013), 114–115. And, as Susan Stewart has argued: 'The collection cannot be defined simply in terms of the worth of its elements. Just as the system of exchange depends upon the relative position of the commodity in the chain of signifiers, so the collection as a whole implies a value—aesthetic or otherwise—independent of the simple sum of its individual members.' Susan Stewart, *On Longing: Narratives of the Miniature, the Gigantic, the Souvenir, the Collection* (Durham, NC: Duke University Press, 1993), 166.

[42] Hanks, *Frank Lloyd Wright*, 17.

[43] William Tronzo, 'Introduction,' in *The Fragment: An Incomplete History*, ed. William Tronzo (Los Angeles: Getty Research Institute, 2009), 6.

[44] Piece of framed glass taken from Frank Lloyd Wright's Fallingwater, Mill Run, Pennsylvania, 1935. Commemorative pieces are given to donors of $500 or more to the Fallingwater Window Legacy Fund. Photo: fallingwater.org.

[45] 'Windows Legacy Fund,' Fallingwater, https://fallingwater.org/more-ways-to-give/windows-legacy-fund/.

seen as part of a novel—if imperfect—process of preservation that is perhaps unique to Wright's work alone.

Elsewhere, valuable furniture, windows, light fittings, and other detachable items have also been removed from Wright buildings by caretakers to protect them from theft,[46] weathering, and daily use.[47] As Abigail Foerstner says regarding Wright's domestic interiors, when a dining table can be worth more than a million dollars, it is usually impractical to keep the original furniture in place and still live in the house—it is simply 'too valuable to use, too expensive to insure and too vulnerable to risk storing in hot attics or damp basements.'[48] One widely accepted solution is to preserve houses as museums. Still, this museumization process can have a significant impact on building fabric, due to the accommodation of visitor services and access requirements. It also has immaterial consequences by freezing buildings in time, and fundamentally changing the experience of visitors by extinguishing use value and the possibility of occupation.[49] An alternative solution advocated by Wright's grandson, architect Eric Lloyd Wright, is to sell valuable items to museums, and to replace them with replicas that extend the useful life of the house.[50] Of course, this too is a compromise, and is often dismissed for sacrificing material authenticity in favor of a visual or phenomenal fidelity.[51]

Still there are those groups of Wright preservationists that insist on the material originality and completeness of his works, often spending large amounts of time and money to recover and reintegrate original pieces of Wright's design—time and funds that arguably would be better spent on other more pressing preservation efforts. This issue of material authenticity, however, needs to be considered more holistically in the context of Wright's work and its preservation.

---

46 In a recent case, several Wright-designed items from the Freeman House were stolen from a storage facility of the University of Southern California. See: Antonio Pacheco, 'Thieves steal Frank Lloyd Wright and Schindler furniture pieces around Los Angeles,' *The Architect's Newspaper*, February 4, 2019, archpaper.com/2019/02/wright-schindler-furniture-thefts/.

47 In the case of the Ward Willits House, a number of windows in a poor state of repair had become too fragile to renovate and keep in place. Several were removed and donated to the Chicago Historical Society, to save them the costly ongoing restoration work required to maintain them with the house. Copies were installed to maintain the integrity of the design. See: Nancy Ryan, 'Making Things Wright,' *Chicago Tribune*, August 9, 1998, www.chicagotribune.com/news/ct-xpm-1998-08-09-9808090225-story.html; Hanks, *Frank Lloyd Wright*, 18.

48 Foerstner, 'Wright of Wrong?,' 1.

49 As Arrhenius points out more generally: 'Conservation even when its aim is to preserve an object or a site in its current form without alteration or restoration, establishes a distance between the present existence of the object and its past. Classified as heritage, buildings turn into "special" objects relocated into the realm of cultural history, as space that can be understood generically, if not always physically, as that of the museum.' Arrhenius, *The Fragile Monument*, 140.

50 Foerstner, 'Wright of Wrong?,' 4.

51 Frank Lloyd Wright, Interior view of Taliesin West, Scottsdale, AZ, 1937. Visitors can be seen seated in reproduction chairs. Photo: author.

[52] Stephen Cairns and Jane M. Jacobs, *Buildings Must Die: A Perverse View of Architecture* (Cambridge, MA: MIT Press, 2014), 64.

[53] Tronzo, 'Introduction,' 4.

It also raises the so far unexamined questions of building maintenance, and the value of maintaining use. Suffice it to say here that architecture is rarely a static assembly of materials, and it is often impractical—if not impossible—to preserve it intact over long periods. Rather, materials have predictable lifespans and must be periodically maintained and replaced to extend the life and use value of a building, which persist as a dynamic amalgamation of new and old fabric. As Cairns and Jacobs note in their provocatively titled book, *Buildings Must Die*, 'durability is not an intrinsic attribute of architecture, it is an attribute of how the social world approaches architecture.'[52]

Acknowledging the inevitability of regular maintenance and material replacement, a few perhaps obvious but important observations might be made. First, that it is only because of, and not in spite of, the regular removal of original materials, and the integration of new ones, that in-situ architectural preservation can occur at all. Second, that the state of wholeness and completion in architecture is a fragile and fleeting condition: wholes begin to fall apart as soon as they are made. As William Tronzo notes, the fragment is in fact architecture's more durable and enduring state.[53] Seen in this context, what is unique about Wright's work is not the fact of its fragmentation. Rather, it is the particular role that museums and markets have played in accelerating the inherently dynamic material life of his architecture.

The turning of Wright's work into fragments, therefore, need not be lamented. Nor does the collection of it in pieces need to be seen as an inherently destructive process. Instead, the removal and substitution of materials, artefacts, and building fragments that are too valuable or fragile to be retained in-situ, can be seen as part of the natural life of buildings—one that allows structures to be occupied longer, and thereby extending and protecting a building's use value. Put another way, one of the unarticulated values of collecting and preserving Wright's fragments in the museum is that it liberates the original structure from the obligation of in-situ preservation, as well as the debilitating effects of economic value on its ability to be occupied. As such, the fragmentation and replacement of material can be seen as giving life to a building, while the fragments themselves can be given a second life—and new value—as parts of collections, marking a new beginning, rather than an end. As Caitlin Desilvey puts it, the challenge is 'to understand change not as loss but as a release into other states, unpredictable and open.'[54]

Given the impossibility of the in-situ preservation of Wright's work in perpetuity, and the teleological drive of all architecture toward the condition of the fragment, a more philosophical—and pragmatic—approach to the conservation of Wright's architecture might therefore accept the fragmentation and dispersal of building fabric over time, and seek to leverage the process to help preserve Wright's architectural legacy. This, however, requires a re-thinking of those predominant systems of value that obstinately seek what is often an unfeasible, if not illogical or entirely impossible, ideal of preserving Wright's work unchanged and in place. It will be no easy task. For one thing, preservation discourses are largely dominated by the idea of originality as a prerequisite condition for authenticity. This is despite the fact that the retention of original fabric is contrary to the predictable material vicissitudes of buildings during their usable lives, suggesting that originality must therefore be rethought as a criterion for architectural authenticity. In other words, to embrace the inevitable fragmentation of Wright's work, and to remain open to its productive possibilities, notions of originality and authenticity need to be disassociated.

[54] Caitlin DeSilvey, *Curated Decay: Heritage Beyond Saving* (London: University of Minnesota Press, 2017), 3.

[55] These include the writing and experimental projects of Jorge Otero-Pailos and Adam Lowe. Also see: Jorge Otero-Pailos, Erik Langdalen, and Thordis Arrhenius, *Experimental Preservation* (Zurich: Lars Müller, 2016).

A small number of preservation theorists and practitioners have recently begun to do just that: fundamentally rethinking the idea of authenticity, and its attendant values in Western culture that fetishize original building fabric and the idea of the architect as artist-author.[55] In this context, the question of authenticity shifts away from whether or not something is original, to focus instead on whether or not the substitution is done well, using the criteria of adequacy and integrity to validate practices of replication, substitution, maintenance, and reconstruction. Hence, the authenticity of Wright's architecture—and, therefore its cultural value—might be better judged not on the originality of his windows, furniture, and furnishings, but on how well their routine substitutions help to prolong the serviceable lives of his buildings in a consistent and recognizable form.

More challenging still is the need to unravel the rhetoric surrounding Wright's work and its pretensions of unity and an 'organic' connection to site—a difficult but not impossible task. After all, Wright developed numerous designs for mass-produced housing and construction systems throughout his long career—including the famed Usonian system houses—which were used and adapted for sites across the United States. Such designs make up a significant number of his extant buildings, and include projects where Wright is known to have never visited the project site or the finished building, raising questions about the significance of site to Wright's practice, and the specificity of his designs to particular settings. He was also wont to re-use and adapt his ostensibly unique 'one-off' designs for new projects. For example, the plan for the 1949 unbuilt house for Robert F. Windfohr in Fort Worth, Texas, was recycled for the later Bailleres House in Acapulco, Mexico from 1952 (also unrealized), and then again for a house project for Arthur Miller and Marilyn Monroe in Roxbury, Connecticut in 1957. In this light, Wright's rhetoric on 'organic' architecture must be seen in a more nuanced way, and his projects not as singular, site-specific creations, but as points in a continuous process of formal development and adaptation.[56] Wright would also change his own buildings, suggesting that he did not see his finished works as static museum pieces but, rather, understood their dynamic nature as buildings and interiors to be lived in, adapted, and changed.[57] Such observations open the door to more permissive attitudes to changes and substitutions in his built works.

Arguably, one of the unspoken values of those fragments of Wright's architecture in museums and collections, therefore, is that they force us to confront and re-assess conventional attitudes towards the preservation of Wright's legacy; to challenge the central rhetoric of site in his work and, perhaps most importantly, to rethink issues of completeness, authenticity, originality, and the values we attach to them in architectural heritage. So, while Hoffmann may be right that a good pot or poem will survive intact longer, the dissolution of architectural wholes need not be feared, only better understood and harnessed for the purposes of preservation.

For Wright's buildings, there is nothing to fear in death. May they rest in pieces.

[56] On this issue, also see: Amanda Reeser Lawrence, 'Spin-Offs: The V. C. Morris Shop and Self-Reflexivity in the Work of Frank Lloyd Wright,' in *Perspecta: The Yale Architectural Journal 49, Quote*, ed. A. J. P. Artmel, Russell LeStourgeon, and Violette de la Selle (Cambridge, MA: Yale School of Architecture, 2016).

[57] Perhaps most strikingly, his home and studio in Oak Park underwent radical changes between 1889 and 1911, and again in c. 1925 and 1956. See: The Frank Lloyd Wright Home and Studio Foundation, *The Plan for Restoration and Adaptive Use of the Frank Lloyd Wright Home and Studio* (Chicago: University of Chicago Press, 1978), ix, 42–43. Also see: Hanks, *Frank Lloyd Wright*, 15.

3000.- 1500.-

ALDO ROSSI

Installation view of *Architecture I*, 1977, with prices. Washington DC, Smithsonian Institution, Archives of American Art, Leo Castelli Gallery records.

Model Values
Architectural Models and the Conceptual Limits of Art Markets

Jordan Kauffman

1 This was not the first time that architectural representations were shown in a private art gallery, though none held from the mid- to late-twentieth-century proved as influential. Perhaps the first dedicated exclusively to architectural material was the 1923 *Les architects du group 'De Stijl'* at Léonce Rosenberg's L'Effort Moderne in Paris, which featured both drawings and models. See also notes 3 and 5.

2 Architects featured in *Architecture I* were Richard Meier, Aldo Rossi, Raimund Abraham, James Stirling, Walter Pichler, Robert Venturi and John Rauch, and Emilio Ambasz.

3 *Houses for Sale* included works from Emilio Ambasz, Peter Eisenman, Vittorio Gregotti, Arata Isozaki, Charles Moore, Cesar Pelli, Cedric Price, and Oswald Mattias Ungers. Precedence for the creation of works (and the design of houses) specifically for a private gallery is found in the 1923 *Les architects du group 'De Stijl'* exhibit. Both the Maison d'Artiste and the Maison Particulière by Theo van Doesburg and Cornelius van Eesteren were developed for this show. See also notes 1 and 5.

On October 22, 1977, the Leo Castelli Gallery in New York opened its doors to an exhibition of work unlike any it had previously mounted. Instead of the contemporary art to which visitors had become accustomed, the gallery was filled with architectural work.[1] Walls beset with architectural drawings and pedestals holding models displayed the work of eight architects representing seven practices.[2] Some drawings were sold, but no models. The success of the exhibition *Architecture I* in attracting the attention of critics—it was reviewed in the *New York Times*, the *Philadelphia Inquirer*, *Artforum*, and other venues of note—in part drove the gallery to hold another exhibition of architecture three years later. *Architecture II: Houses for Sale* enlisted eight architects to design houses to be sold through the gallery.[3] Each responded by sending drawings of buildings that, depending on the project, ranged from abstract to construction drawings, and models. This show was Castelli's most popular of the year; 25,000 people reportedly came through the doors during its four-week run. Notably, neither houses nor models were sold through the gallery, though some drawings were.

Though a commercial failure, the show garnered widespread attention from critics and the press, with reviews published across the US and Europe, and proved a resounding success in driving public conversation about architecture and its representations in the art market. A third and final architectural show, *Follies: Architecture for the Late-Twentieth-Century Landscape*, was held three years after *Houses for Sale*. Nineteen architects designed garden follies which could be purchased for construction, or one could acquire the drawings or models themselves as collectible artifacts for display.[4] Again, a few drawings sold, but no models, and no follies were ever realized.

These three shows are important among the myriad architecture exhibitions held in galleries during the postmodern period—a time when architectural representations became firmly entrenched within the economics of the art world—for three key reasons. First, the Castelli Gallery was the preeminent art gallery in the United States and an acknowledged trendsetter in the art world. It therefore had immense influence on how architectural representations were received within the art world and perceived by others, such as collectors, critics, and other gallerists. Second, in all of these shows, unlike most others during this period, models were featured alongside drawings, which highlighted the relationship of these forms of representation within the gallery world.[5] Finally, across the three shows, the drawings and models demonstrated the diversity of techniques employed at that time to display these forms of representations in private galleries.

While I have elsewhere explored the place that these shows occupied within the larger art market, and their influence in shifting the general perception of architectural drawings in particular—from working documents to autonomous

4 *Follies* consisted of projects from Raimund Abraham, Agrest and Gandelsonas, Emilio Ambasz, Gae Aulenti, Batey and Mack, Ricardo Bofill, Peter Cook, Eisenman/Robertson, Frank Gehry, Michael Graves, Hans Hollein, Christian Hubert, Arata Isozaki, Machado-Silvetti, Raphael Moneo, Paul Rudolph, Joseph Rykwert, Quinlan Terry, and Bernard Tschumi. Quinlan Terry's contributions were the only follies that were not designed specifically for the show, having been commissioned previously by Alistair McAlpine for his West Green House in Hampshire, England.

5 The Max Protetch Gallery was another private gallery that often exhibited models alongside drawings. However, it opened only one year prior to this second show at the Castelli Gallery. For more on the Protetch Gallery, see especially Jordan Kauffman, *Drawing on Architecture: The Object of Lines, 1970-1990* (Cambridge: MIT Press, 2018), 223–245. Precedence for this can be found again in *Les architects du group 'De Stijl'*, where seven models were shown. See also notes 1 and 3.

6 See Jordan Kauffman, *Drawing on Architecture: The Object of Lines, 1970–1990* (Cambridge: MIT Press, 2018).

objects, to aesthetic ones, and finally to ones representative of architecture's history—this article focuses on the other significant, but overlooked, form of architectural representation at these shows: the models.[6] Although architectural drawings emerged within this context as objects imbued with new sets of values—aesthetic, artistic, commercial, conceptual, and cultural—architectural models proved resistant; the perceptual shifts and attendant values affecting the drawings did not impact the models in the same way. This chapter will explore and illuminate why models followed such a different path.

In order to parse the effects of the art market and the art world on these forms of representations, a number of important factors must be emphasized. Chief among these are the galleries in which they were shown, the techniques used to display the works, and the reception and contextualization of the works by critics, potential buyers, and the public. Also important are the intentions of the works' creators. The extent to which their aims affected display, and thus conditioned reception, was highly variable. This will be investigated in detail below, but generally it can be observed that for drawings, the architects' intentions had little influence on display, while for models, their objectives were much more impactful.

Displaying Architectural Models

The techniques mobilized to display architectural representations reveal much about the particular values that the gallery wished to promote. Most directly, the intention was that the works be understood to have monetary value. By bringing representations into the gallery, it was the hope that they would be appreciated and subsequently purchased. There are also broader social and cultural values that works might attain if displays are successful and economics are favorable, which is precisely what happened with architectural drawings. In the shows at the Castelli Gallery, drawings were, with few exceptions, displayed uniformly: on the wall; matted, framed, and behind glass; and largely consistently within each show. In *Architecture I*, all original drawings were framed in either white or light wood frames, while *Houses for Sale* used dark frames, as did *Follies*. In all three shows, the drawings were hung at eye level. To emphasize the importance of this, it is worth noting that this was not the only option available. There was no particular reason the architectural drawings *had* to be framed. They could, for instance, have been placed on tables or pinned to walls. In the art world, the use of frames had even been challenged since early in the century, and Castelli himself had previously held numerous shows in which art was not or could not be framed. Further, within architecture, there are notable examples of shows at other galleries that did not frame drawings. For instance, at George Collin's *Visionary Drawings of Architecture and Planning* exhibit at the Drawing Center in 1979, some were hung directly on walls, and at the Aedes Gallery in Berlin, the decision was made not to frame works after its first shows in 1980, as frames were then seen as antithetical to the nature of the documents themselves, which was as part of a process. The frame, it was understood, both literally and figuratively framed the work, cutting it off from its referents and isolating it as a singular object to be appreciated. Its consistent use, therefore, must be seen as a conscious decision, rather than simply a convention or requirement of display.

    The consistent presentation of the drawings, however, contrasts with the variability in the display of architectural models. Although models were most often displayed on white cuboid pedestals, flush with exterior dimensions of the model's base, in each show there were notable deviations that challenged this standard. In *Architecture I*, this was found in the projects of Raimund Abraham, James Stirling, Emilio Ambasz, and Robert Venturi and John Rauch. The most straightforward departures occurred in the displays for Venturi and Rauch and Ambasz. With Venturi and Rauch's model for the Marlborough-Blenheim Hotel, the model appreciably overhung its pedestal such that the scale of the plinth was diminished in relation to the model.[7] Since the model itself contained a wide base, this proportion evoked a table, which is the more standard placing for an architectural model as a useful object. The pedestal on which Ambasz's model for the Center for Applied Computer Research and Development sat had a substantial gap on the bottom.[8] Because the model was low to the ground, this gap allowed visitors to approach the model and view it from above more easily. Consequently, the model and the pedestal together promoted active engagement more so than some alternative display methods. Abraham's 9 Houses were a series of models—evident because of separate, adjoined bases displayed on one pedestal.[9]

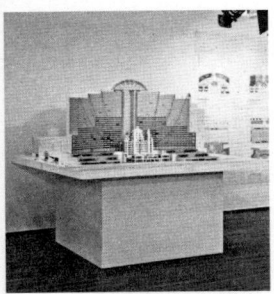

More extreme deviations appeared in the displays of Abraham's House Without Walls[10] and Stirling's University of Cambridge History Faculty Building[11]. House Without Walls and its pedestal were conjoined. Where the model was cut

7 Installation view of Venturi and Rauch, Marlborough-Blenheim Hotel, *Architecture I*, 1977. Washington DC, Archives of American Art, Smithsonian Institution, Leo Castelli Gallery records, c. 1880–2000.

8 Installation view of Emilio Ambasz, Center for Applied Computer Research and Development, *Architecture I*, 1977. Washington DC, Archives of American Art, Smithsonian Institution, Leo Castelli Gallery records, c. 1880–2000.

9 Installation view of Raimund Abraham, 9 Houses, *Architecture I*, 1977. Washington DC, Archives of American Art, Smithsonian Institution, Leo Castelli Gallery records, c. 1880–2000.

10 Installation view of Raimund Abraham, House Without Walls, *Architecture I*, 1977. Washington DC, Archives of American Art, Smithsonian Institution, Leo Castelli Gallery records, c. 1880–2000.

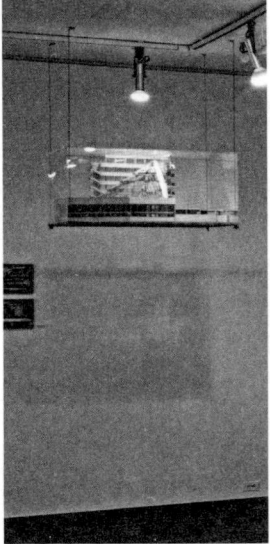

11 Installation view of James Stirling, University of Cambridge History Faculty Building, *Architecture I*, 1977. Washington DC, Archives of American Art, Smithsonian Institution, Leo Castelli Gallery records, c. 1880–2000.

away to reveal the house's subterranean elements, the plinth was also cut on a bias defined by the corners of the model's sectional cut, which continued the model's imaginary cut into the earth. At their intersection, the model and pedestal were connected, and the cut in the pedestal was painted with the same paint that covered the model. On all other sides, however, a shadow gap between the model and the platform emphasized their disconnect as the model seemed to hover above it. The model and pedestal were at one point merged together as a singular object, while at another moment disconnected. This critical relationship highlighted the possible ambiguities of using pedestals for the display of models: while being distinct elements, one edifying the other—the pedestal emphasizing the model as a form of sculpture—they could also be understood as a part of the same mutually supportive structure. This relationship was familiar in art at this time, having been initiated in sculptural practices at the beginning of the twentieth century, but prior to this had little impact in thinking about architectural models.

James Stirling's model for the Cambridge University History Building exemplified the most radical diversion from conventional techniques: it was hung from the ceiling. Four cables, each attached to a corner of the thin base upon which the model sat, held the model in a Perspex case above head height. A hole was cut into the bottom of the base through which one gazed in order to see the model from below. The model would have been, in effect, viewed as something akin to the worm's-eye axonometric drawings for which Stirling became known. While challenging standard modes of displaying models, this hanging technique also challenged visitors to experience a model in a non-normative mode, and instigated a collapse of the model and the drawing into something hybrid and indeterminate.

As with *Architecture I*, *Houses for Sale* had some models that challenged typical modes of display. There were also some drawings that pushed assumed boundaries. Arata Isozaki produced a series of lead bas-reliefs from drawings that he had made. These were hung on the wall, unframed, and gave some three-dimensionality to the drawings. Charles Moore developed a series of four shadow boxes that contained multiple layers, with each layer representing a different distance from the picture plane, something only implied in a drawing, thus pulling apart the collapse of dimension that occurs in drawings. Moore's shadow boxes had depth and were hung on the wall. Their frames were Perspex boxes, with the cutline of the landscape defining the inner edge.

In this second show, there were two significantly non-conventional displays. One was Cedric Price's model for his project, Platforms, Pavilions, Pylons, and Plants.[12] While this model was displayed on a standard plinth and was encased in Perspex, it was shown just above head height. A mirror was suspended from the ceiling directly above it and at an angle. This arrangement required a visitor to stand at an appropriate distance from the model in order to look at the mirror to see the model from above. Hence, this three-dimensional model could only be viewed as an image on a two-dimensional surface. Aided by the apparatus on which it was displayed, this model blurred the distinction between the model and a drawing of it.

The second unconventional display involved Eisenman's model for House El Even Odd, which represented perhaps the most extreme disparity with the normative display of models.[13] Two models were part of this project and both were hung on the wall. The true significance of this emerges when one realizes that the models are 'axonometric models,' a form first pioneered by Eisenman in his previous house

12 Installation view of Cedric Price, Platforms, Pavilions, Pylons, and Plants, *Houses for Sale*, 1980. Washington DC, Archives of American Art, Smithsonian Institution, Leo Castelli Gallery records, c. 1880–2000.

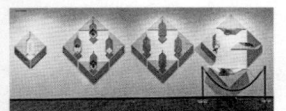

13 Installation view of Peter Eisenman, House El Even Odd, *Houses for Sale*, 1980. Washington DC, Archives of American Art, Smithsonian Institution, Leo Castelli Gallery records, c. 1880–2000.

project, House X. With all verticals tilted by 45 degrees, these models are readable only at one moment, when they appear as an axonometric drawing. By mounting these models on the wall with the two-dimensional axonometric drawings of the project, the ambiguity between model and drawing was enhanced. Further emphasizing this, the models were mounted so that the only strong indications that the left and bottom works of the last display were three-dimensional models, were the shadows they cast on the wall from the gallery's overhead lights and a rope barrier preventing visitors from getting too close.

In *Follies*, the third show, many of the pedestals were augmented in some way. The four pedestals for Diana Agrest and Mario Gandelsonas's models for The Forms of a Legend were of unfinished wood; Frank Gehry's model for The Prison was also set on an unfinished wooden pedestal; Ricardo Bofill's model for The Temple-House was likewise placed on an unfinished wooden pedestal and its roof was suspended from the ceiling at a height that allowed the interior layout of the model to be seen; Joseph Rykwert's Janus with His Head in the Clouds was positioned at an angle to the gallery space to accommodate the design of the model;[14] Andrew Batey and Mark Mack's The Tent was displayed on a pedestal made from sheet metal; and the pedestal for Graves's model for Castelli Leone had a base and registration line near the top. Eisenman and Jacquelin Robertson's Fin d'Ou T Hou S had four models in Perspex cases mounted to the wall of the gallery.[15] Rather than having them viewed straight on as with House El Even Odd, however, these were oriented to be looked down at from above. The models were not the axonometric models of the previous project and, therefore, did not create the same ambiguities between drawings and models. Thus, even though they were mounted on

14 Installation view of Joseph Ryckwert, Janus with His Head in the Clouds, *Follies*, 1983. Washington DC, Archives of American Art, Smithsonian Institution, Leo Castelli Gallery records, c. 1880–2000.

15 Installation view of Eisenman/Robertson, Fin d'ou T Hou S, *Follies*, 1983. Washington DC, Archives of American Art, Smithsonian Institution, Leo Castelli Gallery records, c. 1880–2000.

the wall, they were more readily interpretable simply as models. The reasons for this variety in the display of models is because the works were designed explicitly for exhibition. While this was also the case with *Houses for Sale*, the greater number of custom pedestals in this show is likely because architects were by this time more conversant with showing their work in galleries and the influence they could have on their presentation.

All of these means of display set the stage for the appreciation of these representations in new ways, and were not neutral. Their purpose was to draw the architectural work into the art world in a way recognizable to those who were likely to invest in the work as art: it was more familiar and more readily understood. Since architecture was a new subject for private sale galleries, there undoubtedly was anxiety that people would be unsure of its value and, therefore, it was believed prudent to endow the work with the familiarity of more traditional art sold in galleries. While this was accomplished with one consistent technique for the drawings, the models were displayed with greater variety. Drawings were framed and under glass; models were hung from ceilings and walls, viewed indirectly in mirrors, rotated with respect to the gallery's layout, raised above plinths, placed directly on plinths, and either encased in Perspex or not.

The aforementioned model for Abraham's House without Walls gives partial insight into the rationale for this variation. The architect designed the pedestal for this project—it was previously displayed in an exhibition with the same pedestal. Thus, the display of this model was not left to the gallery, but to the architect. In other ways, each display of the models discussed above was configured through some influence of the architect, whether directly or indirectly through the form of the model itself. The architectural models then, rather than architectural drawings, were the means through which the architects' desires more forcefully pushed back on gallery standards. As a result, the model and its display mechanisms emerged as a site of confrontation between the gallery's purposes and the architect's desires in a way that drawings, more easily encapsulated in normative means of display, did not.

The Reception of Architectural Models

While drawings and models were displayed differently and can be analyzed for the ways they physically incorporated or resisted the gallery's objectives, and while the displays make evident how galleries were aiming to promote the objects, whether the objects were actually perceived and valued differently outside of that immediate context is another matter altogether. To ascertain this, a number of other factors must be examined that influenced the perception of these objects, and the analysis that follows will illustrate the differences in values associated with drawings versus models in a broader context.

One factor is the reporting on and critiquing of these and other gallery shows of architectural material. Criticism was abundant in newspapers, magazines, and journals of record, and these assessments introduced new frameworks for thinking about architectural representations that cohered with gallery objectives. Headlines proliferated emphasizing architectural drawings as art: 'Architecture Drawings as Art,' 'Architectural Drawings as Art Gallery Art,' 'The Revealing Art of Architectural Drawings,' 'Architectural Drawings as Works of Art,' 'Art: The Drawings of Architecture,' 'Architectural Drawings Raised to an Art,' and 'The Art of Building on Paper.'[16] It was 'Architectural Drawings,' that

16 Ada Louise Huxtable, 'Architectural Drawings as Art,' *The New York Times*, June 12, 1977; Ada Louise Huxtable, 'Architectural Drawings as Art Gallery Art,' *The New York Times*, October 23, 1977; Ada Louise Huxtable, 'The Revealing Art of Architectural Drawings,' *The New York Times*, December 19, 1976; John Harris, 'Architectural Drawings as Works of Art,' *Apollo* (February 1990); Vivien Raynor, 'Art: The Drawings of Architecture,' *The New York Times*, September 12, 1982; Paul Goldberger, 'Architectural Drawings Raised to an Art,' *The New York Times*, December 12, 1977; Paul Goldberger, 'The Art of Building on Paper,' *The New York Times*, June 5, 1977.

17 Victoria Donahoe, 'Architectural Drawings Suddenly Sought-After Items,' *Philadelphia Inquirer*, December 25, 1977; Grace Glueck, 'Architects' Drawings Lure Collectors,' *The New York Times*, February 6, 1986.

18 Arthur Drexler, 'Engineer's Architecture: Truth and Its Consequences,' in *The Architecture of the École des Beaux-Arts*, ed. Arthur Drexler (New York: Museum of Modern Art, 1977), 15.

19 Kenneth Frampton and Silvia Kolbowski, eds., *Idea as Model* (New York: Rizzoli, 1981), 1.

20 See for instance, Henry A. Million and Vittorio Magnago Lampugnani, eds., *The Renaissance from Brunelleschi to Michelangelo: The Representation of Architecture* (New York: Rizzoli, 1994), and Henry A. Million, ed., *The Triumph of the Baroque: Architecture in Europe, 1600–1750* (New York: Rizzoli, 1999).

were the 'Suddenly Sought-After Items,' and it was 'Architects' Drawings [that] Lure Collectors.'[17] Not one review mentioned the architectural models in the exhibitions more than in passing. This was despite some theorization by influential people that architectural models had value in themselves, as 'generat[ing] their own truth' (Arthur Drexler)[18] and as having 'an artistic or conceptual existence … independent of the project they represented' (Peter Eisenman)[19]. Critics had thrust drawings, not models, to the forefront of popular discourse about architectural representation; models were almost completely ignored.

Part of what influenced critics to focus so heavily on drawings points to a second reason architectural models were overlooked: there were many contemporaneous events outside of the gallery world that focused solely on architectural drawings. Among the best known are the *Architecture of the École des Beaux-Arts* exhibition held at the Museum of Modern Art in New York (MoMA) in 1975. This exhibition brought widespread attention to architectural drawings and was a key influence on the attentiveness to drawing within Postmodern architectural practice. Additionally, between 1975 and 1989 there were at least thirty other major exhibitions at various institutions in the United States and Europe devoted entirely to architectural drawings. The only notable exhibitions during this period exclusively highlighting models were two that were held in 1976–1977 and 1980 at the Institute of Architecture and Urban Studies, New York, a smaller institution with more narrow appeal; both exhibitions were titled *Idea as Model*. It was only in the nineteen-nineties, after the markets contracted, that major exhibitions of architectural models were mounted.[20] Given the limited number of events and exhibitions centered on models, the impetus to criticize and to theorize about them as completely as drawings was not there.

Another reason drawings were more easily incorporated into the art world is connected to the general understanding that drawings, more than only those by the old masters, had value in themselves, a concept that developed in art just before this moment in architecture. The attention to drawings in architecture was partly an outgrowth and continuation of this established trend in the art world. Related to this, many of the contemporary architectural drawings on display in galleries experimented with art practices by invoking at various times Cubism, Futurism, Pop, Conceptual Art, and Constructivism, and by using techniques such as collage, pastiche, axonometry, and, importantly, color, on a variety of substrates. These were familiar aspects to art critics and the art-going public because of previous developments in drawing within art. Additionally, in 1975, just after MoMA mounted *The Architecture of the École des Beaux-Arts*, it opened a retrospective about drawing in the arts, *Drawing Now*, which drew further attention to drawing practices. Architectural drawings, hence, appealed not only to those interested in architecture, but also to those interested in art.

Since architectural drawings grew to be considered within the context of art, one might question why architectural models also ultimately would not have been construed in the same terms, as a form of sculpture. After all, the use of pedestals derives from display practices of sculpture. It may have been because, by this time, the trend within sculpture of critiquing or abandoning pedestals was well established. Thus, the display of contemporary practice on pedestals was anachronistic in a way that framing drawings was not. Models were therefore less relevant and less desirable to those interested in contemporary practices.[21]

An additional factor influencing why architectural models were not understood as sculpture relates to materiality.

21 While framing within painting had been subject of critique for some time, drawings, at least ones made with more transitory materials and on more delicate substrates, as architectural drawings were, necessitated greater protection.

Sculpture was often made from durable substances, while materials used for the architectural models in these shows were more fragile: cardboard, light wood, and thin plastics predominated. Even though all models were presentation models, they were likely not intended and constructed to have the extended lifespan associated with most investable sculpture. The employment of these more delicate materials relates to the model's use primarily as a representation of an envisioned building (none were process models) for advertisement purposes. Sculpture, in contrast, would often be an end product.

Further insight as to why architectural models were not interpreted as sculpture may have to do with the seeming ease of comprehending them. Whereas architectural drawings require knowledge and work to understand, models that stand in for buildings and fail to explore their capacities to reveal other facets of architecture, do not. At a time when conceptual art was favored, that is, an artform esteemed for the intellectual work driving its creation and required to appreciate it, the ease of reading models as derivative representations curtailed their acceptance as a form of art.[22]

A further factor in the neglect of models relates to debates that permeated within architecture concerning the general understanding about the relationship between Postmodern practice, which the representations in these shows demonstrated, and Modern architectural practice. Historian and critic Richard Pommer hinted at this in a review of a museological exhibition of architectural drawings, *Drawing Towards a More Modern Architecture*. Pommer stated, 'The recent exhibitions cast much light, but in unexpected directions, on the current debate in architectural circles over the significance of drawings versus models in the move away from conventional modern architecture.'[23]

The refrain, still commonplace today, was that Modernism

---

[22] A particular irony must be noted here, as in some instances, the perceived accessibility of architectural drawings was an important factor in them being collected. This was the case, for instance, with the corporate Gilman Collection of Architectural Drawings, which was assembled to be more accessible to employees than the conceptual and minimal art the Gilman Paper Company had previously collected.

[23] Richard Pommer, 'Architecture: Structures for the Imagination,' *Art in America* (March-April 1978), 79.

focused on models, so Postmodernism, in reaction, focused on drawings. Even as Pommer was critical of this generalization, he recognized that general discourse at this time centered on drawings because of the desired break with perceived modes of modern production.

While critics essentially ignored models for all these reasons, collectors also largely disregarded them. No major private collections of architectural models were assembled during this time, while collections of drawings proliferated. Among the most notable was the Gilman Collection of Architectural Drawings—a collection for the Gilman Paper Company that today forms the bulk of MoMA's drawing material produced in this period. Additionally, the major repositories of architectural materials of this period, such as the Canadian Center for Architecture, and the Deutsches Architekturmuseum, all acquired drawings through commercial galleries.

Only collectors already involved in architecture, and thus with a vested interest in acquiring evidence of architects' practices, acquired models. These included the Deutsches Architekturmuseum, which collected singular models and even had a number made for their collection; the Canadian Centre for Architecture, which accumulated them primarily as parts of archives; and the Nederlands Architectuurinstituut, which acquired mainly through donation. This collecting by institutes, however, was not motivated by a perceptual shift driven by the same factors—and did not give rise to a similar shift in conceptualization—that the galleries had induced with drawings.

One reason for this, beyond the critical attention given to drawing, is practicality. It is far easier, and cheaper, for both individuals and institutions to collect works that are typically smaller, less cumbersome, and more easily conserved.

However, this should not be considered in isolation, as collections of sculpture and of minimalist and conceptual art had already been established, and those works were often much larger than any of the architectural models for sale. It is that both the critical response and the collecting practices of individuals, companies, and institutions, so necessary to frame and drive perception during this moment, did not accompany the display of models. So, while in some instances models became understood as valuable objects within architecture, they resisted autonomy outside of the discipline and never fully emerged as a form of aesthetic art in their own right.

That architectural models, made by architects, resisted incorporation into the discipline of art is further emphasized by a number of events outside the gallery world that brought architects and artists together in attempts to bridge the perceived gap between architecture and art. Among these were *Architectural Analogues*, which was held at the downtown branch of the Whitney Museum in 1978, *Collaborations: Artists & Architects*, which held at the Architectural League of New York in 1981, and *Art + Architecture*, a series of exhibitions and conferences that was held throughout the nineteen-eighties at the Institute of Contemporary Arts in London.

In these events and exhibitions, many of the artists chosen were well known for producing architectonic works and sculptures at both small (model) and habitable scales. Unlike architectural models, however, these did not have difficulty being perceived as art. Additionally, many of those who participated were on the rosters of the galleries that showed architecture. So, while these events brought these two disciplines closer than they perhaps would have been otherwise, at the same time they reaffirmed and made visible the fissure between architecture and art by recognizing a distinct realm to which each participant and their contributions belonged.

Conclusions

Why architectural models resisted reconceptualization as art, and why they did not attain the same values as drawings, is explained by this multitude of factors: the social and economic circumstances of the art world, which includes the contexts in which works were shown; how work was displayed; how work was critiqued; whether and how work was collected; and how models related to cognate practices within art. While galleries attempted to align both forms of representations, it was drawings that emerged as most consequential. Models were secondary. However, as noted above, models were not completely disregarded. Though they never attained value as artworks, and though they were never collected in as great a number or as systematically, models were still of interest to architectural repositories and had historical value within the discipline as evidence of past practices. It is because of this recondite situation that architectural models in the postmodern era—and this is part of their importance— force a nuanced consideration of how architectural representations, within the context of art markets, attained particular values at this time. That models resisted this transformation in ways that drawings did not, and were not inscribed with the same values, points to conditions that limit the conceptual shifts that art markets provoke.

Shifting Values of Architectural Heritage at Open-Air Museums

View of Main Street precinct at Sovereign Hill. Photo: Maksym Kozlenko, 2012. commons.wikimedia.org/wiki/File:Sovereign_Hill_-_Main_Street_S_from_near_Normanby_-_2012-04-08.jpg.

Shifting Values of Architectural Heritage at Open-Air Museums

Amy Clarke

Open-air museums are commonplace in many parts of the world, with hundreds dotting the landscapes of Europe and North America, and a smaller but not insignificant assortment throughout Asia and Oceania. These are places in which a selection of buildings, often with an overarching theme, are curated in a landscaped environment and then exhibited to the visiting public. While this may seem a relatively niche format, there is a surprising degree of variety among open-air museums. They can be understood as both museum collections and heritage sites, which reveals the difficulty in categorizing them in museological terms, as well as in differing approaches to conservation and display. Some are based on an original group of in-situ structures in an historic landscape and may have added replicas or reconstructions of other buildings and infrastructure to the site in order to create a fuller 'picture.' Others comprise relocated buildings and replicas, brought together in a staged outdoor environment to form a collection that illustrates a particular theme, while others still are complete reconstructions of an earlier environment, sometimes based on remnant archaeological or documentary evidence. Villages, forts, gold mining towns, and rural settlements are common forms of open-air museums, as is the organization of the museum around buildings and structures of a specific time period, or those associated with a particular culture. The underlying purposes of open-air museums vary too, though in recent decades they have generally had conservation, education (and/or research), or entertainment—or some combination of these—as their focus. All of these factors must be considered when attempting, as this chapter does, to make generalized observations about the evolving relationship between open-air museums and architectural heritage, particularly with regards to the value of architecture itself to open-air museum operations. Despite the great variety of open-air museums, there are some obvious common issues and trends that warrant greater reflection, and all revolve to some extent around the growing desire of these museums to attract visitors.

In a notable departure from the architectural focus of early open-air museums, increasing concern for the visitor experience has forced a shift in the ways such institutions manage and showcase their architectural collections, to the point that many now provide minimal information on the structures themselves (either on site, or in published form). What appears to draw people—and certainly what many such institutions are now heavily promoting—is 'edutainment'. Visitors come seeking opportunities to 'travel back in time'; to suspend reality and experience life as it was in a different era or place. Though open-air museums still rely on collections of architectural forms to create the setting and underlying narrative or theme for their operation, these structures are, in many cases, relegated to the status of a stage. This does not necessarily mean that architectural value is absent or that architectural research has ceased, but that these elements now jostle for recognition alongside manifold other museum services, institutional agendas, and visitor expectations. The examples discussed here—Colonial Williamsburg (Virginia, U.S.), Fortress Louisbourg (Nova Scotia, Canada), and Sovereign Hill (Victoria, Australia)—illustrate the competing values attributed to architectural heritage in this setting, and how the goals of conservation, education and entertainment intersect in a particular way that challenges how architectural heritage is defined and valued.

Evolving Role of Architecture at Open-Air Museums

Some of the earliest examples of open-air museums emerged out of Scandinavia and northwest Europe in the late nineteenth and early twentieth centuries, and these were primarily driven by a desire to preserve regional vernacular architectural forms in the face of rapid industrialization. Places such as Skansen in Sweden (1891), the Norwegian Folk Museum in Oslo (1902), and the Holland Open Air Museum in Arnhem (1912)—were intended to serve as repositories for vernacular building forms. Indeed, Anderson notes that these early museums were founded with an ambition to collect and preserve architecture, and showed little concern for public education or entertainment.[1] Often instigated by wealthy men with antiquarian instincts, such museums took several years to develop, as specific architectural specimens took time to be found, purchased, and relocated to the museum site. Once settled in their new environment, necessary repairs would be undertaken, and an emphasis—at least at places with a regional vernacular focus, like Skansen—was placed on using traditional materials and techniques. In taking such an approach, pre-industrial skill sets were preserved and

[1] Jay Anderson, 'Living History: Simulating Everyday Life in Living Museums,' *American Quarterly* 34, no. 3 (1982), 292.

regional architectural forms and materials were promoted; indeed, Anderson and Gailey have argued that one of the primary goals of early open-air museums was the valuing and championing of folk identities.[2] Architecture played a central role, as it provided overt visual signifiers of the regional cultures being promoted, and as such, it is not surprising that it was a prominent focus of the collector-curators of this era.

By the late nineteen-fifties, however, the focus of open-air museums shifted towards the research and representation of everyday lives. Acquiring a particular type of structure—a doctor's surgery, a bank, a butcher's shop or a haberdashery, for example—was less to do with valuing the architectural form from a material or design perspective, and more with having the appropriate setting in which to demonstrate a specific component of that society's operation. The value of the buildings as architecture was diminished. In this period, archaeologists, ethnographers, and historians utilized open-air museum environments for experimentation, particularly for filling gaps in knowledge that required lived experience in order to be rediscovered or revived.[3] Conservation was still a priority, but had progressed into research and education and what the buildings could reveal about the past more generally. Open-air museums were places where twentieth-century researchers and visitors could get a little closer to understanding and perhaps empathizing with the daily realities of those who had come before them. The educational capabilities of open-air museums continue to be promoted in this way in the twenty-first century, though some institutions emphasize this far more than others.

Today, open-air museums are sometimes referred to as 'living history' museums, reflecting the expectation of visitors for some degree of 'activation' or 'interpretation' of history. These are the terms used by open-air museums to describe

[2] Ibid.; Alan Gailey, 'Domesticating the Past: The Development of Open-Air Museums,' *Folk Life* 38 (1999–2000), 10.

[3] Anderson, 'Living History,' 291.

[4] Edward N. Kaufman, 'The Architectural Museum from World's Fair to Restoration Village,' *Assemblage* no. 9 (1989), 28; Gailey, 'Domesticating the Past,' 11.

costumed tours and demonstrations, the presence of working machinery or historic breeds of animals, and opportunities for visitors to try activities for themselves. Visitors to these institutions are more likely to witness costumed staff re-enacting an historical event or activity, than to have in-depth conversations with guides about construction techniques and materials.[4] Architecture continues to be present, but in many cases, it now serves as a backdrop for a performance that is either watched by or participated in by visitors.

In order to explore the changing place of architecture in open-air museums in greater detail, it is helpful at this point to turn to the three aforementioned examples: Colonial Williamsburg, Fortress Louisbourg, and Sovereign Hill. These are generally well-regarded examples within the open-air museum field, and are significant tourist attractions in their own right. Their origin stories and modes of construction, particularly relating to architecture, serve as points of contrast. As this discussion will demonstrate, however, despite their different institutional histories, the touristic agendas of the three museums have grown increasingly prominent in recent decades. This is perhaps attributable to the era of mass-tourism, which blossomed from the late nineteen-fifties across the Western world. Increasing numbers of middle- and working-class travelers have sought out destination-based entertainment that offers something distinct. Theme parks, package holidays, and family-friendly infrastructure and services have risen to prominence, forcing all other public-facing attractions—open-air museums included—to adapt in order to remain financially viable. Moreover, by the postwar period, open-air museums had ceased to be the domain of wealthy benefactors, and had transitioned towards not-for-profit models that relied upon visitor admission charges, on-site businesses (e.g. retail, hospitality, small-scale manufacturing), and the occasional government grant or charitable donation. As the three examples will highlight, by the mid twentieth century, architecture alone was unlikely to attract significant numbers of paying customers. People expected an 'experience'—something that would entertain, hold their attention, evoke nostalgia or bestow a sense of personal improvement—when they parted with their money. While there is still architectural value to be gained at such institutions, the details that are of interest to architectural/heritage professionals and enthusiasts have been increasingly minimized in favor of socio-cultural narratives, costumed performances, and seasonal programs pitched at families.

Colonial Williamsburg

Colonial Williamsburg's restored eighteenth-century townsite sits across 175 acres (seventy ha) (with an additional 3,000-acre (1200 ha) green belt), and comprises over 400 restored or reconstructed buildings, of which around fifty are open to the public.[5] The Colonial Williamsburg Foundation uses the remainder of the buildings as workspaces and private accommodation, strictly maintaining their historic appearance so as to enhance the surrounding streetscape, whilst giving the site the feeling of being 'alive' throughout the year.[6] Attracting approximately 1.7 million guests annually (with around 700,000 purchasing general admission tickets), Colonial Williamsburg is undoubtedly one of the best-known open-air museums globally.[7] Its fame stems from its historical connections to significant figures and moments in eighteenth-century American history: it was the capital of Virginia during the time of George Washington and Thomas Jefferson,

[5] A. S. Travis, *Planning for Tourism, Leisure and Sustainability: International Case Studies* (Wallingford, Oxfordshire: CABI, 2011), 214; Taylor Stoermer et al., eds., *Colonial Williamsburg: The Official Guide* (Williamsburg: Colonial Williamsburg Foundation, 2014), 130–176; Mary Miley Theobald, *Colonial Williamsburg: The First Seventy-Five Years* (Williamsburg: Colonial Williamsburg Foundation, 2001), 41.

[6] Stoermer et al., *Colonial Williamsburg: The Official Guide*, 130–176.

[7] Colonial Williamsburg Foundation, *Annual Report 2015* (Williamsburg: Colonial Williamsburg Foundation, 2015), 13; *Annual Report 2011* (Williamsburg: Colonial Williamsburg Foundation, 2011), n.p.

8 The reconstructed Capitol building at Colonial Williamsburg. Photo: author, 2018.

The reconstructed Governor's Palace at Colonial Williamsburg. Photo: author, 2018.

9 Anders Greenspan, *Creating Colonial Williamsburg* (Washington, D.C.: Smithsonian Institution, 2009), 23; Theobald, *Colonial Williamsburg: The First Seventy-Five Years*, 19.

10 Ivor Noel Hume, 'Resurrection and Deification at Colonial Williamsburg,' in *The Constructed Past: Experimental Archaeology, Education and the Public*, ed. Peter G. Stone and Philippe G. Planel (London: Routledge, 1999), 93; Michael Wallace, 'Visiting the Past: History Museums in the United States,' in *A Living History Reader: Volume One*, ed. Jay Anderson (Nashville: American Association for State and Local History, 1991), 190.

11 James S. Miller, 'Mapping the Boosterist Imaginary: Colonial Williamsburg, Historical Tourism, and the Construction of Managerial Memory,' *The Public Historian* 28, no. 4 (2006), 58; *Colonial Williamsburg, the First Twenty-Five Years; a Report by the President as of December 31, 1951* (Williamsburg: Colonial Williamsburg, 1952), 11.

and the setting for numerous political events that contributed to the American Revolution (1765–1783) and the United States' Declaration of Independence (1776).

Having lost much of its prestige following the loss of the status of Virginia state capital to Richmond in 1779, Williamsburg slept through the nineteenth and early twentieth centuries with minimal disruption to its built environment. When the amateur historian and local Minister, William A. R. Goodwin, began targeting wealthy benefactors in the mid nineteen-twenties to fund the town's restoration, there were substantial eighteenth-century architectural remains suitable for retention. Nevertheless, key structures including the Capitol, the Governor's Palace, and Raleigh's Tavern had been lost to the ravages of time, fire, and unsympathetic landlords. A major project of archaeological excavation, architectural research, and reconstruction was deemed necessary in order to return the town to the height of its eighteenth-century glory.[8] As part of this scheme, numerous post-eighteenth-century structures were deemed anachronous, and as a result, around 400 were demolished; many residents were moved out of the historic center altogether.[9] Prior to his involvement in the Colonial Williamsburg project, John D. Rockefeller Jr. had shown an interest in architectural conservation, having donated to projects at Versailles, Reims, and Fontainebleau in France as well as offering US$10 million for the reconstruction of the Egyptian Museum in Cairo in the early nineteen-twenties.[10] He proved to be a willing partner (with very deep pockets) for Goodwin in the Williamsburg project. Beginning with an initial donation of US$3 million in 1926, it is estimated that he donated over US$50 million to the restoration by the early nineteen-fifties; his extended family have remained closely involved—both financially and in a managerial sense—since his death in 1960.[11]

Since 1937, Colonial Williamsburg has run a merchandising enterprise, which gives manufacturers the opportunity to license and sell designs under the 'WILLIAMSBURG' label. Scholars such as Sten Rentzhog and Charles Alan Watkins have suggested that this commoditization of the Colonial Williamsburg aesthetic was partially responsible for the 'Colonial Revival' trend in architectural and interior design from the late nineteen-thirties onward.[12] This influence showed no sign of dissipating in the postwar era: by the late nineteen-sixties Colonial Williamsburg had grown into an extraordinarily popular tourist destination, complete with a range of accommodation, golf courses, conference facilities and retail outlets in addition to the 'restored' historic town. Despite this commercialization—which continues unabated in the twenty-first century—Colonial Williamsburg has operated as a charitable enterprise since its foundation, and profits have always been invested back into site operations. Financial and Annual Reports from the past twenty-five years reveal the considerable costs involved in maintaining the site's numerous buildings, artefact collections, exhibition spaces, historic trades, interpretative/education programs, and overarching infrastructure. In 1996 the Foundation posted an annual financial loss of over US$6 million, and the situation worsened after September 11, 2001: in 2002 the Foundation reported a deficit of US$35.5 million.[13] By 2018, the balance sheet had improved somewhat, though an operating deficit of US$2 million was still recorded.[14] Moreover, very few 'new' historic buildings have been added to Colonial Williamsburg in recent decades; exceptions include the Public Hospital (opened in 1985), and R. Charlton's Coffeehouse (completed in 2009).[15] Existing structures are reinterpreted semi-regularly, however, to provide new trade or retail spaces that will appeal to customers. A much stronger emphasis on

[12] Sten Rentzhog, *Open Air Museums: The History and Future of a Visionary Idea*, trans. Skans Victoria Airey (Carlssons: Jamtli Forlag, 2007), 146–147; Charles Alan Watkins, 'The Tea Table's Tale: Authenticity and Colonial Williamsburg's Early Furniture Reproduction Program,' *Journal of Decorative Arts, Design History, and Material Culture* 21, no. 2 (2014).

[13] Cary Carson, 'Colonial Williamsburg and the Practice of Interpretive Planning in American History Museums,' *The Public Historian* 20, no. 3 (1998), 43; Colonial Williamsburg Foundation, *Annual Report 2002* (Williamsburg: Colonial Williamsburg Foundation, 2002), n.p.

[14] Colonial Williamsburg Foundation, *Annual Report 2018* (Williamsburg: Colonial Williamsburg Foundation, 2018), 20.

[15] Theobald, *Colonial Williamsburg: The First Seventy-Five Years*, 61–62; Colonial Williamsburg Foundation, *Annual Report 2016* (Williamsburg: Colonial Williamsburg Foundation, 2016), 11; *Annual Report 2009* (Williamsburg: Colonial Williamsburg Foundation, 2009).

entertainment—including themed tours and hands-on activities, seasonal festivities, and evening events—has been hailed as the solution to Colonial Williamsburg's financial challenges.[16] It would seem architecture is presently understood by the Foundation as something to be maintained in the background as part of the site's aesthetics, which in turn helps visitors to have a 'thought-provoking, moving, and entertaining' experience that could also be 'relaxing, even rejuvenating.'[17] This is in contrast to the way the open-air museum was described by an early staff-member, who in 1942 regarded Colonial Williamsburg as 'an educational and architectural adventure of the first magnitude.'[18]

Fortress Louisbourg

Like Colonial Williamsburg, the Fortress of Louisbourg open-air museum (on the island of Cape Breton in Nova Scotia, Canada), was built upon its original site. One of the key differences in Louisbourg's case, however, was that there were no surviving structures from the eighteenth-century fortress when the reconstruction project began in the nineteen-sixties.[19] Moreover, the historical significance of Louisbourg is rather more subtle, in that it tells a peripheral part of Canada's story. From 1713 it was an impressive French fortified settlement situated at a convenient point on the trade and fishing routes of North America's north Atlantic coast; after a siege in 1758 it fell to British forces and was abandoned.[20] It was not associated with any particular national heroes, but was recognized by Canadian authorities in the early twentieth century as an important national heritage site due to its links to Canada's French and British colonial histories.[21] Fortress Louisbourg's archaeological excavation and reconstruction

---

[16] Colonial Williamsburg Foundation, *Annual Report 2018*, 3–4; *Annual Report 2016*, 3–5.

[17] Colonial Williamsburg Foundation, *Annual Report 2015*, 7.

[18] Alfred C. Bossom, 'How Americans Handle a Restoration,' *Journal of the Royal Society of Arts* 90, no. 4621 (1942), 634–644.

[19] A. J. B. Johnston, *Louisbourg: Past, Present, Future* (Halifax, NS: Nimbus, 2013), 92–93, 97.

[20] Bruce W. Fry, 'Reaching out to the Bureaucracy and Beyond: Archaeology at Louisbourg and Parks Canada,' in *Past Meets Present*, ed. John H. Jameson Jr. and S. Baugher (New York: Springer, 2007), 19.

[21] Erna L. Macleod, 'Decolonizing Interpretation at the Fortress of Louisbourg National Historic Site,' in *Canadian Cultural Poesis: Essays on Canadian Culture*, ed. Garry Sherbert, Annie Gerin, and Sheila Petty (Wilfrid Laurier University: Wilfrid Laurier UP, 2006), 361–362.

was funded by the Federal Canadian Government from 1961 as part of a regional scheme intended to provide jobs for recently unemployed laborers from the failing Cape Breton mines.[22] In addition, converting a site with a strong French identity into a 'national' heritage tourist attraction made sense to politicians in this period, as French Canadian nationalists continued to question their place in the Federation. Fortress Louisbourg was a reminder that the French influence spread beyond Quebec, and moreover, that the French had played a fundamental role in the creation of modern Canada.[23] The architecture and interior décor of the fortress buildings was crucial to achieving this goal, as it would serve as a visual representation of the 'French' identity of the site.

The Government's initial goal of reconstructing the entire fortress town—covering sixty-five acres (twenty-six ha)—was quickly revised when the costs, time, and labor involved became clear. The modified plan marked out a partial reconstruction (approximately one-third of the original site), with the remainder being conserved as a nationally significant archaeological landscape.[24] Given the lack of physical remnants with which to begin, the Fortress Louisbourg team deployed a rapid-fire approach of excavation that was undertaken almost simultaneously with reconstruction; Taylor and Fry recall how engineers and local laborers waited impatiently on site as the archaeologists carried out hurried surveys.[25] This was a cause of frustration for many of the archaeologists and historians involved, as the pace of building—itself dictated by the expectations of the Federal Government for completion of the project for the 1967 Bicentennial celebrations—forced hasty decisions. The King's Bastion,[26] the Dauphin demi-bastion[27] and Block One were the first parts of the site to be rebuilt.[28] As Fry notes, however, within only a short time of their completion, further research revealed the

22 Bruce W. Fry, 'Designing the Past at Fortress Louisbourg,' in *The Reconstructed Past*, ed. John H. Jameson Jr. (Lanham: Altamira, 2004), 199; Carol Corbin, 'Symbols of Separation: The Town of Louisbourg and the Fortress of Louisbourg,' *Environments* 24, no. 2 (1996), n.p.

23 Macleod, 'Decolonizing Interpretation at the Fortress of Louisbourg National Historic Site,' 361-362; Corbin, 'Symbols of Separation,' n.p.

24 Fry, 'Reaching out to the Bureaucracy and Beyond: Archaeology at Louisbourg and Parks Canada,' 20; 'Designing the Past at Fortress Louisbourg,' 203-204.

25 Fry, 'Designing the Past at Fortress Louisbourg,' 201-203; C. J. Taylor, *Negotiating the Past: The Making of Canada's National Historic Parks and Sites* (Montreal: McGill-Queen's UP, 1990), 177-178.

26 The reconstructed King's Bastion at Fortress Louisbourg. Photo: author, 2012.

27 The reconstructed Dauphin demi-bastion at Fortress Louisbourg. Photo: author, 2012.

28 Fry, 'Designing the Past at Fortress Louisbourg,' 203-204.

King's Bastion rampart walls had been built too high, and the belt course that separated the ramparts from the parapet was too thick; construction teams were forced to undertake remedial work whilst other structures remained half-finished.[29] Despite this external pressure, the official opening of the Fortress in 1969—two years later than hoped—was a rather subdued affair, as only the King's Bastion (including its barracks, chapel, and governor's quarters) had been completed. It was not until 1980 that all reconstruction from the nineteen-sixties program was concluded.[30] Over sixty structures had been rebuilt, though many were finished to the exterior only in order to give a more complete sense of the streetscape.[31] This in itself reveals a shift in the underlying agenda of the project: the superficial appearance of building facades was deemed more valuable or important to visitors than the architectural and historic elements that might have been captured with the completion of a smaller number of buildings in greater detail, inside and out.

No further buildings were planned from this point, as by the late nineteen-seventies the Federal Government had dramatically reduced its expenditure on such projects.[32] Instead, the museum staff found they had an opportunity to focus on closer research of their existing findings, which totaled over five million artefacts and tens of thousands of documents.[33] This certainly helped to improve the accuracy with which the reconstructed buildings were displayed (including period-appropriate fabrics, furnishings, and paint colors).[34] But it also meant that the overall emphasis shifted from architecture and engineering to socio-cultural history: who had lived in the buildings, what their lives had been like, and how best to portray these narratives to visitors. This trend gained hold at Louisbourg at the same time that it began to influence the interpretative and research programs at many other North

---

29 Fry, 'Designing the Past at Fortress Louisbourg,' 205.

30 Corbin, 'Symbols of Separation,' n.p.; Fry, 'Designing the Past at Fortress Louisbourg,' 199–200.

31 Terry MacLean, *Louisbourg Heritage: From Ruins to Reconstruction* (Sydney, NS: University College of Cape Breton Press, 1995), 108; Jay Anderson, *Time Machines: The World of Living History* (Nashville: American Association for State and Local History, 1984), 62.

32 Fry, 'Reaching out to the Bureaucracy and Beyond,' 29–30.

33 Ibid.; John Fortier, 'Louisbourg: Managing a Moment in Time,' in *A Living History Reader: Volume One*, ed. Jay Anderson (Nashville: American Association for State and Local History, 1991), 39.

34 Fry, 'Designing the Past at Fortress Louisbourg,' 205–206.

American open-air museums. Thus, while the Canadian Government and the Fortress's management had already decided that there would be no additional phases of large-scale architectural reconstruction, it was convenient that this decision aligned with the new era of 'edutainment'-driven heritage site management. This was an approach that could be achieved with less funding, and would arguably attract higher numbers of tourists; and indeed, this remains the priority for Fortress Louisbourg in the present day. The approximately 75,000 visitors who pay admission each year have become a vital component of the site's financial viability in the medium and long term.[35] The 2011 Parks Canada heritage management plan for the Fortress—which is a nationally protected site under Federal jurisdiction—stressed the centrality of 'visitor experience' and in particular the ambition to 'stimulate all of the senses' and appeal to teens and young adults.[36] As at Colonial Williamsburg, historic architecture contributes greatly to the overall image of Fortress Louisbourg as a cultural heritage attraction, but it is clear that management have come to believe that far more is needed to 'sell' the site to the public.

[35] MacKellar Cunningham & Associates Ltd., *Louisbourg 300: Economic Analysis & Return on Investment (ROI)* (Louisbourg: Parks Canada, 2014), 3.

[36] Parks Canada, *Fortress of Louisbourg National Historic Site of Canada: Management Plan 2011* (Louisbourg: Parks Canada, 2011), 18–19.

Sovereign Hill

The final example to be discussed comes from more humble origins, in the sense that it did not have a wealthy benefactor or a federal government willing to invest millions of dollars in its creation. Sovereign Hill, in Ballarat (Victoria, Australia), was the initiative of a group of local historical enthusiasts and Apex Club members in 1966–1967, who believed the creation of a gold-rush-themed historical park would greatly benefit the region.[37] From the outset their goal was to attract tourists

[37] Mary Akers, *Your Introduction to Sovereign Hill: Background Information on Buildings and Equipment at the Sovereign Hill Goldmining Township*, 2nd revised ed. (Ballarat: Ballarat Historical Park Association, 1981), 84.

38 Sovereign Hill Museums Association, *The Traveller's Guide to Sovereign Hill* (Ballarat: Sovereign Hill Museums Association, 1999), 10; Nina Valentine, *First Act: Sovereign Hill, and How It All Began* (Ballarat: Ballarat Historical Park Association, 1980), 20.

39 Valentine, *First Act*, 8.

40 View of Main Street precinct at Sovereign Hill. Photo: Maksym Kozlenko, 2012. commons.wikimedia.org/wiki/File:Sovereign_Hill_-_Main_Street_S_from_near_Normanby_-_2012-04-08.jpg.

41 Peter Cuffley, *A Golden Vision: The Story of Sovereign Hill* (Ballarat: Sovereign Hill Museums Association, 2006), 87.

42 Valentine, *First Act*, 7.

to Ballarat by offering a 'time travel' experience, one that would give people an opportunity to learn more about life in an eighteen-fifties mining town, and offer a sense of the energy that surged through Australian settler societies upon the discovery of gold. Unlike Colonial Williamsburg and Fortress Louisbourg, the Sovereign Hill open-air museum was not based around extant remains as such. A thirty-six-acre site was chosen in the area of historic nineteenth-century mines including those of Normanby North, Llanberris No. 2 and Speedwell Quartz Mining Company, but there was no usable architecture in the vicinity, nor does there appear to have been any archaeological surveys carried out as part of the reconstruction.[38]

Early records from the Ballarat Historical Park Association (later renamed Sovereign Hill Museums Association) reveal a shopping list of period buildings intended for construction on the site. Nina Valentine, an original member of the Interiors Committee for the museum, recalls one meeting in the late nineteen-sixties at which over thirty different commercial and industrial/manufacturing buildings were planned for the Main Street precinct alone.[39, 40] These were to be based upon buildings that were known to have existed in the early days of Ballarat's history, or—in the absence of sufficient visual or documentary evidence relating to a specific structure—to instead be developed as representations of the architectural styles and forms that would have been used in the area at that time.[41] A local architect, Ewan Jones, was brought in to the Sovereign Hill project early on, and most of the structures built on site were the products of his practice.[42] Occasionally, the Sovereign Hill team would be offered an existing building for relocation to their site. An early-nineteenth-century slab hut from nearby Raglan and a mid-nineteenth-century cottage from Greendale were donated in

1969–1970, for example, and were reinterpreted as a pre-1851 pioneer's hut and a wealthy settler's cottage, named 'Bright View.'[43] Curatorial staff acquired period-appropriate materials, fittings, and fixtures from historic buildings scheduled for demolition, and would then integrate these components into the reconstructions at the museum. Sovereign Hill's Apothecaries' Hall utilized cedar fittings from Mowatt's Pharmacy of Port Melbourne, constructed in 1853 and demolished c. 1970, while the museum's United States Hotel incorporated bar fittings taken from the ruinous nineteenth-century Cherry Tree Hotel near Bendigo.[44]

Five years after its official opening in 1970, Sovereign Hill had around thirty-five structural exhibits on site; this has since increased to more than sixty-five, with several of the early reconstructions being redesigned and sometimes moved to a different location within the museum.[45] Moreover, the building program has never completely stopped. Recent examples include a Wesleyan Day School added in 2018; St Alipius Diggings School, and Eyres Brothers & Newman Hardware and Ironmongers, opened in 2007; and in the mid-two-thousands, a major redesign and expansion of the museum's Chinese Camp.[46] Importantly, when decisions have been made at Sovereign Hill regarding which buildings to add, the senior staff appear to have been influenced by visitor experience as the first priority, with available records and existing research being a secondary factor.

Over the past twenty years, numerous nineteenth-century trades and retail outlets have been added to those already on site, and the introduction of more stimulating methods of engaging with the mining landscape—which now includes an artificial creek for gold-panning, an underground network of tunnels and shafts, and a wide range of working machinery—has been a focus since the mid-two-thousands.[47] Thus,

[43] Michael Evans, 'Historical Interpretation at Sovereign Hill,' *Australian Historical Studies* 24, no. 96 (1991), 143; Sovereign Hill Museums Association, *The Traveller's Guide to Sovereign Hill*, 46; Barbara Glover, *Sovereign Hill: Goldmining Township, Ballarat* (Moorabbin: Scancolor, 1985), n.p.

[44] Cuffley, *A Golden Vision*, 92, 96.

[45] Austin McCallum, *Sovereign Hill, Ballarat, Australia: Walk into Living History: Tour Guide*, rev. ed. (Ballarat: Ballarat Historical Park Association, 1975).

[46] Sovereign Hill, *Annual Report 2017-18* (Ballarat: Sovereign Hill, 2018), 23; *Annual Report 2006-07* (Ballarat: Sovereign Hill, 2007), 12.

[47] Sovereign Hill, *Annual Report 2007-08* (Ballarat: Sovereign Hill, 2008), 27; *Annual Report 2013-14* (Ballarat: Sovereign Hill, 2014), 26.

while Sovereign Hill remains more active in its additions of architectural reconstructions when compared with Colonial Williamsburg and Fortress Louisbourg, these additions are not being made for the sake of architectural conservation, but instead for the opportunity these structures bring to generate further experiential value as part of a tourist attraction. This is not surprising, as Sovereign Hill relies entirely on visitors—of which the museum achieved a record 512,751 in the 2014–2015 financial year—to remain financially viable.[48] The tourist dollar extends beyond admission charges: these are customers who will purchase products from the numerous on-site historic trades and businesses, patronize the museum's working bakeries and restaurants, and stay in the on-site accommodation (designed to look, at least from the exterior, like mid-nineteenth century barracks and cottages). This had been a remarkably successful approach for Sovereign Hill until 2018–2019, when it recorded its first-ever operating loss of AUD$128,640 (which it attributed to a decrease in operating activity revenue and the writing down of an asset valuation).[49] It remains to be seen whether this loss will have an impact on the museum's medium- and long-term development agendas, and whether further architectural additions will be halted in favor of projects that might generate additional income.

Historical Architecture as a Touristic Experience

Despite the diversity of themes, funding models, and operating motivations of the hundreds of open-air museums that extend around the globe today, it is pertinent to remember that they share a common ancestor: the vernacular architectural museums of north-west Europe of the late nineteenth

[48] Sovereign Hill, *Annual Report 2014–15* (Ballarat: Sovereign Hill, 2015), 5.

[49] Sovereign Hill, *Annual Report 2018–2019 (Including Financial Report)* (Ballarat: Sovereign Hill, 2019), 2.

century. Arguably, these pioneering open-air museums were themselves inspired by the displays of architecture at world's fairs and expositions, as historians such as Gailey and Kaufman have noted.[50] At least in this initial stage, architecture was being collected and conserved *because* it was valued as architecture: specific combinations of style, form, material, construction method, and so on. These were structures that were perceived not only as representing innovations in design and technology over time, but also as vital material evidence of regional identities that were becoming increasingly homogenized in the industrial era. Less than a hundred years after the first open-air museums opened their gates, however, the prevailing mood had shifted. Certainly, architecture is still a fundamental part of these sites: it provides the aesthetics that sets a museum apart from the outside world, assists in the creation of a 'time travel' experience, and gives a setting for artefacts and historic demonstrations. But is architecture—or to be even more precise, the conservation of historic architecture—the main event? For the majority of open-air museums today, the answer to this question is simple: no, nor has it been for some time. This does not mean that architectural heritage value and tourism are mutually exclusive, but that in the case of many open-air museums such as those described here, the need to engage in exploratory architectural conservation and reproduction has ceased to be driven by research for its own sake, and has instead been supplanted by the aesthetic and performative values of architectural heritage for (non-expert) visitors. Perhaps, as Emma Waterton has recently observed of Sovereign Hill, this trend reveals yet another type of value for open-air museums, whereby their role as indicators of shifting cultural values and tastes could be more closely explored for the benefit of the wider heritage field.[51]

50 Kaufman, 'The Architectural Museum,' 22–24; Gailey, 'Domesticating the Past,' 8.

51 Emma Waterton, 'Curating Affect: Exploring the Historical Geography-Heritage Studies Nexus at Sovereign Hill,' *Australian Geographer* 49, no. 1 (2018), 219–235.

52 A rare example of an interpretive information sign on display at Colonial Williamsburg. It is painted the same color as the building's exterior, and affixed in a position off to one side of the front entrance so as to avoid distracting 'time traveling' visitors. Photo: author, 2018.

53 Stoermer et al., *Colonial Williamsburg: The Official Guide*.

When we reflect upon the trajectories of the three case studies—Colonial Williamsburg, Fortress Louisbourg, and Sovereign Hill—it is clear that the pressures of competing on the open market have played a central role in the increasing prioritization of 'visitor experience'. While it is true that these museums were not established with as strict a focus on architectural conservation as Skansen, for example, all three *were* begun with ambitious rebuilding and restoration programs that drew from (and contributed to) the expertise of architects, archaeologists, and historians. Despite this early work, twenty-first-century visitors to the museums will find it difficult to locate detailed architectural histories or conservation reports for individual buildings. At face value, this is likely a result of contemporary interpretive practice, which calls for minimal signage on-site as a way of enhancing the 'time travel' experience.[52] On a visit to Colonial Williamsburg in late 2018, the most detailed architectural information I could find came in the form of brief building descriptions in the glossy 2014 *Official Guide*, which I quite accidentally stumbled across in a bookstore off-site.[53] The free pamphlet provided upon admission included a basic labelled map, and while some of the costumed staff were well informed on general architectural matters, it was rare that they had time to speak at length without being interrupted by visitors with more banal queries. Visits to Fortress Louisbourg in 2012, and to Sovereign Hill before that, garnered even less information.

If the primary reason for this absence of historical detail has been a desire to limit obtrusive signage on site, and the cost of providing such information in the form of brochures has been deemed prohibitive, one could be forgiven for assuming that the museums' websites would fill this void. While Colonial Williamsburg's site does offer some information after a bit of digging, the other museums' websites leave significant room for improvement. In abundance across all three websites, however, are 'edutainment' promotions including child-friendly tours and hands-on activities, seasonal events, period-themed shopping and dining opportunities, and accommodation packages. The logical conclusion to draw is that managers of popular open-air museums such as these believe that their target audience is the experience-driven consumer who expects a certain degree of architectural staging, but has little interest in the design and conservation histories of the buildings themselves. This does not mean that open-air museums have ceased to hold any value from an architectural perspective (though this value might perhaps be conceived of as sitting in reserve), but it does highlight how vulnerable this segment of the heritage/museums sector has become to forces of commercialization.

Value on Display

Installation view of the Robin Hood Gardens fragment, part of *Robin Hood Gardens: A Ruin in Reverse*, Victoria and Albert Museum. Exhibition presented at the 16th International Architecture Exhibition of the Venice Biennale, May 26–November 25, 2018. Exhibition curated by Christopher Turner and Olivia Horsfall Turner. Installation of fragment by ARUP and muf architecture/art. Photo: Susan Holden.

Susan Holden and Rosemary Willink

Value on Display
Curating Robin Hood Gardens

Susan Holden and Rosemary Willink

1 'The V&A Is Acquiring a Section of Robin Hood Gardens: A Defining Example of Brutalist Architecture and Social Housing,' Victoria and Albert Museum, London, 2017, www.vam.ac.uk/articles/robin-hood-gardens (accessed April 12, 2020). The V&A ultimately salvaged a three-story section of the street and garden facades and the interior fittings of two flats.

In late 2017, the Victoria and Albert Museum (V&A) announced that it would acquire a three-story section—a whole maisonette measuring almost nine meters in height—of the Robin Hood Gardens housing estate by Alison and Peter Smithson (London, completed 1972) on the eve of its demolition to make way for a higher-density residential development, and after two failed attempts to list the Brutalist icon.[1] The building's demolition became a *cause célèbre* in the architecture world, cast as a failure of the heritage framework to protect modernist architecture, and epitomizing the wider loss of social housing in Britain over previous decades. In the debates that occurred during the heritage campaigns, claims for the building's historic, aesthetic, and social value butted up against arguments that its architectural and material obsolescence was in fact a burden on society and stood in the way of the delivery of more and better housing. The case certainly exemplifies the familiar and often intractable contest between the intrinsic cultural value of architecture as heritage, and its value as real property, and in this case as a public asset. A contest that in the moments before a building's demolition is fully on display.

The V&A's acquisition—'representing a full section of the [estate's] repeating pattern of prefabricated parts'[2]—while impressive in its scale, doesn't mitigate the loss of the building. Instead, the ex-situ collected fragment, salvaged during the building's demolition, becomes a permanent reminder of the building's destruction. The museum deploys its institutional authority to stake a claim for Robin Hood Gardens' ongoing cultural value, while exposing differences between the categories of immobile and mobile heritage, and their administration. At the same time, the acquisition, as both object and event, opens up new curatorial opportunities that keep larger questions around the cultural value of architecture in play. In 2018, it was a catalyst for the V&A's contribution to the 16th International Architecture Exhibition of the Venice Biennale, in a display that foregrounded the building's demolition while showcasing new methods of digital documentation that are expanding heritage conservation practices. Due to its scale, the fragment will likely be housed in the V&A's planned new outpost located at Queen Elizabeth Olympic Park,[3] only a few kilometers from the building's original East London site, as part of a larger creative industries precinct that highlights recent investment in cultural and knowledge economies as a basis for future urban prosperity. Such changes in cultural administration in the twenty-first century that emphasize the monetary value of cultural and creative industries, certainly add another layer of complexity to this contest of values.

The discussion in this chapter explores the significance of the V&A's decision to collect a fragment of Robin Hood Gardens, to better understand the changing remit of the museum in culture- and city-making. It also explores some of the effects on architectural heritage as the cultural economy becomes a

2 Jessica Mairs, 'V&A Acquires Entire One-bedroom Flat from Robin Hood Gardens,' *Dezeen*, 9 November 2017, www.dezeen.com/2017/11/09/va-museum-acquires-robin-hood-gardens-flat-alison-peter-smithson-news-london-uk-architecture/.

3 Ibid.

prominent subject of cultural administration. First, it considers the acquisition in relation to the V&A's expansion in East London as part of a new creative industries precinct. It explores its significance as both a contested relic of the area's gentrification and as an example of the kind of spectacular object demanded by the experience economy that underpins such urban precincts. The discussion then shifts focus to explore how the acquisition was a catalyst for the V&A's contribution to the 2018 Venice Architecture Biennale, and the influence of curatorial agendas in shaping collections policies. It discusses the V&A's exhibition in Venice in relation to a longer history of the V&A's engagement with the topic of heritage, the changing place of architecture in its collection, and the museum's changing interface with cultural policy.

Gentrification, Museum Expansion and the Cultural Economy: Values of Heritage in Flux

4 Robin Hood Gardens, Poplar, London, 1972. © Sandra Lousada/Mary Evans Picture Library/The Smithson Family.

Completed in 1972, Robin Hood Gardens housing estate was a relatively late example of this kind of Brutalist and megastructural approach to social housing, but was nonetheless a significant built manifestation of the work of the Smithsons who were pioneers in advancing new ideas about living in the city.[4] Developed by the Greater London Council to replace tenement housing, the Smithsons sought to incorporate their knowledge of East London communities, while applying the design ideas of Team X and their critical uptake of Le Corbusier's modernist tenets. 213 flats were spread across two buildings that echoed the Smithsons' influential competition proposal for the Golden Lane Estate (1952, unbuilt). The building's signature 'streets in the sky' manifest the interrelationship of people and their environment and the 'gradations between domestic and public space' that the Smithsons saw as intrinsic to community, while its landscaped heart provided a contrast to the fortified perimeter that sheltered the estate from surrounding traffic noise.[5] As noted by Mark Crinson, the scale of the estate 'was important to the assertion that housing was as heroic a part of the area as the docks or the Blackwall Tunnel.'[6] However, the construction of the project coincided with the economic decline of this area as the docks were closed, and its reception was plagued by changing value regimes as both 'modernism and … the welfare state [came] under concerted attack.'[7]

The building was first slated for demolition in 2007, as Tower Hamlets Council began to consider the redevelopment of a larger area of the borough that included the Robin Hood Gardens site. The first campaign to list Robin Hood Gardens was launched by *Building Design* magazine after English Heritage (later renamed Historic England)—the organization responsible for making recommendations to the Department of Media, Culture and Sport on the status of England's historic buildings—issued Tower Hamlets Council with a certificate of immunity from listing.[8] Owing to the high-profile nature of the estate, English Heritage published a short film online, explaining factors that weighed on the decision against listing, emphasizing how the estate did not meet its original brief at the time of completion, the compromises made to its design in the final stages of construction and how it 'failed … to create a housing development which worked on human terms.'[9]

For several years, its fate was unclear until plans to demolish and replace it with a new residential complex, Blackwall Reach, were announced in 2014, and Tower Hamlets Council sought an extension on the certificate of

5 Mark Crinson, *Alison and Peter Smithson* (London: Historic England, 2018), 72–73.

6 Crinson, *Alison and Peter Smithson*, 71.

7 Crinson, *Alison and Peter Smithson*, 78.

8 A certificate of immunity is a legal guarantee that the building or buildings named in the certificate will not be considered for listing for five years. See: 'Robin Hood Gardens Estate,' *Historic England*, August 4, 2015, historicengland.org.uk/whats-new/news/robin-hood-gardens/.

9 *Robin Hood Gardens*, film by Historic England, 2009, www.youtube.com/watch?v=A3OKrWrkC4U.

10 'Robin Hood Gardens Estate.' The Head of Designation at Historic England, Emily Gee, explained: 'The building has some interesting qualities, such as the landscape, but the architecture is bleak in many areas, particularly in communal spaces, and the status of Alison and Peter Smithson alone cannot override these drawbacks.'

11 Still from video footage of the demolition of the Robin Hood Gardens. © Amy Frearson/Dezeen. See: Jessica Mairs, 'Bulldozers Move In on Robin Hood Gardens,' *Dezeen*, 25 August, 2017, www.dezeen.com/2017/08/25/bulldozers-demolition-robin-hood-gardens-alison-peter-smithson-brutalist-estate/.

12 'Robin Hood Gardens Estate.' Hunstanton was Listed at Grade II* in 1993. The Economist Group was Listed at Grade II* in 1988 and amended in 2013. Park Hill (995 flats and maisonettes) was Listed at Grade II* in 1998, and has undergone extensive renovation since the early two-thousands.

13 Examples including Park Hill in Sheffield and Grand Parc in Bordeaux have sought to maintain the provision of affordable housing. Park Hill was re-developed by Urban Splash in partnership with English Heritage with a mixed-tenure model. It was short-listed for the RIBA Stirling Prize in 2013. Grand Parc (530 dwellings) was transformed by Lacaton & Vassal in 2016. It received the EU Mies Award for Contemporary Architecture in 2019.

14 Nicholas Thoburn, 'Concrete and Council Housing,' *City* 22, no. 5–6 (2018), 612–632.

15 The housing estate suffered extensive vandalism after completion. Critical views of residents also formed part of the recent heritage campaigns, see: Michael Parker, 'Robin Hood "Homes vs Heritage": Residents and Architects Clash,' *The Docklands and East London Advertiser*, March 14, 2008, www.eastlondonadvertiser.co.uk/news/robin-hood-homes-v-heritage-residents-and-architects-clash-1-665585.

immunity. This was the catalyst for another campaign, spearheaded by the Twentieth Century Society and supported by high-profile architects including Sir Richard Rogers and Dame Zaha Hadid. This campaign was eventually defeated in 2015, with Historic England upholding its 2009 decision concluding that 'as no new information has come to light on the building, we stand by our assessment that Robin Hood Gardens does not meet the high threshold for listing.'[10] Demolition of the complex began in August 2017.[11]

In defending their response, English Heritage highlighted the work of the Smithsons that had already been listed, including the Hunstanton School and Gymnasium, Norfolk (1950–1954) and The Economist group, City of Westminster, London (1960–1964); as well as their commitment to listing postwar housing estates, including the Smithson-inspired Park Hill development, Sheffield (1967–1972) by Jack Lynn & Ivor Smith for Sheffield City Architects' Department.[12] However, the fate of modernist housing complexes in the twenty-first century has been mixed. The increasingly popular appeal of Brutalism (as demonstrated by other contributions to this book) has not necessarily translated into heritage conservation, particularly for social housing and institutional building types that present challenges in terms of complex ownership structures and typological obsolescence, and require extensive investment and re-imagining to be retained.[13] As Nicholas Thoburn has described: 'Brutalist form is either turned against itself as "concrete monstrosity" or refashioned as class-cleansed "modernist masterpiece."'[14] In fact, the open hostility towards the architecture of Robin Hood Gardens by some residents and segments of the public has been one aspect of the argument put in favor of the redevelopment of the site.[15] To complicate matters further, London is in dire need of affordable housing, a situation that Blackwall Reach claims to ameliorate. However, as part of a broader plan to develop East London, it is also contributing to London's soaring rents and housing prices.[16]

In November 2017, with destruction of the building underway, the V&A announced it would acquire a section of the building salvaged during the demolition process.[17] The idea was originally posed by architect Liza Fior of muf architecture/art during a residency with the museum, which focused on developing architectural strategies for the expansion of the V&A on the former London Olympic site.[18] The timing of the announcement provoked some critics to condemn the V&A for not engaging in the earlier campaigns to list the building—a criticism discussed in more detail later in this chapter.[19]

Known as V&A East, this new outpost is proposed to be part of a new cultural, education and innovation precinct, East Bank, that includes branches of London College of Fashion, BBC studios, and Sadler's Wells Theatre. V&A East is also part of a larger architectural renewal and expansion campaign of the museum underway since 2001, branded FuturePlan, with a list of projects that includes the completed urban renewal of the Exhibition Road Quarter, refurbishment of the Photography Centre, and the transformation of the Museum of Childhood at Bethnal Green.[20] Indeed, the construction of V&A East is intended to be a landmark of FuturePlan, following the opening of a substantial new branch of the museum in Dundee designed by Kengo Kuma in 2018.[21]

The ambition to create a new urban precinct based on co-location of cultural institutions is by no means a new idea. Nor is the linking of institutional collections to the economy of design industries. The V&A, first conceived as the

16 S. Elmer and G. Dening, 'The London Clearances,' *City* 20, no. 2 (2016), 271–277.

17 © Victoria and Albert Museum, London.

18 Oliver Wainwright, 'Will This Three-storey Slice of Brutalism Be the Toast of Venice?,' *The Guardian*, May 15, 2018, www.theguardian.com/artanddesign/2018/may/15/robin-hood-gardens-three-storeys-british-brutalism-venice-biennale. Fior's question to the V&A was: 'Given the museum engages with the world through objects, can Robin Hood Gardens prompt engagement with east London?'

19 Ella Braidwood and Will Hurst, 'Critics Round on V&A's Acquisition of Robin Hood Gardens Section,' *Architect's Journal*, November 13, 2017, www.architectsjournal.co.uk/news/critics-round-on-vas-acquisition-of-robin-hood-gardens-section/10025178.article?v=1. In its defense, a spokesperson for the V&A explained that as a non-departmental public body 'it was not legally able to sign [Building Design's] petition of 2008 to save Robin Hood Gardens.'

20 'Futureplan,' Victoria and Albert Museum, n.d., www.vam.ac.uk/info/futureplan (accessed April 12, 2020). The V&A boasts that the first phase of FuturePlan (2001–2009) involved over fifty architectural, design and engineering practices. See: 'Completed FuturePlan projects,' Victoria and Albert Museum, www.vam.ac.uk/info/futureplan-completed-projects/.

21 'V&A Dundee Visitor Numbers Hit Half a Million,' news release, Victoria and Albert Museum, March 31, 2019, www.vam.ac.uk/dundee/info/va-dundee-visitor-numbers-hit-half-a-million.

22 Anthony Burton, *Vision & Accident: The Story of the Victoria and Albert Museum* (London: V&A Publications, 1999), 46.

23 John Gold and Margaret Gold, 'Olympic Futures and Urban Imaginings: From Albertopolis to Olympicopolis,' in *The Handbook of New Urban Studies*, ed. John Hannigan and Greg Richards (London: Sage, 2017), 3.

24 Internal renders of proposed V&A Collections and Research Centre, Here East. © Diller Scofidio + Renfro, 2018.

25 A similar design strategy is evident at The Broad, a Los Angeles museum also by Diller Scofidio + Renfro (2011–2015), where collection storage is positioned midway in the building, shaping the lobby below and the exhibition spaces above, and is visible to visitors through a series of windows. 'The Building,' *The Broad*, n.d., www.thebroad.org/about (accessed July 3, 2020).

26 Elizabeth Diller quoted in: Tom Ravenscroft, 'Designs Revealed for V&A East Buildings by O'Donnell + Toumey and Diller Scofidio + Renfro,' *Dezeen*, November 2, 2018, www.dezeen.com/2018/11/02/v-a-east-odonnell-tuomey-diller-scofidio-renfros-olympicopolis-london/.

Museum of Manufactures (1852), was part of a larger project envisaged by Prince Albert to serve as a permanent reminder of the *Great Exhibition of the Works of Industry of All Nations* held in London in 1851. With the purchase of a Georgian mansion, Gore House, along with twenty-eight hectares of surrounding land, South Kensington was created. Albertopolis, as the new quarter colloquially became known, was an entire precinct devoted to 'schools of instruction' aimed at improving the design standards for English manufacturing and, as was Albert's ambition, the appreciation of good design in the general population, and included an architectural collection that demonstrated new building materials.[22] In a more contemporary sense, it is also a precedent for the way host cities of major events leverage the associated investment for new social and cultural infrastructure—a pattern that is now taken for granted. It was certainly at play in London's 2012 Olympics, and today continues with the development of V&A East.[23]

V&A East is proposed to include a new museum building designed by O'Donnell + Toumey at Stratford Waterfront, and a Collection and Research Centre designed by Diller Scofidio + Renfro in the refurbished former Olympic Broadcast Centre, Here East.[24] The latter is based on the concept of open collection storage and promises new opportunities for the display of large-scale architectural installations.[25] As Elizabeth Diller has described:

> Planned from the inside out, this project will be like stepping into an immersive cabinet of curiosities—a three-dimensional sampling of the eclectic collection of artefacts, programmed with diverse spaces for research, object study, workshops, and back-of-house functions.[26]

Diller's formulation of the museum as an 'immersive cabinet of curiosities' evokes one of the origin stories of the museum typology, while acknowledging advances in art museum design brought about by developments in art practice in the late twentieth century towards large-scale and immersive works.[27] There is a promise that the building will not only accommodate, but display, the v&a's growing collection of full-scale architectural fragments, which includes the intact plywood interior of Edgar J. Kaufmann's office from 1930 designed by Frank Lloyd Wright, as well as a range of vernacular architectural fragments such as the sixteenth-century timber facade of a house in Bishopsgate.[28] In contrast to the 'high threshold' for listing demanded by architectural heritage legislation that constrains in-situ conservation, the museum's collecting remit can be broader and perhaps more flexible, but it is nonetheless constrained by the limitations of museum display and storage facilities and the complexities of collecting architecture at full-scale. v&a East goes some way towards mitigating this constraint.

What is new in this re-formulation of the cabinet of curiosities, however, is its combination with the display of back-of-house functions. This in itself is not a new idea, but in the context of the larger intent of the precinct it has the effect of expanding the idea of the 'exhibitionary complex' theorized by Tony Bennett, as audiences are sought for every aspect of the museum's operations, and new opportunities found for the display of creative exchange, reflecting the elevation of such activities in cultural administration that has come about as a result of the focus on creative industries.[29] Cultural economist David Throsby points out that 'architecture has a double role to play in an urban context, … as a major determinant of the quality of urban environments' but also 'as one of the

27 Rosalind Krauss, 'The Cultural Logic of the Late Capitalist Museum,' *October* 54 (1990), 3–17.

28 A fifteenth-century marquetry ceiling, preserved from the now destroyed Altamira Palace near Toledo, Spain, is planned to be integrated within the center's architecture, above a public space for displays and events. See: 'The V&A East Project,' Victoria and Albert Museum, n.d., www.vam.ac.uk/info/va-east-project (accessed April 12, 2020).

29 Tony Bennett, 'The Exhibitionary Complex,' *New Formations* 4 (1988), 73–102.

cultural industries."[30] Throsby played a significant role in the development of the field of cultural economics in the early two-thousands, and his theorization of the interrelationship between so-called high arts, which have high intrinsic value, and the creative industries, which commercialize creative content, has been central to the subsequent focus on the creative industries in cultural policy. In *The Economics of Cultural Policy*, Throsby addresses some of the challenges of accounting for the multiple values of architecture in this value chain—where it might be considered a creative industry, cultural infrastructure, cultural heritage, or indeed any combination of these. The V&A East project exemplifies this entanglement.

In the East Bank creative industries precinct, the reputation of the V&A as a leading design museum is intended to contribute explicitly to the cultivation of a robust creative economy in East London. The emphasis is on fostering creative activity in such a way that it can be translated into economic activity, through entrepreneurship and growth in production and consumption of cultural goods, services, and experiences. A key part of this is the development of soft and hard infrastructure, and the cultivation of audiences that will sustain a creative industries sector of the economy. What remains unresolved in this entanglement is the status of architectural heritage as a category of cultural administration. And to what extent, in its acquisition of a fragment of Robin Hood Gardens, the V&A's authoritative voice in debates about the cultural value of architectural heritage is at odds with its explicit aim to support British creative industries and its stake in the cultural and knowledge economies.[31]

[30] David Throsby, *The Economics of Cultural Policy* (Cambridge, UK: Cambridge University Press, 2010), 132.

[31] *V&A Strategic Plan 2018–2020* (London: Victoria and Albert Museum, n.d.), www.vam.ac.uk/info/reports-strategic-plans-and-policies (accessed 25 May 2020).

Robin Hood Gardens at Venice: Exhibiting Destruction

At the time of the announcement of the acquisition, the V&A contextualized it as part of a longer history of collecting full-scale architecture: an association that echoes the immersive cabinet of curiosities idea that underpins the design of V&A East, as discussed earlier.[32] However, this emphasis on the collection as the determining context for the acquisition does not fully account for the museum's engagement with the concepts and politics of heritage. In the words of Laurajane Smith: 'Heritage is heritage because it is subjected to the management and preservation/conservation process, not simply because it "is."'[33] Increasingly, the agency of the museum is being played out through its exhibition and curating activities, as much as through its acquisitions and collections. In the case of Robin Hood Gardens, this can be seen in relation to the V&A's contribution to the 2018 Venice Architecture Biennale, which was devised to showcase the newly acquired fragment, and capitalized on the public's attention to the building's demolition. This approach reflects the focus of the V&A's Design, Architecture and Digital department on 'contemporary collecting' and their recent emphasis on 'urbanism and ... the role architecture plays in shaping society.'[34] Within a longer historical trajectory, it shows how the collections policies and exhibition practices of the V&A have changed over time, revealing the changing agency of the museum, and the role of curatorial practices, in defining heritage.

In March 2018, as the demolition of Robin Hood Gardens was proceeding in earnest, the V&A announced that its acquisition of a fragment of the building would be the impetus for its contribution to the 2018 Venice Architecture Biennale.[35] This was the third iteration of the V&A's special

[32] 'The V&A Is Acquiring a Section of Robin Hood Gardens.' See also: Mark Brown, 'V&A Acquires Segment of Robin Hood Gardens Council Estate,' *The Guardian*, November 10, 2017, www.theguardian.com/artanddesign/2017/nov/09/va-buys-three-storey-chunk-robin-hood-gardens-council-estate-alison-peter-smithson-brutalist-architecture.

[33] Laurajane Smith, *Uses of Heritage* (London and New York: Routledge, 2006), 3.

[34] *Collections and Development Policy* (London: Victoria and Albert Museum, 2019), 9, 11, www.vam.ac.uk/info/reports-strategic-plans-and-policies.

[35] 'V&A to present *Robin Hood Gardens: A Ruin in Reverse* at the 16th International Architecture Exhibition, in collaboration with La Biennale di Venezia. Korean artist Do Ho Suh film commissioned to document the architecture and interiors of the internationally recognised London estate currently under demolition,' press release, Victoria and Albert Museum, [2018], www.theculturediary.com/sites/default/files/2018_pavilion_of_applied_arts_press_release_embargoed_until_6_march_cw.pdf (accessed 25 May 2020). See also: Jessica Mairs, 'V&A to Recreate Robin Hood Gardens' Streets in the Sky at Venice Architecture Biennale,' *Dezeen*, March 17, 2018, www.dezeen.com/2018/03/07/victoria-albert-va-museum-robin-hood-gardens-venice-architecture-biennale/.

36 The V&A's contributions span both the Art and Architecture Exhibitions of the Venice Biennale. The previous two contributions were: *A World of Fragile Parts* (2016) and *Display – Between Art and Arts & Crafts* featuring Jorge Pardo (2017). *Fragile Parts* explored the role of copies in conservation and preservation practices. One of the exhibited pieces *Infractus: The taking of Robin Hood Gardens* by Smout Allen with Scanlab Projects used 3D digital scanning to capture elements of the estate that reflected human occupation including curtains. See: 'La Biennale di Venezia 2016,' Victoria and Albert Museum, www.vam.ac.uk/articles/la-biennale-di-venezia-2016; and '#fragileparts,' hashtag twitter.com/hashtag/fragileparts.

37 See: 'Values of Design: 2017.12.02–2019.08.04,' *Design Society*, www.designsociety.cn/en/category/exhibition-list/detail!Exhibition-Values-of-Design.

38 On the penultimate day of the Venice Architecture Biennale, the V&A in London opened a small display on UK housing estates entitled, *A Home for All: Six Experiments in Social Housing*.

39 *Robin Hood Gardens: A Ruin in Reverse*, Victoria and Albert Museum. Exhibition presented at the 16th International Architecture Exhibition of the Venice Biennale, May 26–November 25, 2018. Installation views showing photograph of Alison Smithson and the *Sticks and Stones* display at the 1976 Venice Biennale. Photo: Susan Holden.

40 This earlier exhibition is discussed as a reference point in: 'The V&A at the 2018 Architecture Biennale,' Victoria and Albert Museum, www.vam.ac.uk/articles/la-biennale-di-venezia-2018 (accessed April 13, 2020).

collaboration with the Venice Biennale, housed in the Pavilion of Applied Arts at the Biennale's Arsenale site, and the only instance of participation by an international museum.[37] It represents a further dimension of the V&A's expansion strategy, which includes other exhibition-based partnerships, such as that with the Design Society at Shekou, Shenzhen, which launched in 2017 with the exhibition *Values of Design*.[37]

In 2018, the International Architecture Exhibition at the Venice Biennale, entitled *Freespace*, was curated by Yvonne Farrell and Shelley McNamara of Grafton Architects whose aim was to draw attention to the notion of generosity and intergenerational equity in the built environment and the role of architecture in this. The V&A's contribution to the exhibition, titled *Robin Hood Gardens: A Ruin in Reverse*, was curated by Christopher Turner and Olivia Horsfall Turner and connected to the larger Biennale theme through the topic of social housing.[38] Its title cleverly paid homage to an earlier exhibition the Smithsons mounted at the 37th Venice Biennale in 1976, entitled *Sticks and Stones*, a small-scale affair centered on a bench that took the form of one of the concrete fins from Robin Hood Gardens positioned in front of a large photograph showing the estate under construction.[39] 'A building under assembly' wrote the architects in the accompanying catalogue, 'is a ruin in reverse.'[40] The exhibition in 2018 of a section of the building saved from demolition brought a new perspective to this sentiment, as stated in one of the didactic panels of the *Ruin in Reverse* exhibition: 'It is too late to save Robin Hood Gardens, but what can we salvage from its ruin?' However, the reiteration of these words in the title of the 2018 exhibition also had the startling effect of collapsing the temporal difference between the construction and demolition of the estate, so that the one condition was somehow immanent in the other, refocusing the heat of the debate over the building's demolition on larger questions of urban change.

The exhibition had three main components: a display of documentary material, a film of the estate by artist Do Ho Suh commissioned by the V&A, and the full-scale building fragment exhibited outside the Pavilion adjacent to the Arsenale Canal. muf architecture/art played a role in the design of the fragment installation, and were recognized as contributors to the exhibition, along wih ARUP Engineers. All aspects of the exhibition accentuated the event of the building's demolition, while engaging with well-recognized curatorial challenges of how to represent the scale and complexity of architecture in the context of an exhibition.

The documentary material presented inside the Pavilion addressed the history of the building's design and occupation, as well as the heritage campaigns mounted to save it. A range of images and textual panels presented well-known excerpts from the Smithsons' oeuvre; explanations of the design features of Robin Hood Gardens, notably its generously-scaled access balconies; photographs of the newly occupied building; and the 1970 BBC television documentary *The Smithsons on Housing*, in which the architects claimed Robin Hood Gardens to be as relevant for London as the first Georgian square. Statements from notable architects that made claims both for and against the building's design, such as by Richard Rogers and Charles Jencks, were included alongside photographs of the building in the process of being demolished.[41] Commentary by leading figures in architectural discourse, including the Smithsons themselves, acknowledged the significance of the building as a polemical project in the history of architecture.

41 *Robin Hood Gardens: A Ruin in Reverse*. Installation views showing photographs by Peter Kelleher of the building in the process of being demolished, 2018. Photos: Susan Holden.

Do Ho Suh's film titled *Robin Hood Gardens, Woolmore Street, London E14 0HG* extended the artist's interest in architecture and the theme of home, utilizing time-lapse photography, drone footage, 3D scanning and photogrammetry—techniques also being used in the emerging field of digital heritage—to document the building's interiors.[42] Suh took hundreds of shots of each room and then 'stitched' them together[43] to create a slow-moving image that pans from one apartment to another, passing effortlessly through the building's concrete walls and floors.[44] The film captures the surfaces and detail of the interior spaces and apartment fixtures including heating panels and toilets, quite literally stripping the building of its brutalist materiality in order to emphasize the 'intangible quality' of the building and the contingencies of personal occupation.[45]

The reconstructed fragment provided a material counterpoint to the film, but in the end, was not the actual piece acquired by the museum, which had not yet been accessioned into the collection.[46] It was described as 'a composite portrait of the Smithson's original vision' and was presented as a mocked-up 1:1 section of an access balcony assembled from concrete balustrade and façade mullion elements salvaged from the demolition site.[47] It had a double role of being indexical to both the building and the acquisition, and provoked questions as to what indeed the acquisition would amount to, beyond segments of the repetitive concrete facade, and its affective potential as a display. The rawness of the defaced concrete captured the rundown state of the building at the time of demolition, and the use of chipboard to sheet the scaffold armature paradoxically echoed the boarded-up appearance of the complex after residents had 'decanted' and demolition was beginning.[48]

---

42 For a description of the film see: 'Robin Hood Gardens,' Victoria and Albert Museum, www.vam.ac.uk/event/RBVAN43y/ldf-2019-robin-hood-gardens.

43 Rachel Spence, 'Do Ho Suh in Venice: The Lives of Others,' *Financial Times*, May 11, 2018, www.ft.com/content/e7cc1056-51e5-11e8-84f4-43d65af59d43; and Paul Laster, 'Do Ho Suh: From sculpture to film,' *White Hot Magazine* November 2019, whitehotmagazine.com/articles/ho-suh-from-sculpture-film/4436.

44 *Robin Hood Gardens: A Ruin in Reverse*. Installation views showing stills of the film *Robin Hood Gardens, Woolmore Street, London E14 0HG*, by Do Ho Suh, 2018. Photos: author.

45 Do Ho Suh quoted in: Spence, 'Do Ho Suh in Venice.'

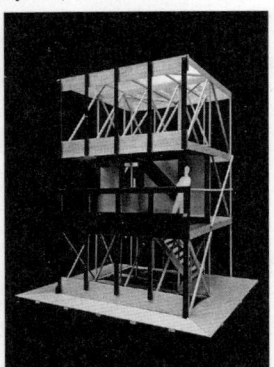

46 Model of the Robin Hood Gardens fragment installation, as proposed for the *Robin Hood Gardens: A Ruin in Reverse* exhibition by muf architecture/art. © muf architecture/art.

47 Ben Luke, 'Podcast Episode 34: Venice Architecture Biennale, and the Brutalist Social Housing Debate,' June 1, 2018, produced by Julia Michalska and David Clack, *The Art Newspaper* www.theartnewspaper.com/podcast/podcast-episode-34-venice-architecture-biennale-and-the-brutalist-social-housing-debate.

Ruin in Reverse did raise debate about the loss of public housing, with architect Sam Jacob saying: 'Even—especially—as a ruin, the issues that surround it remain a provocation … to find new ways to create housing and a more equitable city.'⁴⁹ However, it was also a catalyst for criticism to be levelled at the V&A for 'art washing' the 'so-called social cleansing taking place in East London.'⁵⁰ In response, Director Tristram Hunt rebuked the idea that museums should be 'vehicles for social justice' and 'organising demonstrations and signing petitions'; instead he declared: 'I see the role of the museum not as a political force, but as a civic exchange: curating shared space for unsafe ideas.'⁵¹

Yet, this was not the first time that the V&A used destruction as the basis for an exhibition about the value of architecture. In 1974, under the directorship of Roy Strong, the V&A mounted *The Destruction of the Country House 1875–1975*, an exhibition designed to bring attention to the hundreds of properties across England of architectural and historical significance that were at risk of deteriorating due to the inability of owners to access funds for their maintenance. The exhibition was a precursor to the European Architectural Heritage Year of 1975 and dramatized this potential loss to the national estate in the Hall of Lost Houses. This was another kind of staging of demolition, a pre-emptive one that was not shy in engaging with the politics of heritage, and arguably had a real impact on foregrounding architectural heritage in public arts policy in Britain in the decades to come. Strong would go on to claim that this was the first time 'a museum exhibition was an exercise in polemic.'⁵² As an activist exhibition *avant la lettre*, the *Destruction* exhibition provides a provocative counterpoint to the V&A's position on Robin Hood Gardens, and to the changing agency of the museum in relation to architectural heritage.⁵³

III

48 *Robin Hood Gardens: A Ruin in Reverse*. Installation views of the Robin Hood Gardens fragment. Photos: Susan Holden.

49 'Biennale 2018: The blog,' *The Architects Journal*, May 23, 2018, www.architectsjournal.co.uk/news/venice-biennale-2018-the-blog/10031353.article.

50 Stephen Pritchard, 'No Breathing Space: V&A, Artwashing and the Theft of Robin Hood Gardens,' *Bella Caledonia*, June 1, 2018, bellacaledonia.org.uk/2018/06/01/no-breathing-space-va-artwashing-and-the-theft-of-robin-hood-gardens/.

51 Tristram Hunt, 'Displaying the Ruins of Demolished Social Housing at the Venice Architecture Biennale Is Not "Art-Washing",' *The Art Newspaper* 302 (June 2018), www.theartnewspaper.com/comment/displaying-the-ruins-of-demolished-social-housing-is-not-art-washing-the-v-and-a-is-a-place-for-unsafe-ideas.

52 Roy Strong, *The Roy Strong Diaries 1967–1987* (London: Phoenix, 1998) quoted in Ruth Adams, 'The V&A: The Destruction of the Country House and the Creation of "English Heritage",' *Museum and Society* 11, no. 1 (2013), 1.

53 Barry Bergdoll introduces the concept of an activist exhibition in a discussion of the Museum of Modern Art, New York (MoMA). See: Barry Bergdoll, 'In the Wake of Rising Currents: The Activist Exhibition,' *Log* 20 (2010), 159–167.

54 For an analysis of rise of the Country House Lobby and the Wealth Tax debate see: Adams, 'The V&A,' 3–5, 11.

55 *The Destruction of the Country House 1875–1975.* Exhibition held at the Victoria and Albert Museum, October 9–December 1, 1974. Installation view of the Hall of Lost Houses. © Victoria and Albert Museum.

56 Adams, 'The V&A,' 7 and Burton, *Vision & Accident*, 225.

57 The scenography can perhaps also be understood as a corollary to the striking image of The Hook at Hants that was included with such prominence in the book publication that accompanied the exhibition. See: John Harris, 'Gone to Ground,' in *The Destruction of the Country House 1875–1975*, ed. Roy Strong, Marcus Binney and John Harris (London: Thames and Hudson, 1974), 15.

58 Strong, *Diaries*, 141, quoted in Adams, 'The V&A,' 7.

Strong's masterstroke in the *Destruction* exhibition was to turn the threat of demolition into a curatorial conceit. The exhibition made an emotive argument for the conservation of the country houses by linking the loss of properties during the twentieth century to the potential future loss of houses due to impositions such as the Wealth Tax proposed by the Wilson Labour Government in 1974.[54] This agenda was couched in what was otherwise a conventional art historical analysis of the architecture, interiors, and gardens of a cross-section of significant country houses.

The most controversial and arguably the most impactful part of the exhibition was the Hall of Lost Houses, an immersive scenography that placed photographs of houses that had been demolished during the twentieth century on crumbling sections of a mock portico, with an accompanying voice-over reading the names of the lost houses against the sounds of burning timber and collapsing buildings.[55] A wrecking ball suspended in mid-air adjacent to this scene of destruction left no ambiguity.[56] Designed by Robin Wade, this scenography was undoubtedly meant to appeal to the emotions, evoking the scale and significance of the country houses themselves, and at the same time representing the threat of loss as a catalyst for action.[57] As Strong recalled:

> The impact on the public was overwhelming, for they alighted upon it turning a corner, having been wafted along by an opening section on country-house glories. And then they came face to face with this. Many was the time I stood in that exhibition watching the tears stream down the visitors' faces as they battled to come to terms with all that had gone.[58]

Although the exhibition was critiqued as propaganda, its impact was undeniable, contributing to the reconceptualization of the country houses as '"treasures" ... worth "saving" ... for the benefit of the "nation."'⁵⁹ While it may not have contributed directly to the shelving of the Wealth Tax in December 1975, it nonetheless was significant in demonstrating the effectiveness of the preservation lobby and the growing public acceptance of the value of national heritage. In subsequent years, government policies made increasing provisions for the financial support of heritage conservation.⁶⁰ As noted by Delafons, the 1975 European Architectural Heritage Year 'was perhaps the beginning of the populist concern for conservation which increasingly supplanted the elitist tradition of conservation in Britain.'⁶¹ While Adams suggests that 'the stately home might be said to be paradigmatic of the uncritical conflation of heritage with national identity,'⁶² in a fundamental way, policy and legislative reform that followed had the effect of making architecture a central aspect of cultural policy in a way it had not been before.⁶³

In contrast to the lobbying activities of Strong, the lack of engagement on the part of the V&A in the campaigns to list Robin Hood Gardens is conspicuous. It marks an historical shift in the geographical locus, and the politics, of conservation in Britain, as noted by Nityanand Deckha:

> While undeniably *conservative* in its endeavours to protect and salvage the old, historic conservation can also function, and has functioned, as an activist practice that attempts to question the logics of speculative urban development. Hence, embedded in conservation is a concern for the everyday spaces as they currently exist and the social memories that have formed them.⁶⁴

59 Adams, 'The V&A,' 2.
60 Adams, 'The V&A,' 12.
61 J. Delafons, *Politics and Preservation: A Policy History of the Built Heritage 1882–1996* (Hoboken: Routledge, 1997), 107, quoted in Adams, 'The V&A,' 12.
62 Adams, 'The V&A,' 10.
63 Adams, 'The V&A,' 12.
64 Nityanand Deckha, 'Beyond the Country House: Historic Conservation as Aesthetic Politics,' *European Journal of Cultural Studies* 7, no. 4 (2004), 404.

[65] 'Venice Biennale 2018: The Blog,' *The Architects Journal,* May 23, 2018.

[66] See: Andrew Dewdney, David Dibosa, and Victoria Walsh, *Post Critical Museology: Theory and Practice in the Art Museum* (London: Taylor & Francis Group, 2012).

[67] *Robin Hood Gardens,* film by English Heritage.

If *Destruction* was axiomatic of the rise of heritage as a category and signaled a claim by the museum to play a role in identifying architecture of significance, *Ruin in Reverse* was symptomatic of the museum's relative impotence in conserving in-situ architectural heritage, and its inevitable complicity with the destruction of heritage in the process of collecting architecture. As candidly put by Paul Finch during the Venice Architecture Biennale: 'culture [is] the consumption of the obsolete.'[65] The ambivalence of *Ruin in Reverse* emphasized the transitory nature of the built environment, and the unresolved role of the post-critical museum in defining and acting on architectural heritage.[66]

Both exhibitions reinforce the difficulty of arguing for the intrinsic cultural value of architecture, which is complicated by the inextricable link between architecture, real property and land speculation, on the one hand, and constrained by the capacity for architecture to be conserved by museums on the other. Destruction becomes a litmus test of the cultural value of architecture. In the museum, it is the point at which the polemic of heritage becomes inscribed in the artefact. Outside the museum, it is a point at which the apparent incommensurability of architecture's economic and cultural value is laid bare. Yet, if the threat of demolition is often a catalyst for heritage listing, listing does not necessarily secure the protection of the complex values of a building.[67]

A *Ruin in Reverse* brought significant exposure to the destruction of Robin Hood Gardens, as well as the V&A's decision to collect a fragment of it. While the V&A has a long history of collecting and exhibiting architecture, it has become a more explicit focus in recent years with the formalization of the Design, Architecture and Digital Department

(DAD, est. 2015), which 'restated' the museum's 'commitment to its architectural collections,' while at the same time embedding 'contemporary collecting' as a clear mandate of the new department.[68] A particular initiative of DAD is Rapid Response Collecting, which seeks the timely collection of designed things 'that articulate important events in the recent history of design and manufacturing,' but also their immediate display.[69] This is a kind of performative collecting, which emphasizes the impact that the immediate display of objects can have in engaging audiences in topical debates that concern society. It foregrounds a more general emphasis in the museum on the activity of collecting as a catalyst for research and engagement. While the Robin Hood Gardens acquisition was not explicitly part of the Rapid Response Collecting strategy, the acquisition and its display in Venice nonetheless reflect some of its parameters and ambitions including the central role of curating, in the way that it became an opportunity to engage with the contest of values surrounding the building's demolition. As described by V&A curator Olivia Horsfall Turner:

> It's not just the object that we're preserving but it's the issues that we want to keep alive. … It's something we feel is really important as the role of [a] public museum to keep those conversations going and provide people with compelling objects that they study and experience in order to make those issues real to them.[70]

Another aim of the Rapid Response Collecting strategy is 'to bring in new and diverse forms of expertise' and 'foster discussion about what the museum should collect.'[71] In the case of the Robin Hood Gardens acquisition, Fior played a central role in suggesting it, and was involved in the exhibition in Venice. More than this, Fior's suggestion becomes a catalyst

[68] *Collection Development Policy*, V&A, 2019, 11. Historically, the collecting of architecture at the V&A has been across diverse departments depending on the material of the object, including Sculpture (plaster casts), Furniture (wooden models), Metalwork (ironwork) and Word and Image (drawings). *Collection Development Policy*, V&A, 2019, 12. The DAD collecting department grew out of a refocusing of the museum's collecting and exhibition programming on twentieth century objects in the nineteen-nineties and two-thousands, which evolved to become the Contemporary Architecture, Design and Digital section in 2012, the precursor to the current DAD, which 'sought to embed the museum's contemporary activities even further within the collections.' *Collection Development Policy*, V&A, 2019, 10.

[69] *Collections Development Policy*, V&A, 2019, 14.

[70] Olivia Horsfall Turner quoted in Mairs, 'V&A Acquires Entire One-bedroom Flat from Robin Hood Gardens.' Similarly, Dr. Christopher Turner, Keeper of the DAD Department described the acquisition as 'an object that will stimulate debate around architecture and urbanism today' while V&A curator Dr Neil Bingham declared that it will 'motivate new thinking and research into this highly experimental period of British architectural and urban history.'

[71] *Collection Development Policy*, V&A, 2019, 14.

to consider how the different collecting strategies and priorities of the museum intersect: how architecture and urbanism might be encompassed in the concept of contemporary collecting, and more generally how the museum might engage with different value regimes associated with architectural heritage.

During her residency at the V&A, Fior became interested in the idea of 'reverse restitution' and how the museum could connect with the situated histories of architectural objects in the collection: 'The V&A is full of bits of buildings that were victims of regeneration,' she said.[72] This was also an idea behind muf architecture/art's contribution to the 2015 exhibition at the V&A *All This Belongs to You*, which included four commissioned installations that were dispersed throughout the museum. muf's installation *More than One (Fragile) Thing at a Time* used VR technology to connect visitors to the afterlife of the places that objects in the Medieval and Renaissance galleries originally came from, to make a 'connection between the past and the present' and 'bring people, object and place closer together.'[73] It was an installation that subtly engaged larger debates about the restitution of cultural property taking place across the museum sector that are challenging the *raison d'être* of the encyclopedic museum in a post-colonial world.[74] In the case of the Robin Hood Gardens acquisition, the continually redeveloped city is the new battle ground for looted objects, and the question of whose interests are served in the treatment of cultural property, and indeed the role of property ownership in the history of heritage conservation, is brought to the fore.

If the museum cannot be a limitless repository of objects, particularly ones as large as the Robin Hood Garden's fragment, how might it engage with architectural heritage? In light of Fior's concept of reverse restitution, the Robin Hood

[72] Liza Fior quoted in Oliver Wainwright, 'Will This Three-Storey Slice of British Brutalism Be the Toast of Venice?' *The Guardian*, May 5, 2018, www.theguardian.com/artanddesign/2018/may/15/robin-hood-gardens-three-storeys-british-brutalism-venice-biennale. In Fior's words: 'There's a staircase from a Florentine palazzo that succumbed to a road-widening scheme, along with the 1930s foyer of the Strand Palace, salvaged when this celebrated London hotel was gutted in the 1960s. … it is the role of the museum to provide a platform for these difficult conversations.'

[73] 'Reverse Restitution, 2015,' muf architecture/art, muf.co.uk/portfolio/more-than-one-fragile-thing-at-a-time/ (accessed May 14, 2020). *The Ethics of Dust: Trajan's Column* by Jorge Otero-Pailos was another commissioned installation in this exhibition that engaged with concepts of heritage and conservation. See: Jorge Otero-Pailos, Erik Langdalen and Thordis Arrhenius, *Experimental Preservation* (Zurich: Lars Müller Publishers, 2016).

[74] Hannah McGivern, '2018 in Museums: Big Ethics Questions Dominate the Field,' *The Art Newspaper* 307 (December 10, 2018), www.theartnewspaper.com/analysis/2018-in-museums.

Gardens acquisition can thus also be understood as a challenge to both the physical and conceptual limits of the museum's collection. The acquisition becomes a provocation, not to government policy, as the 'Destruction' exhibition was, but to the museum's own collections policies, and through this, its very attitude towards the imbrication of culture and the built environment.

In this respect, the Robin Hood Garden acquisition puts the question of value, and its place in cultural administration, itself on display. Not only does the acquisition highlight the many tensions associated with articulating the cultural value of architecture through established frameworks such as those of heritage and museum collections; it also highlights the disjunctions that come about by bringing the values of architecture as heritage, and the expanding role of the museum in urban regeneration and as part of the creative economy, into direct dialogue.

Critical discourse on cultural value rightly points out the problems of attempting to reconcile different values into a one value system, and similarly the instrumentalization of cultural value at large.[75] And yet, as this analysis of the Robin Hood Gardens acquisition by the V&A shows, prevailing models of the cultural economy are nonetheless revealing of the complexities in accounting for architecture's cultural value, and the role of cultural institutions and administrative frameworks in determining them. While the demolition of Robin Hood Gardens was a decisive conclusion to the contest between the economic and cultural value of architecture at stake in the heritage campaigns, for the V&A the question is to what extent the acquisition can keep debates about cultural value, and the imbrication of the conservation, curating and commissioning activities of the museum in defining architectural heritage, productively in play.

[75] Geoffrey Crossick and Patrycja Kaszynska, *Understanding the Value of Arts and Culture: The AHRA Cultural Values Project* (Wilshire: Arts and Humanities Research Council, 2016). See also: Robert Phiddian, Julian Meyrick, Tully Barnett and Richard Maltby, 'Counting Culture to Death: An Australian Perspective on Culture Counts and Quality Metrics,' *Cultural Trends* 26, no. 2 (2017), 174–180.

On the Architecture of the Late-Capitalist Museum

Tod Williams Billie Tsien
Architects, American Folk Art
Museum, New York, NY, 2001.
Photo: Michael Moran / OTTO
/ Raven & Snow.

Philip Goodwin and Edward Durell Stone, Museum of Modern Art, New York, NY, 1939. Photo: Museum of the City of New York.

On the Architecture of the Late-Capitalist Museum
The Museum of Modern Art and the Demolition of the American Folk Art Museum

Joanna Merwood-Salisbury

1 Tod Williams Billie Tsien Architects, American Folk Art Museum, New York, NY, 2001. Photo: Michael Moran/OTTO/Raven & Snow.

In 2014 the Museum of Modern Art in New York (MoMA) demolished its next-door neighbor, the American Folk Art Museum, to accommodate an expansion. Designed by architects Tod Williams and Billie Tsien, the award-winning Folk Art Museum was only thirteen years old.[1] The demolition was highly controversial: prominent architects and critics implored MoMA to find a way to preserve Williams and Tsien's building, arguing that the rules of obsolescence do not apply to cultural monuments in the same way they do to commercial buildings. Marshaling its influence, the art and architecture press created a narrative in which MoMA, with its corporate sensibility, insatiable desire for growth, and bland modernist aesthetic, had betrayed its mission to promote good architecture. This chapter places these events within the history of architecture at MoMA as both the institution that established the canon of 'modern architecture' and as a built form that slowly expanded within a single New York City block. It asks, how does this fraught episode illustrate the value of architecture to the museum in a broader sense?

The construction of the Folk Art Museum and a concurrent extension to MoMA were part of an explosion of museum construction and expansion that began in the final decades of the twentieth century.[2] In her essay, 'The Cultural Logic of the Late Capitalist Museum,' Rosalind Krauss argued that many museum directors had begun to think of their collections in terms of 'assets'; not unique and irreplaceable embodiments of cultural knowledge but forms of cultural capital.[3] Many saw the architecture of the museum in similar terms. When they gambled on expensive buildings designed by high-profile architects, directors exchanged the traditional authority of architecture, which comes from stability and permanence, for the capricious value of the spectacle.[4] Since the nineteen-nineties, scholars and critics have reacted to this phenomenon with ambivalence, citing the Centre Pompidou in Paris (1977) and the Guggenheim Museum in Bilbao, Spain (1997) in particular.[5] On the one hand, the trend of investing heavily in prominent buildings appeared to raise the cultural value of architecture; on the other, it risked reducing architecture to little more than an extension of the museum's marketing campaign. Tracing the history of architecture at MoMA (including its original curatorial agenda, its later attitude towards expansion, and its actions in demolishing the Folk Art Museum) allows us to reconsider the terms of millennial anxiety about museum architecture.

Since its founding in 1929, MoMA has promoted architecture as a form of aesthetic expression equal in importance to the fine arts. Indeed, it is one of the few major museums to give modern and contemporary architecture prominence. Through its influential early-twentieth-century exhibitions MoMA defined what it called the International Style, established a canon of examples primarily from Europe, and constructed a linear narrative of stylistic progression that

2 Victoria Newhouse, *Towards a New Museum* (New York: Monacelli Press, 1998); Wim de Wit, 'When Museums Were White: A Study of the Museum as Building Type,' in *Architecture for Art: American Art Museums 1938–2008*, ed. Scott J. Tilden (New York: Harry N. Abrams Inc., 2004), 11–16; Raul A. Barreneche, *New Museums* (London: Phaidon, 2005).

3 Rosalind Krauss, 'The Cultural Logic of the Late Capitalist Museum,' *October* 54 (1990), 3–17.

4 Guy Debord, *The Society of the Spectacle* (Detroit: Black & Red, 1970).

5 Jean Baudrillard, 'The Beaubourg Effect: Implosion and Deterrence,' in *Simulacra and Simulation*, trans. Sheila Faria Glaser (Ann Arbor: University of Michigan Press, 1994), 61–74; Hal Foster, 'Master Builder,' in *Design and Crime and Other Diatribes* (London and New York: Verso, 2002), 27–42; and Michael Sorkin, 'Brand Aid or, The Lexus and the Guggenheim (Further Tales of the Notorious B.I.G.ness),' *Harvard Design Magazine* 17 (Fall 2002–Winter 2003), 4–9. See also: Anthony Vidler, 'Introduction,' in *Architecture Between Spectacle and Use*, ed. Anthony Vidler (New Haven and London: Yale University Press, 2008), vii–xiii.

remained fixed for decades. Architects Philip Goodwin and Edward Durell Stone designed the Museum's original 1939 building to represent the potential of the new style for the United States. Reinforcing its early ideological positioning, MoMA utilized the modern style as a mechanism of both continuity and renewal in its mid- to late-twentieth-century expansions. As an aesthetic system and reference point, the use of the style guaranteed the stability of the institution's image, even as the physical form of the building expanded through a process of *assemblage*. By contrast, the contemporary museum as a form of spectacle generally depends on an understanding of its architecture as singular and novel. In this context, a study of MoMA's demolition of the Folk Art Museum is instructive. Comparing these projects allows us to re-examine the modes of relationship between architecture, the museum, and the processes of capitalist renewal.

Two Museums, One Block

MoMA and the Folk Art Museum have several similarities. Both were founded by wealthy collectors and supported initially by philanthropy. Both occupied (at different times), townhouses on West Fifty-Third Street belonging to members of the Rockefeller family. But as institutions and institutional buildings, they are very different. In narratives accompanying the Folk Art Museum's demolition, this difference contributed to the smaller institution's demise. MoMA began as a temple to a new category of 'modern' art based around a core collection of European works of fine art. When the Folk Art Museum opened in 1963, its focus was deliberately American, grounded in eighteenth-century vernacular arts and crafts.[6] As art historian David Brody has noted, the

6 'Museum Director's Statement: Gerard C. Wertkin,' in *Architecture for Art*, 18.

invention of an academic category of 'folk' art arose in opposition to the concept of the 'fine' arts and as a critical reaction to the culture of modernity.[7] In contrast to the era of mass production, it represents a nostalgia for a pre-modern era in which hand-crafted goods were lifelong treasured possessions. In this way, the Folk Art Museum's collection presents a clear contrast to that of its prestigious next-door neighbor. In subsequent years, however, these institutions expanded their collections to accommodate broader definitions of 'modern' and 'folk' art. Soon after its founding, MoMA began to exhibit photography, film, architecture, and design, disciplines that art historians had not traditionally considered within the realm of the fine arts. MoMA established its interest in the cultural value of modern architecture in two early exhibitions: *Modern Architecture: International Exhibition* (1932) and *Early Modern Architecture: Chicago 1870–1910* (1933). With these exhibitions the Museum identified a new style of architecture appearing in Europe, and argued for the American origins of that style in the commercial vernacular of the late nineteenth century.[8] In turn, the Folk Art Museum expanded its scope beyond the United States, exhibiting a more diverse range of folk artists from around the world, including the work of 'outsider' or self-taught artists.

Both museums commissioned significant building works in the late nineteen-nineties, during a short-lived but frenetic real estate boom. Williams and Tsien's new Folk Art Museum opened in 2001, and Yoshio Taniguchi's addition to MoMA opened in 2004. Conceived in the late twentieth century and completed in the early twenty-first, these architectural reinventions reinforced, in formal terms, the differences between the two institutions as representatives of 'modern' art and 'folk' art, respectively. In 1997 the Folk Art Museum hired Williams and Tsien to design a more

[7] David Brody, 'The Building of a Label: The New American Folk Art Museum,' *American Quarterly* 55, no. 2 (June 2003), 257–276.

[8] Henry-Russell Hitchcock and Philip Johnson, *The International Style* (New York: W. W. Norton, [1932] 1995), 29. See also: Terence Riley, *International Style: Exhibition 15 and The Museum of Modern Art* (New York: Rizzoli, 1992); Henry Matthews, 'The Promotion of Modern Architecture by the Museum of Modern Art in the 1930s,' *Journal of Design History* 7, no. 1 (1994), 43–59; and Sybil Gordon Kantor, *Alfred H. Barr Jr. and the Intellectual Origins of the Museum of Modern Art* (Cambridge, MA: MIT Press, 2002). I discuss the ideological agenda of 'Early Modern Architecture: Chicago 1870–1910,' in Joanna Merwood-Salisbury, 'American Modern: The Chicago School and the International Style at the Museum of Modern Art,' in *Chicagoisms: The City as Catalyst for Architectural Speculation*, ed. Alexander Eisenschmidt and Jonathan Mekinda (Chicago: Park Books/University of Chicago Press, 2014), 116–129.

substantial, permanent building on two adjacent townhouse sites, at 45 and 47 West 53rd Street. The architects had a rare real estate advantage with which to work. Though the site was small, it faced a gap in the urban fabric of the Manhattan grid, a mid-block arcade between Eero Saarinen's CBS Building (1961) and Roche Dinkeloo's Deutsche Bank Building (1988). Unlike any of its neighbors on West 53rd Street, the new building could be seen from afar. Even before work on the Museum had begun, rumors surfaced that MoMA had offered to swap sites in exchange for a site it owned further west on the same block, allowing the larger institution to occupy the highly desirable location. This swap did not eventuate. Williams and Tsien took advantage of this unusual axial approach, creating a striking sculptural facade made of three panels of Tombasil, a bronze alloy created by casting the metal onto a concrete and stainless steel formwork. With its tactile, handcrafted appearance, this particular feature (labeled a 'Midtown icon' by New York Times architecture critic Herbert Muschamp) became the focus of debate when the Museum's fate became uncertain.[9]

When the Folk Art Museum opened with an exhibition of the works of outsider artist Henry Darger in December 2001, it presented a distinct contrast to its larger next-door neighbor. High real estate prices had limited the Folk Art Museum to a small footprint, at least by institutional standards. While the facade was visually arresting, the narrow site made it difficult for Williams and Tsien to accommodate the functions of a museum in the traditional linear circulation pattern. Instead, its organizational strategy echoed Sir John Soane's labyrinthine house-museum in London, with its intimate scale, small rooms, and eclectic arrangement of objects. Inside, the architects had little choice but to emphasize verticality.[10] Rather than the neutral and self-contained gallery

[9] Herbert Muschamp, 'Fireside Intimacy for Folk Art Museum's New Home,' *New York Times* (December 14, 2001), E35.

[10] 'Architect's Statement: Billie Tsien,' in *Architecture for Art*, 18.

spaces seen at MoMA, they organized their building around a grand central stair, which anchored a series of small galleries arranged over four floors. Lit by a skylight, this stair had niches for the display of objects built into its structure, allowing visitors to encounter pieces in the collection through a pleasurable experience of peripatetic discovery. These differences were even more apparent on the exterior. Where the Folk Art Museum was massive, weighty, and handcrafted, MoMA displayed the lightness and sleekness of machine precision. Where the Folk Art Museum was a vertically-oriented single volume, MoMA was horizontal and iterative. In a series of successive additions, various architects engaged with the language of modernity in different ways, overlaying formal accretions next to and over each other to create a sort of architectural palimpsest along the street front. Immediately apparent, these formal differences served to fuel the protest when the smaller building came under threat.

In 1997, the same year that the Folk Art Museum hired Williams and Tsien to design its new premises, MoMA organized an invited competition for an expansion that doubled its size, restoring and enlarging the famous sculpture garden, and adding gallery spaces and a research and education wing.[11] This expansion was made possible by the purchase of the Dorset Hotel and two townhouses on West 54th Street, allowing MoMA to fill up yet more of the block and expand even further west. The Museum invited ten prominent architectural firms (including Williams and Tsien) to submit proposals. In its competition program, MoMA noted the difficulty of the brief. Because the museum was 'the work of various architects,' competitors were asked to, 'demonstrate a sensitivity to the history and culture of this institution.' At the same time, proposals should be 'a great achievement in architectural design.'[12] Given the complicated nature of the

[11] Joanna Merwood, 'Ten Projects for the MoMA,' *Lotus International* 95 (1997), 27–45.

[12] 'Issues and Criteria of the Charette for the New Museum of Modern Art,' *Lotus International* 95 (1997), 34.

site and the requirement to respect the existing fabric with its illustrious history, competitors tended to shy away from grand statements. Rem Koolhaas' entry, featuring a giant 'MoMA Inc.' sign emblazoned on the facade, was a notable exception. This pointed critique of MoMA's corporate image conformed to the scholarly critique of the contemporary museum as a major driver of the culture economy, operating according to the logic of business and utilizing aesthetics for financial profit. Koolhaas' irreverent proposal exchanged the 'high' art of modern architecture for the 'low' art of advertising graphics, of signage, and the language of the glass-clad steel frame for that of a sans-serif typeface. However, as the complex history of the institution shows, MoMA had long since moved on from such a crude branding strategy.

The Museum as Object and Medium

At the turn of the twenty-first century, academic criticism of new museum architecture rested on its extravagant image-ability. Utilizing the two categories of late modernism set out by Robert Venturi and Denise Scott-Brown, this criticism applied equally to museums conceived as elegantly reconfigurable 'decorated sheds' (signified by the Centre Pompidou) or as sculpturally complex 'ducks' (such as the Guggenheim Bilbao). No matter which approach they employed, museum directors and architects were charged with exploiting the architectural image in pursuit of effect. The design of the original 1939 MoMA building prefigured that strategy. While the architects employed a modern aesthetic that is now familiar and unremarkable, this aesthetic was so different from other cultural buildings that it offered a unique brand identity. Built on the site of a townhouse at no.11 West 53rd

Street, the MoMA building was designed by MoMA trustee Philip Goodwin working in collaboration with Edward Durell Stone, a member of the team of architects working on the Rockefeller Center complex rising two blocks further south.[13] The Museum intended the building to be an exemplar of the International Style it had introduced in the famous 1932 exhibition. MoMA's Director, Alfred H. Barr Jr., was never happy with the choice of architects or the resulting building. Barr had traveled to Europe to consult with Ludwig Mies van der Rohe, Walter Gropius, and J. J. P. Oud. However, the Museum's President and trustees, including Nelson Rockefeller, preferred American architects. Cantilevered over the sidewalk, the sleek, semi-transparent cubic building Goodwin and Stone designed represented not the Bauhaus aesthetic of machine precision, but a version palatable to the American public. It was undoubtedly a pointed contrast to the brownstones that flanked it, and to the Art Deco commercial buildings and Neoclassical cultural monuments of New York City.[14] The interior, however, was more traditional, featuring galleries that replicated the scale and arrangement of the rooms in the original townhouse, with décor more *moderne* than modern. In this way, the Goodwin-Stone Building represented not the shock of the new, but a supremely urbane image of American modernism.

The MoMA building succeeded in cementing the International Style in the public consciousness. But, before long, it became too small to accommodate the Museum's growing collection and activities. During the Second World War and in the following years, the Museum commissioned prominent architects, including Marcel Breuer, to design exemplary modern houses for display at full-scale in its rear courtyard.[15] When it came to expanding the Museum building itself, however, MoMA continued its tradition and hired

13 Rona Roob, '1936: The Museum Selects an Architect: Excerpts from the Barr Papers of the Museum of Modern Art,' *Archives of the American Art Journal* 23, no. 1 (1983), 22–30; and Dominic Ricciotti, 'The 1939 Building of the Museum of Modern Art: The Goodwin-Stone Collaboration,' *The American Art Journal* 17, no. 3 (Summer 1985), 50–76.

14 Philip Goodwin and Edward Durell Stone, Museum of Modern Art, New York, 1939. Photo: Museum of the City of New York.

15 Mirka Beneš, 'Inventing a Modern Sculpture Garden in 1939 at the Museum of Modern Art, New York,' *Landscape Journal* 13, no. 1 (Spring 1994), 1–20; Beatriz Colomina, 'The Media House,' *Assemblage* (August 1995), 59.

16 On this period of Johnson's career, see: Joan Ockman, 'The Figurehead: On Monumentality and Nihilism in Philip Johnson's Life and Work,' *Philip Johnson: The Constancy of Change*, ed. Emmanuel Petit (New Haven: Yale University Press, 2009), 82–109.

17 Daniel M. Abramson, *Obsolescence: An Architectural History* (Chicago: University of Chicago Press, 2016), 80–87.

18 Philip Johnson, Museum of Modern Art Annexe, New York, 1964.

19 *The Museum of Modern Art Builds* (New York: Thirtieth Anniversary Committee of the Museum of Modern Art, 1962). See also: Thomas S. Hines, *Architecture and Design at the Museum of Modern Art: The Arthur Drexler Years, 1951–86* (Los Angeles: Getty Research Institute, 2019).

not an independent architect but another trustee, Philip Johnson. After the war, Johnson returned to the Museum as a member of the advisory committee following a controversial foray into politics.[16] Between 1953 and 1964 he designed a series of deliberately anti-monumental additions which became the model for future expansions.

Daniel Abramson has argued that, in its purest form, the high modernist style promoted by MoMA in its early exhibitions, represented an attempt to deal with obsolescence.[17] This design response depended on a technically sophisticated structural system, in theory capable of endless expansion and providing an infinitely flexible interior, all housed in a suitably monumental and permanent exterior. While such a system could accommodate almost any function or program, it was particularly well-suited to the museum type, with its ever-increasing collection and ever-changing displays. The iconic example of this approach, Abramson argues, is Mies' New National Gallery in Berlin (1961). While Johnson worked hard to emulate Mies in this period, in his MoMA additions he utilized not the form of Miesianism but its reproducible image.

Completed in 1964, Johnson's MoMA Annexe added two new wings on either side of the original building.[18] Each four bays wide and six bays high, the two wings were the same height as the Goodwin-Stone Building and articulated via an expressed steel frame with tinted windows. Johnson's restrained Miesianism suited MoMA's brief. The Annex was built to accommodate not only traditional galleries, but also a Department of Education, a film library, and a program of circulating exhibitions. Explicitly stated in a booklet MoMA sent to potential donors announcing the expansion, the goal was to produce not a new urban landmark, but rather to facilitate MoMA's function as a global taste-maker.[19] In the second half of the twentieth century, MoMA saw its role primarily as a publicity generator, producing and disseminating the image of modern art and architecture in the United States and internationally. Propelled by the Rockefeller family, the image of modern architecture that the Museum had helped create in the nineteen-thirties had become an all but ubiquitous signifier of modernity.

As its influence and premises grew, the imageability of MoMA as a unique object-building diminished. Although the Museum continued to promote architecture as an essential medium of modernity—not only in exhibitions but also in publications, films, and radio broadcasts—over time, its brand came to rest not on the originality of its architectural form but the ubiquity of its house style. Hence, in the nineteen-sixties and seventies, as MoMA's curators broadened their perspective to mount exhibitions of alternative strands of modern design, as well as shows featuring vernacular and historicist architecture—notably *Architecture Without Architects* (1964) and *The Architecture of the École des Beaux-Arts* (1976)—the MoMA building maintained allegiance to high American modernism. On the street facade, these additions were complementary rather than synthetic. Different architects, including Johnson and later Cesar Pelli, offered their interpretations of the modern style, layering one on top of the other. Within the volume of the block, and dictated by local practices of real estate development, these additions contributed to the general delirium of the Manhattan grid rather than lending it rational order. None were intended to usurp the supremacy of the now historic Goodwin-Stone original. As Alan Wallach has noted, where the 1939 building had once represented the idealized future, by the mid-twentieth century it had come to signify the idealized past.[20]

This complex history formed the background to the 1997

20 Alan Wallach, 'The Museum of Modern Art: The Past's Future,' *Journal of Design History* 5, no. 3 (1992), 211.

21 Glenn D. Lowry, *Designing the New Museum of Modern Art* (New York: Museum of Modern Art, 2004), 37.

22 'Architect's Statement: Yoshio Taniguchi,' in *Architecture for Art*, 228.

23 Yoshio Taniguchi, Museum of Modern Art addition, 53rd Street entrance, New York, 2004.

competition. How did the competitors deal with it? Most reveled in the 'non-objecthood-ness' of the MoMA campus, seeking to open it up, literally and metaphorically, to the city around it, and creating multiple pathways through it. This strategy aligned with a new curatorial stance adopted by MoMA's Director Glenn D. Lowry. Rejecting the rigid narrative of the evolution of modern art that had defined the Museum since its inception, Lowry argued for a more open curatorial approach.[21] The Museum might be considered a laboratory, he claimed, one in which a collective of curators continually re-wrote the history of modern art, taking the objects in its collections and displaying them in new exhibitions, testing out new narratives. Lowry used the metaphor of weaving; curators add threads, creating new patterns to the cloth of art history, which is continually expanding and growing. In spatial terms, this meant less prescribed circulation paths and more opportunities for visitors to find their way through the objects in the collection.

The metaphor of weaving aligned with the dominant theoretical paradigm of the nineteen-nineties: influential architects imagined the city as a field rather than an object, a plane for the performance of events. When Yoshio Taniguchi was named the winner of the competition, he wrote later, 'I approached the plan for the new MoMA as if it were an urban design. As opposed to designing a single new building, I treated the museum like a city within a city.'[22] The question is, to what kind of city was he referring? Opened in 2004, Taniguchi's expansion introduced a through-block lobby, visually connecting West 53rd and West 54th Streets for the first time, and an enormous, six-story high atrium for the installation of contemporary art.[23] Outside he took a contextual rather than synthetic approach, responding to the different characters of the two sides of the site. To the south, he created what he called a 'collage of milestones in the history of the museum's architecture ... restoring or preserving the existing buildings.'[24] To the north, he applied a monolithic grey, horizontal wall.[25] This wall was perhaps the least successful aspect of the addition, appearing less like a serene, unifying element as he intended, and more like an overscaled, high-end construction hoarding.

In an inversion of the terms of the criticism of the late-capitalist museum, critics disparaged Taniguchi's MoMA not because it was a memorable image created by a culturally revered author-designer, but because it was all but indistinguishable from the built vernacular of midtown Manhattan. The brand MoMA had created had become devalued. By the turn of the twenty-first century, it had long ceased to represent the avant-garde. The large, minimalist interior spaces Taniguchi had created attracted unflattering comparisons to a shopping mall and an airport. In place of the Goodwin-Stone Building's metropolitan urbanity, the Taniguchi addition seemed less an expression of architecture as a 'field condition,' and more of the aesthetically incoherent late-twentieth-century condition Koolhaas had labeled 'BIGNESS.' BIG buildings, Koolhaas argued, were dictated by the prosaic requirements of crowd circulation via elevators and escalators, and industrial-scale environmental conditioning via climate control and fluorescent lighting. A singular architectural gesture or even a combination of gestures could not control such buildings.[26] Neither good nor bad, they were beyond assessment in traditional aesthetic terms. Doubled in size by Taniguchi's addition, had MoMA become the first BIG museum? This possibility spurred a sense of dread when the Folk Art Museum came up for sale.

24 See 'Architect's Statement: Yoshio Taniguchi,' in *Architecture for Art*, 228.

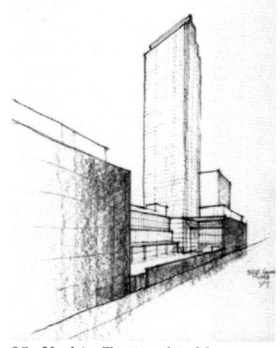

25 Yoshio Taniguchi, Museum of Modern Art addition, 54th Street entrance and courtyard, New York, 2004.

26 Rem Koolhaas and Bruce Mau, 'Bigness, or the Problem of Large,' in O.M.A, Rem Koolhaas, Bruce Mau, *S, M, L, XL* (New York: Monacelli Press, 1995), 494–516.

Creative Destruction

27 See, for example: C. J. Hughes, 'Sale of Folk Art Museum Sparks Demolition Fears,' *Architectural Record* 199, no. 6 (June 2011), 26, and Bonnie Rosenberg and Helen Stoilas, 'Don't Blame the Building,' *Art Newspaper* 20, no. 225 (June 2011), 18.

28 Martin Filler, 'MoMA: A Needless Act of Destruction,' *The New York Review of Books* 60, no. 9 (May 23, 2013), 4. See also: Barry Schwabsky, 'MoMA's Demolition Derby,' *The Nation* 296 (May 20, 2013), 5; and Michael Lewis, 'MoMA Adrift,' *The New Criterion* 32 no. 9 (May 2014), 1–6.

29 Michael Webb, 'For Folk's Sake,' *The Architectural Review* 233, no. 1396 (June 2013), 15–16.

While the Folk Art Museum had received a positive critical reception and several architectural awards, the timing of its opening in late 2001 was terrible. Following the attack on the World Trade Center, New York City experienced a steep drop in tourist visitors. The financial crisis that followed led to a worldwide recession. These events made it difficult for the Folk Art Museum to sustain its $32 million debt. In 2011 the Museum moved into smaller premises near Lincoln Center and put its nearly new building up for sale. The Folk Art Museum site was especially attractive because MoMA owned the site immediately to the east. In collaboration with a developer, MoMA planned to construct an apartment tower with ground floor exhibition galleries designed by Jean Nouvel. When newspaper reports announced MoMA was the purchaser, rumors circulated that the larger institution considered its smaller neighbor expendable.[27]

MoMA announced its demolition plan in 2013; critics labeled it a 'tragic turn of events' and a 'mistake of epic proportions.'[28] They accused MoMA of failing its institutional responsibility, and even of committing a crime.[29] Journalistic outrage was partly caused by the closeness of the parties involved. Despite the size of the city, the architecture world is small. Some published criticism came in the form of personal attacks, accusing those in charge of MoMA of acting vindictively, of exacting revenge for the Folk Art Museum's earlier refusal to swap sites. This heated opposition came from a sense of betrayal. Arguably, more than any other institution in the country, MoMA had promoted architecture as a product of exceptionally high cultural value, equivalent to the fine arts. The Museum had been responsible for introducing modern architecture to the United States, via the

International Style exhibition, and for promoting the careers of key practitioners for eighty years. How could this prestigious institution fail to support a building that the architecture world had declared so worthy?

As critic Jorge Otero-Pailos has noted, at the root of the debate was a disagreement about MoMA's responsibility toward the critically-acclaimed thirteen-year-old building.[30] The Folk Art Museum did not qualify for the protections given to buildings recognized for their heritage status, and MoMA had no legal obligation to preserve it. However, its champions argued that the building's exceptional quality and architectural value, legitimated by architectural awards, gave it an inherent cultural significance and a claim to longevity. In these terms, critics argued that MoMA was morally obliged to conserve at least part of it. But what kind of preservation would be acceptable? Reacting to the possibility of the Folk Art Museum's demolition, several critics raised the possibility of 'adaptive re-use' as a solution, suggesting that the smaller building be incorporated somehow into MoMA's extension, possibly even re-designed by Williams and Tsien themselves.[31] Some argued that this solution was in keeping with the history of the MoMA building. Given that Taniguchi's addition and renovation had recognized the museum campus' patchwork nature, critics suggested that Williams and Tsien's building might be successfully absorbed into the *assemblage*. Ironically, it was MoMA that now exhibited the characteristics of vernacular or folk art: retrofitted, recycled, and adaptable. MoMA hired the New York firm Diller Scofidio + Renfro to assess this possibility. But as Elizabeth Diller noted, the Folk Art Museum suffered from its singularity. The particularity of its design made adaptation difficult and expensive. Ultimately, Diller concluded, it could not usefully function as part of the MoMA extension.

[30] Jorge Otero-Pailos, 'Remembrance of Things to Come,' *Artforum International* 52, no. 8, (April 2014), 115–116.

[31] Michael Sorkin, 'Big MoMA's House,' *The Nation* 298, no. 10–11 (March 10–17, 2014), 36.

[32] Aaron Betsky, 'Modern Folk,' *Architect* 100, no. 6 (June 2011), 82.

[33] Sorkin, 'Big MoMA's House,' 36.

Likening the finely-crafted facade of the Folk Art Museum to a painting by Pablo Picasso or Gerhard Richter, advocates of preservation argued that to destroy it was akin to destroying a work of fine art. Several argued that it be removed and preserved for future installation elsewhere. This suggestion points to the liminal status of the Folk Art Museum in particular and architecture in general. When considered in commercial terms, architecture devalues over time; when understood as one of the fine arts (a position MoMA advocated), it retains its value and even gains in value as it ages. But while critics lauded the Folk Art Museum as a work of fine art, imbued with a precious aura, in practice this same quality rendered it highly vulnerable to the cycle of renewal. Tailor-made for its original purpose, it had become obsolete in only a dozen years.

For the art and architecture press, Williams and Tsien's building was not only a finely crafted container for, and symbol of, American folk art culture, a design perfectly adapted to its program and site. It also represented a corrective to MoMA's presentation of the canon of modern architecture. The critic Aaron Betsky suggested that MoMA preserve the building's facade within the new structure as 'memory of the particular brand of reaction to modernity.'[32] As another critic, Michael Sorkin, put it, while MoMA favored architecture

> ... in the Bauhaus tradition, with its aura of functionalist architecture, craft, and performance. Williams and Tsien, on the other hand, are more clearly linked to a branch that includes Frank Lloyd Wright, Louis Kahn, Carlo Scarpa and, perhaps especially, Paul Rudolph—known for his brilliantly unyielding interiors—and other exponents of a thicker sense of materiality and of a specific style of complex orthogonality.[33]

As Abramson argues in his contribution to this book, while functionalist architecture resisted the imperative of obsolescence by absorbing the principle of continual change in the form of an adaptable and expandable system, these architects' work symbolized resistance to obsolescence differently, recalling the archaic and timeless.

Besides representing an alternative legacy of modernism, Sorkin suggested that feelings about the Folk Art Museum ran high, in part, as a rebuke to the kind of urban architecture culture that MoMA had played a role in creating and validating: the compatibility of modern architecture with processes of expansion and renewal. In demolishing the Folk Art Museum, MoMA had acted like a real estate developer with an 'insatiable territorial imperative' rather than a cultural institution. (Donald Trump was referenced here, reinforcing an implied connection between real estate development and lack of morals and good taste).[34] In these terms, beyond its material and spatial qualities, the Folk Art Museum had value as a form of built critique, a finely sculpted counter-point to its refined but bland next-door neighbor.

This episode offered critics the opportunity to question MoMA's destructive actions in the present and its historical influence. MoMA's demolition of the Folk Art Museum seems unjustifiable according to many of the principles of contemporary architecture culture. In demolishing its neighbor, MoMA failed to recognize the worth and quality of a celebrated building. Acting against the principles of sustainability and adaptive re-use, it also wasted costly building resources. Finally, in destroying an example of an alternative strain of modern architecture, MoMA maintained the hegemony of Bauhaus-inspired, high-modern architecture when stylistic and cultural pluralism is considered desirable. Besides illustrating the clash of values between MoMA and

34 Webb, 'For Folk's Sake,' 15.

architecture culture, however, this episode is also useful in problematizing academic criticism of the architecture of the late-capitalist museum.

According to the logic of the spectacle, architecture is supplementary to the museum as an institution. Its value is as a billboard for the museum, giving it a visual identity. Williams and Tsien's Folk Art Museum serves as an example of this approach. As with the Guggenheim Bilbao, the Folk Art Museum believed that by commissioning internationally recognized architects to create a high-quality building, they would significantly increase the institution's profile and visitor numbers. Like the Guggenheim Bilbao, a large part of the resulting building's appeal lay in its sculpted facade. Involving enormous capital expenditure, this strategy is always risky and, in the case of the Folk Art Museum, it was not successful. The publicity benefit accrued by the impressive and eye-catching building was not enough to offset the Museum's precarious financial position.

However, as the example of MoMA reveals, other modes of relationship between architecture, the museum, and the processes of capitalist renewal are possible. Architecture is not a supplement to MoMA: it has always been a core part of the Museum's identity. In one its earliest exhibitions, MoMA brought architecture into the museum not only as a sub-discipline of the fine arts, but as the discipline most representative of modernity. Influenced by its founders and trustees, MoMA's curators translated the formal impermanence, transparency, and reliance on industrial production of the European avant-garde into a system of modern architecture ideally suited for the ongoing cycle of capitalist development. MoMA has diversified its curatorial strategy significantly since the International Style exhibition. At the same time, additions to the iconic 1939 Goodwin-Stone Building exemplify the Museum's continued belief, backed up by investment, in the ongoing value of its particular brand of modernism to the institution. MoMA's early investment in architecture as a vital part of its collection has ensured its ongoing importance for architecture culture, even as the architectural figure of the institution recedes into the ground of the ubiquitous corporate modernism it helped create.

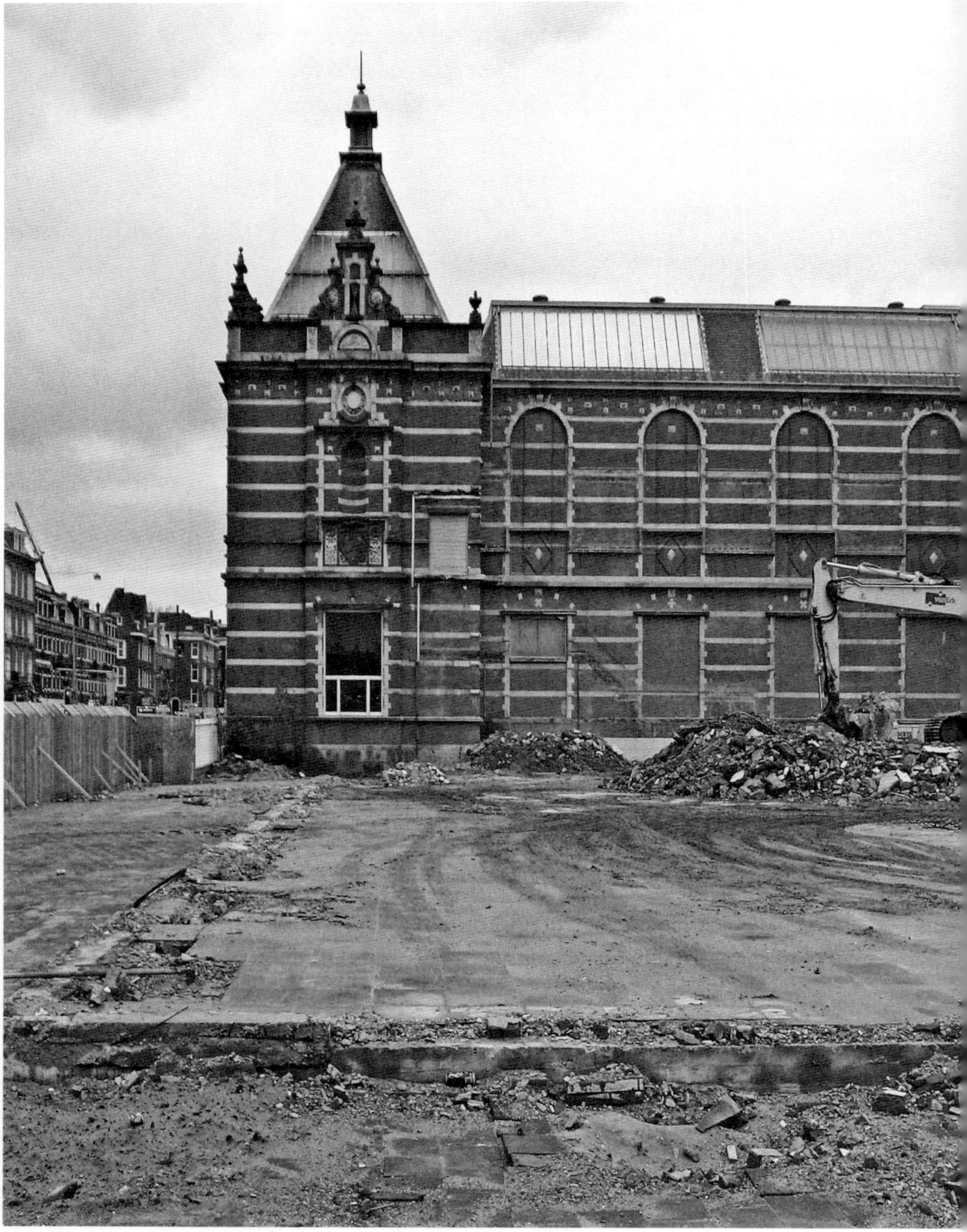

The demolition of the Sandberg wing, Stedelijk Museum Amsterdam, 20 December 2006. Photo: Stadsarchief Amsterdam/ Martin Albers.

Debasing The Collection

AMO, Rem Koolhaas, and the Art and Architecture Heritage of the Stedelijk Museum Amsterdam

Wouter Davidts and
Anton Pereira Rodriguez

1 Ank Leeuw-Marcar, *Willem Sandberg: Portrait of an Artist* (Amsterdam: Valiz, 2013), 105.

A museum is simply not a subject for a competition. You may perhaps be able to create a multiple commission by calling for idea sketches so that you can choose the architect, but the whole execution of the museum plan has to be done by the architect and museum man [sic] together. As long, of course, as the museum man [sic] is able to read architectural drawings, which is not always the case.
—Willem Sandberg, director of the Stedelijk Museum Amsterdam (1945–1963)[1]

On December 16, 2017, the Stedelijk Museum Amsterdam unveiled Stedelijk BASE, the new presentation of its permanent collection, designed by Rem Koolhaas and Federico Martelli of AMO (the research-focused branch of Koolhaas' architectural practice OMA). With Stedelijk BASE the museum collection is no longer displayed in the galleries of the main building (A.W. Weissman, 1895), but in the basement gallery of the museum's newest wing (Benthem Crouwel, 2012). Whereas a chronological arrangement of works runs along the perimeter of the gallery, thematic arrangements are presented with a system of thin, freestanding, irregular grey walls, made of fifteen-millimeter-thick steel plates, clad with two layers of birch plywood, painted white, scattered by Koolhaas and Martelli throughout the space. The result is a maze-like layout of zones and areas within which approximately 700 works from the museum's world-class collection are put on view.² Apart from the largest collection of works by Kazimir Malevich outside Russia and a significant ensemble of De Stijl and Cobra works, the museum also possesses an impressive ensemble of postwar American art and a vast collection of applied arts and design. The new collection display aims to highlight the variety and richness of the museum's holdings by combining works of art with graphic, textile, household and furniture design, prints, and photography.

Koolhaas was brought in by director Beatrix Ruf in 2016. When the German curator took the helm of the Stedelijk in 2014, being only the second director working with the new building, she immediately voiced her discontent regarding the routing through the museum and the overall experience of the galleries. When she revealed the plans for a revised layout of the Stedelijk in 2016 and the appointment of Koolhaas, she did not beat around the bush:

> For an ambitious museum such as the Stedelijk, redesigning the building's layout is indispensable. Our goal is not to be a static museum, but to be a dynamic, perpetually self-renewing institute, and always maximize our visitors' experience. The revised spatial design allows us to use our collection to tell the stories relevant to today, with even greater impact.³

2 AMO and Rem Koolhaas, Display system for Stedelijk BASE, Stedelijk Museum Amsterdam, 2017, installation view. Photo: Ossip van Duivenbode.

3 'New Layout of the Building,' press release, Stedelijk Museum Amsterdam, September 6, 2016, www.stedelijk.nl/en/news/new-layout-of-the-building.

It speaks much of Ruf that she did not give in to the expansionary impulse of new museum directors, whereas the majority of her colleagues time and again opt for a scenario of growth when voicing the wish to dramatically change the museum.[4] Her solution was to resolutely flip the script. In the new director's vision the entire newly built extension, both the galleries in the basement and the galleries on the first floor, would be devoted to the display of the permanent collection, featuring a mix of disciplines (BASE). Art from 1880 to 1980 would be on display in the vast, column-free lower level gallery (Part 1), while a presentation of art after 1980 was going to be located in the more traditional, medium-sized galleries on the first floor (Part 2). The ground floor of the old building would present the collection in topical and thematic presentations (TURNS). Finally, the first floor of the old building with its renowned enfilade of galleries of different size and modes of lighting would host temporary exhibitions (NOW).[5] Ruf thus suggested to use the old building for contemporary art and the new building for the historical collection—a 'drastic reversal', which Koolhaas, as he declared in a Dutch newspaper, found 'irresistibly interesting.'[6]

Invariably, Stedelijk BASE has been portrayed in the press as a remarkable architectural experiment for the presentation of an art collection. It is seen as a new episode in the Stedelijk Museum's rich history of innovative display systems and radical exhibitions. Once we digest the usual rhetoric of novelty and experiment, however, we will argue here, AMO and Koolhaas' design is in fact unexpectedly conventional and vexed. It can be considered as not only another unfortunate milestone in the institution's rather ill-advised treatment of its architectural heritage, but also as an architectural intervention with dramatic consequences for its art patrimony. The so-called 'drastic reversal' in essence has filled the

---

[4] In 2017, Beatrix Ruf edited a volume of essays that specifically dealt with the scenario of (de)growth of 21st century museums. See: Beatrix Ruf and John Slyce, eds., *Size Matters! (De)Growth of the 21st Century Art Museum: 2017 Verbier Art Summit* (London: Koenig Books, 2017). As early as 1995 Stephen E. Weil, former director of the Smithsonian's Hirshhorn Museum and Sculpture Garden, wondered: 'When was a museum director last honored for a twenty-year record of consistent resistance to every expansionary impulse?'

[5] Cross section of the Stedelijk Museum Amsterdam, 'Stedelijk BASE Opens 16 December 2017,' press release, September 13, 2017.

[6] Rem Koolhaas in: Jan Pieter Ekker and Rob Malasch, '"Een parade van greatest hits? Nee", Stedelijk Museum. Vaste Collectie voortaan in de kelderruimte te zien,' *Het Parool*, December 18, 2017; see also: '"Je kunt focussen op meerdere beelden tegelijk": Interview met Rem Koolhaas,' *NRC Handelsblad*, December 14, 2017.

expansive gallery in the basement of Benthem Crouwel's extension—originally designed to host large-scale contemporary art commissions—with an immoveable wall system that in fact annuls the envisioned flexibility of the space, debasing the value of the art collection in the process.[7] Ultimately, it is the integrity of the art collection that suffers the most from the new mode of display.

7 Installation of the freestanding walls designed by AMO and Rem Koolhaas, 2017. Photo: DSL Studio.

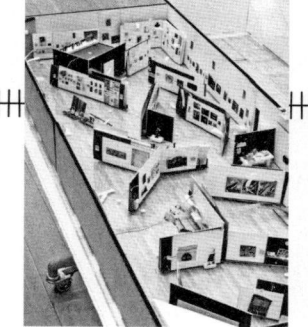

AMO and Rem Koolhaas, Design model for Stedelijk BASE, 2017, oma.eu/projects/stedelijk-base.

Shocking Secrets

Traditionally, a museum's collection is thought of as an array of artefacts that the institution, on behalf of society, considers valuable enough in cultural terms to keep, conserve, study, and display for the benefit of present-day and future publics. Invariably then, a collection also reflects the values a society stands for, and how these are negotiated and change over time, through and with the art that has been amassed. No wonder that most museum collections are as diverse as they are different. Every museum collection delivers, at once, an approximation of art history and an account of the institution's own history. It incorporates a record of the institution's development, the interests of its directors, as much as traces of past exhibitions and the larger cultural and societal trends these were expected to respond to. All too often, however, when the expansionary impulse hits a museum, that heritage—regardless of its inherent qualities and deficiencies—is put at risk.

In the mid-nineteen-nineties Koolhaas professed that 'architecture reveals the deepest and sometimes most shocking secrets of how the values of a society are organized.' At the time the architect even went as far as to discern a renewed belief in an architect's 'power to physically articulate new

8   Rem Koolhaas, as cited in: Douglas Coupland, 'Rem Koolhaas, Post-Nationalist Architect,' *The New York Times*, September 11, 1994.

9   Benthem Crouwel Architects, New extension of Stedelijk Museum Amsterdam, 2012. Photo: Jannes Linders. For a discussion of the 2012 architecture competition and the previous phases, see: Wouter Davidts, 'Nostalgia and Pragmatism: The New Stedelijk Museum Amsterdam,' in *Triple Bond: Essays on Art, Architecture, and Museums* (Amsterdam: Valiz, 2017), 185–200. For a discussion of the winning design of Benthem Crouwel, see: Hans Ibelings, *Stedelijk Architecture* (Amsterdam: Stedelijk Museum, 2012).

visions.'[8] To this day these words still sound prophetic and haven't lost any of their critical resonance. They express a fundamental belief in the imaginative powers of the discipline of architecture to grant its practice a critical grounding.

If we follow Koolhaas' proclamation then, any renewal of a permanent collection display and the associated exhibition architecture, contains the inherent capacity to 'reveal the deepest and sometimes most shocking secrets' of the organization of societal values—such as those of art—that every museum collection entails. In other words, it provides the opportunity to assess the importance and virtue of art, and of culture at large, within contemporary society. Even more, it presents the occasion to foster truly imaginative responses to the challenges twenty-first-century museums are facing when dealing with the vast collections of artefacts that are held in storage, waiting to be put on display. Which objects are to be selected from the invariably large holdings of museums, and subsequently, what 'stories relevant to today' can be told with them?

Sweet Revenge and Homecoming

The commission to design the exhibition architecture for the permanent collection at the Stedelijk Museum must have been sweet revenge for Koolhaas. Twice his office OMA missed out on the opportunity to expand his beloved museum. In 1992 the design of Venturi Scott Brown was selected over theirs in the first architecture competition for an extension of the Stedelijk. In 2003 they weren't even shortlisted for the second architecture competition. Eventually the design of Benthem Crouwel was awarded first prize: the so-called 'bathtub' that opened in 2012.[9] Ruf's invitation in 2016, however, finally granted the Dutch architect an opportunity to leave his mark. While Koolhaas initially advised Ruf on the new routing through the building, the architect and AMO were later commissioned to develop the exhibition architecture for the basement galleries, that is, to develop a structure to showcase highlights from the permanent collection from 1880 to 1980. To this end they worked intensely with Ruf and the team of Stedelijk curators, to the extent that Federico Martelli, AMO's project architect, even acted as an 'embedded collaborator' of the museum.[10] The architects were, in other words, not just contracted to conceive an architectural support for the artefacts selected by the director and her curatorial team, but also to co-determine with the latter the overall conceptual thrust of the new collection display.[11] This situation was in many respects unique. In most, if not all of the recent revisionist rearrangements of the permanent collection at peer institutions of the Stedelijk such as Centre Pompidou in Paris, Tate Modern in London, or The Museum of Modern Art in New York, architects were not invited to the table from early on.[12] Never did an architect receive so much responsibility and decision-making power in both the mode of display and the selection of works from the collection as with Stedelijk BASE.

Apart from a revenge of sorts, the commission was first and foremost a homecoming for Koolhaas. Growing up in Amsterdam, he allegedly frequented the museum on an almost daily basis between the age of twelve and eighteen. 'The Stedelijk Museum was my university, really,' the architect stated on the eve of the opening of Stedelijk BASE. 'I can say that my entire aesthetical sense has been determined by the history of the Stedelijk.'[13] Two shows that Koolhaas vividly remembered from his visits as a youngster are *Bewogen Beweging* (Moving Movement, 1961) and *Dylaby* (1962), two

10 Rem Koolhaas in: Ekker and Malasch, '"Een parade van greatest hits? Nee".'

11 This situation became all the more pressing as Ruf was forced to step down in October 2017, two months prior to the opening of BASE, leaving Koolhaas in fact as the main author of the enterprise. She resigned following allegations of a lack of transparency in her external activities as a private art advisor and accusations of failing to disclose details around a large donation of 200 works to the contemporary and modern art museum by German collector Thomas Borgmann, which also involved the purchasing of works. In June 2018 an independent investigation cleared her of any wrongdoing.

12 When the Tate Modern opened in 2000, it surprised both the critics and the larger public with a thematic organization of the collection: yet the architects Herzog & De Meuron had no hand in it. Some years later, the Centre Pompidou presented a feminist and non-occidental perspective on its collection, respectively with elles@centrepompidou (2009–2011) and *Modernités plurielles* (2013–2015). At both the Tate Modern and Centre Pompidou the exercise was done first and foremost by curators and art historians. The revising of the historical canon that every museum collection invariably relates to and to a certain extent represents, as well as the search for formulas to make the collection more attractive and accessible to larger publics, were at both institutions approached as principally museological exercises. The architecture within which the new narrative had to be deployed, either existed (Tate) or came second (Pompidou). In the recent rehanging of the collection at the Museum of Modern Art in New York, following the major renovation by Diller Scofidio + Renfro (2019), once again the responsibility rested fully with the museum curators. The architects were not involved.

13 Rem Koolhaas in video *Stedelijk Base / The Making of*, Stedelijk Museum Amsterdam, 2018.

14 Daniel Spoerri, Installation for *Dylaby*, 1962. Photo: Ed van der Elsken.

15 Rem Koolhaas, as cited in: Claire Wrathall, 'Cultural Capital: The Spectacular Stedelijk Base Calls for an Arty Weekend in Amsterdam,' *Telegraph*, January 31, 2018.

16 Alice Twemlow, 'Museum With Walls,' *DISEGNO* 18 (July 2018). In fact, in his keynote speech delivered at the opening of the museum Koolhaas made references to the 'rather cheap looking' displays used by Sandberg. See: Domeniek Ruyters, 'Base Values: De nieuwe vaste opstelling van het Stedelijk,' *Metropolis M*, December 14, 2017.

17 For a sincere account of the Sandberg wing see: Paul Kempers, *Binnen was buiten: De Sandberg-vleugel Amsterdam* (Amsterdam: Valiz, 2010).

groundbreaking and legendary exhibitions in the museum's history. In the late nineteen-fifties and early nineteen-sixties the museum gained international fame with radical experiments in display and exhibition architecture, instigated by the flamboyant and visionary director Willem Sandberg. *Bewogen Beweging*, curated by the artist Daniel Spoerri, is considered as the first exhibition to bring together artists working in kinetic art, performance, happenings, and film. Widely popular with the public it was a Neo-Dadaist experience of movement and audience participation. In a similar way, *Dylaby*—an abbreviation of dynamic labyrinth—radically defied the traditional experience of museum visitors. Conceived in close dialogue with the participating six artists—Per Olof Ultvedt, Robert Rauschenberg, Martial Raysse, Niki de Saint Phalle, Daniel Spoerri, and Jean Tinguely—the various artist's installations in the rooms of the Stedelijk challenged the static encounter with art. The artists presented artworks on both the floor and the ceiling to create a disorientating effect.[14]

Stedelijk BASE, according to Koolhaas and Martelli, can be considered at once a continuation of and homage to these historically novel modes of display.[15] Additionally, their design references a remarkable piece of the museum's architectural heritage. During the design process, for which they explored the different strategies that the museum used over the years, the architects became particularly interested in a system of freestanding exhibition partitions they called the 'Stedelijk wall.'[16] This modular wall system had been used extensively between 1955 and 1979 in the expansion at the back of the old building, the so-called Sandberg wing (J. Sargentini and F. Eschauzier, 1954) that was sadly destroyed in 2006 to announce the construction of the new extension by Benthem Crouwel.[17] With its open floor plan and windows from floor to ceiling, this modest yet groundbreaking building materialized Sandberg's radical ideas about a democratic, accessible, and living museum. Contrary to the robust and stately building from the nineteenth century, this modern pavilion spoke the language of both transparency and flexibility.[18] Pedestrians and cyclists could look straight into the museum and see what was on view, 'without paying any entrance fee.'[19]

According to the Belgian art critic writing for the arts magazine *L'œil*, Michel Seuphor, in 1956, no other exhibition space responded so well to the modern spirit and use of space. It delivered an ideal answer to the demands of contemporary art and museum practice.[20] Sandberg indeed conceived of the building as an outright flexible space that could be rearranged according to the needs of every new exhibition. To that end he developed a system of freestanding walls that could be easily rearranged to create new spatial conditions for display:

> Then there was my plan for free-standing partitions that you could move around, standard partitions so that you could have the paintings at right angles to the windows and never needed to hang them opposite a window. In that way, you wouldn't get very much reflection and you could, in my opinion, easily create a route.[21]

Sandberg's schematic floor plan of the new museum space of 1954 shows the underlying aims.[22] Visitors could wander freely through the exhibition space, creating their own routes according to their natural sense of orientation.[23] As the freestanding walls were supported by slender legs, the visitor could also retain an overview of the general layout of the exhibition.[24]

18 The Sandberg wing, 2000. Photo: Stadsarchief Amsterdam/Martin Albers.

19 Leeuw-Marcar, *Willem Sandberg*, 105–106.

20 Michel Seuphor, 'Un musée militant (Stedelijk Museum Amsterdam),' *L'oeil* 2, no. 19/20 (1956), 35. 'C'est la plus belle réussite du Musée et je ne crois pas qu'il y ait, actuellement, dans aucun endroit au monde un lieu d'exposition plus idéal, mieux adapté à l'esprit moderne et aux multiples usages de l'espace.' (This is the most beautiful achievement of the Museum and I don't believe that there is, actually, anywhere in the world a more ideal exhibition space, better adapted to the modern spirit and the multiple usages of space. Translation by the authors.)

21 Leeuw-Marcar, *Willem Sandberg*, 101.

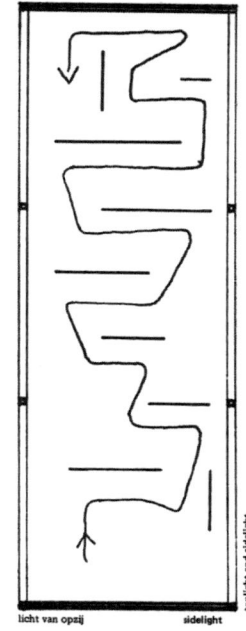

22 Willem Sandberg, Schematic floor plan of the new museum wing, 1954. From: Carel Blotkamp, *Museum in ¿Motion? The Modern Art Museum at Issue* (The Hague: Govt. Pub. Office, 1979), 330.

23 Kempers, *Binnen was buiten*, 49.

24 *4 Amerikanen*, Stedelijk Museum Amsterdam, 1962, installation view. Photo: Nederlands Fotomuseum/Jaap d'Oliveira.

Urban Density and Visual Synchronicity

At first sight, Stedelijk BASE presents itself as a smart merger of the labyrinthine set-up of such exhibitions as *Bewogen Beweging* and *Dylaby* and the free arrangement of walls of the Sandberg pavilion, with a contemporary twist. For Koolhaas, the design for the permanent collection display had to provide a multiplicity of spatial possibilities. 'We did not want to create a rigid circuit for visitors,' the architect pointed out. 'They'll have the freedom to explore in different directions, and choose their own route, as adventurous as circulation through any city.'[25] For Ruf, the permanent collection display had to respond to the new forms of visual literacy that have arisen in the present-day era of digital data and communication. 'The widespread use of the Internet has given us a new way to gather information,' Ruf claimed, 'We browse, see masses of images in one go, connect them and make combinations.'[26]

The resulting scheme for Stedelijk BASE combines both views: Koolhaas' model of urban density and Ruf's model of visual synchronicity. The architect's predilection for metropolitan life and an urban culture of congestion conveniently doubles up with the curators' wholehearted embrace of the continuous coexistence and potential exchangeability of images in the digital sphere. The collection presentation no longer aims to offer a concise, authored story, but an open-ended, multifarious field of possible linkages.[27] Triumphantly the press release states:

> The lay-out understands the collection as a network of relations rather than as a presentation of individual artworks. To capture these networks, very thin walls define an almost urban environment of free association and multiple relations.[28]

---

25 Rem Koolhaas, as cited in: 'Stedelijk BASE opens,' Stedelijk Museum Amsterdam, December 14, 2017, www.stedelijk.nl/en/news/stedelijk-base-opens (accessed June 11, 2019).

26 Beatrix Ruf, as cited in: 'Stedelijk BASE Opens 16 December 2017,' press release, Stedelijk Museum Amsterdam, September 13, 2017, www.stedelijk.nl/en/news/stedelijk-base-the-new-collection-presentation-of-the-stedelijk-museum-amsterdam-will-open-on-16-december-2017-2.

27 Rem Koolhaas and AMO, Concept-drawing of the Stedelijk collection, 2017. oma.eu/projects/stedelijk-base.

28 'Stedelijk BASE Opens,' press release, Stedelijk Museum Amsterdam, December 14, 2017, www.stedelijk.nl/en/news/stedelijk-base-opens (accessed June 11, 2019).

However, despite such pronouncements, and the deep affinity demonstrated between the architects and the museum, Koolhaas' and Martelli's reference to the Stedelijk's rich art and architecture patrimony and exhibition history is as empty as it is false. The walls may be thin, but they are heavyweights. In the end no less than 180 tons of steel were rigged into the basement space. The plates may only be fifteen millimeter thick, but their very weight prevents them from being moved or rearranged. In the end, Koolhaas and Martelli delivered a most stable and irreplaceable structure—given the unexpectedly high expense it is very unlikely that it will be taken out soon. Moreover, the thin plaster wall boards that are omnipresent in museum buildings and which the architects attempted to avoid, sort of made a ghostly return. In order to be able to affix any work onto the steel walls, two layers of birch plywood, painted white, had to be glued onto the steel surfaces.[29] Yet, even more importantly, the very spatial set-up the walls provide, ultimately has troublesome effects on the display of the collection, the very *raison d'être* of the whole enterprise.

29 Martelli, as cited in: Twemlow, 'Museum With Walls.'

Innovative or Conservative

In essence, the collection display of Stedelijk BASE follows a double logic. A timeline with works strictly arranged in order of date from 1880 to 1980, runs along the perimeter of the gallery, boasting representative masterpieces, mostly paintings, from the respective decades. Thematic arrangements of historic movements (Amsterdam School, Abstract Expressionism, Post-Minimal), societal themes (The First and Second World War, Utopia and Dystopia) and influential artists (Malevich, Mondrian, Kandinsky) inhabit different

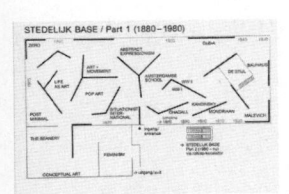

30 Rem Koolhaas and Frederico Martelli, Schematic floorplan of 'Stedelijk BASE,' 2017. Courtesy Stedelijk Museum Amsterdam.

31 'Stedelijk BASE', installation view, 2018. Barnett Newman's *Cathedra* (1951) next to a series of chairs by Charles & Ray Eames. Photo: Wouter Davidts.

32 Christophe Van Gerrewey, 'Stedelijk Base: De nieuwe collectieopstelling,' *De Witte Raaf* 191 (January–February 2019) (our translation).

33 Ibid.

corners and zones within the maze of thin and grey walls of steel, without being allotted to discrete areas.[30] The collection display, moreover, is not limited to works of fine art. The curators and architects also picked artefacts from the Stedelijk's rich collection of design, graphic design, and applied arts, subsequently dispersing them throughout the already dense arrangement. One can find, for example, three Eames' chairs on protruding wall elements along Barnett Newman's *Cathedra*,[31] or Dieter Rams and Hans Gugelot's iconic 1956 Braun Phonosuper (model SK 4)—also known as 'Snow White's Coffin'—flanked on the left by Sedje Hémon's 1961 black-and-white music-referencing linocut, *Pas de Quatre, and* Pablo Picasso's 1956 large oil painting *Femme nue devant le jardin*, on the right. Further down the timeline one can spot Ettore Sottsass and Perry King's 1969 plastic portable typewriter, *Valentine S*, right below Jagoda Buić's 1967 hanging sculpture in sisal and textile, *Fallen Angel*.

As a result, Stedelijk BASE not only offers a different type of museum space, but a museum experience that is, as Belgian art and architecture critic Christophe Van Gerrewey rightfully noted, 'defined by simultaneity, superficiality, supreme individual impressions (and the absence of authority), aura-less objects, irreducible plenitude and not so much the possibility as the transience of interpretations.'[32] Traditionally, the museum has been held to function as a stronghold against such phenomena: in a society where experience has become ever more commercialized, mediatized, and fleeting, the museum is often promoted as a rare site of focus, concentration, deceleration, and reflection. Koolhaas, however, intervenes in such a fashion, Van Gerrewey remarks, that any critique on a project like his is deemed 'irrefutably conservative.'[33] Why could one have anything against Stedelijk BASE's inherent promise of free exchange, assessment, association, multiple meanings, and individual agency?

At the start Ruf claimed that the revised spatial design would aim to use the Stedelijk's collection to 'tell the stories relevant to today.'[34] Yet does Stedelijk BASE live up to this promise? What is the larger narrative about art collections in general, and about the collection of the Stedelijk Museum in particular, that is being advanced by the mode of display that Koolhaas inserted in the basement of the Stedelijk?

The larger narrative advanced by Stedelijk BASE, we would like to argue here, is that there is no larger narrative (possible)—only smart diagrams of dynamic relations.[35] The very refusal to tell an overarching story has become a story in and of itself. And architecture plays the leading role in this. The maze-like set-up of Stedelijk BASE, Van Gerrewey insightfully notes, indeed makes clear, at any point in the exhibition, that 'there is always more, that other objects, timeframes, genres or artistic choices are also begging for attention, and that—in the end—every museological construction is precisely that: a construction, a fabrication of historians and curators.'[36] History is no longer deemed singular, but plural. On an ideological level very few will disagree with such arguments. No museum today can still claim to present an authoritative account of art history, and very few actually still do. Stedelijk BASE's architecture however dramatically exemplifies the moment at which this revisionist urge turns into a rhetorical void. In Amsterdam the pluralist narrative is at once institutionalized and built. The curators' and architects' shared belief in a set-up that is predicated on surprising connections and exciting associations has turned into a self-fulfilling prophecy. The principle sounds very promising rhetorically, but utterly fails on the level of experience and understanding.

[34] 'New Layout of the Building,' Stedelijk Museum Amsterdam.

[35] For their analysis of the collection of the Stedelijk Museum, AMO produced a large set of schemes mapping the potential relationships between the various parts of the collection in both historically and thematically informed 'clusters'. These schemes then informed the dispersed display of the artworks. See: 'Projects: Stedelijk BASE,' oma.eu/projects/stedelijk-base (accessed May 1, 2020).

[36] Van Gerrewey, 'Stedelijk Base' (our translation).

Conformist and Reactionary

The timeline with works on the perimeter of the gallery schoolishly reduces history to a scroll bar—amplified by the dumbfounding fact that all works are, literally, installed on one neat, straight line, precisely on the horizontal middle of each work.[37] The display system and arrangement of works within the gallery in turn transmute the collection into a curious mix of a Pinterest board and a high-end flea market—especially when viewed from the 'urban' observatory on top of the reconstruction of the Gerrit Rietveld and Truus Schröder-Schräder's 1926 Harrenstein Bedroom.[38] A local newspaper fittingly headlined that the Stedelijk turned 'looking at art into googling,' whereas another described it as 'a presentation for instagramming millennials.'[39] The artworks appear as mere interchangeable 'hits,' juxtaposed without any decipherable logic. On the level of singular artworks, the possibilities for 'free association and multiple relations' are often as simplistic as they are reductive, if not detrimental to the visual appearance and aesthetic understanding of the artworks. What does one gain for example by presenting three Eames' chairs on protruding wall elements alongside Barnett Newman's *Cathedra*—apart from reducing the latter's painting to fancy wall decoration, not unlike the better vintage store? Stedelijk BASE doesn't offer unexpected combinations or though-provoking insights, but only the clichéd confirmation of the present circumstances of the image economy.

Instead of adventurous and thought-provoking, Stedelijk BASE is as conformist as it is reactionary. If the exhibition architecture reveals to any extent the societal organization of value at stake in the museum, it does so by a sheer affirmation of shallowness: it merely accommodates the meaningless juxtaposition and the facile interchangeability that mark the

37 Stedelijk BASE, installation view, 2018. Photo: Wouter Davidts.

38 Stedelijk BASE, installation view, 2017. Courtesy Pictoright Amsterdam. Photo: Gert Jan van Rooij. 'The Collection: Stedelijk BASE,' press release, Stedelijk Museum Amsterdam.

39 Bianca Stigter, 'Stedelijk Museum maakt van kunst kijken googlen,' *NRC Handelsblad*, December 13, 2017; Kees Keijer and Sophie Zürcher, 'Nieuwe presentatie Stedelijk: Liefdeloos, of juist zó 2017?,' *Het Parool*, December 18, 2017.

presence and use of images in the digital realm. The accompanying claim that visitors themselves will discover the connections, make associations, and eventually do the interpretation, is a weak bid. In present-day times of societal uncertainty and polarization people are increasingly in search of larger narratives, while simultaneously extremists of all sorts highjack public debates with simplistic catchphrases. In this precarious situation it's far from a conservative call to expect a museum to take up the societal responsibility and embrace its own agency as a public institution to test out what Ruff's self-professed commitment 'to tell the stories relevant to today' can mean. Internationally, museums go to great lengths to rewrite the canonized story of art, to decolonize the established narratives of art, that is, to redefine the potential value and significance of their art patrimony by expanding the perspectives they portray beyond those of the dominant cultural group. These attempts are grounded in the shared belief that there is indeed no longer one over-arching story of art to be told, but they don't forfeit the responsibility to find out which stories can nonetheless be told, about and with the collection they safeguard. If anything, they are aimed at disclosing the historical intricacies and specificities of the coming into being of that heritage—as contested as such stories often may be. There's very little narrative to contest at Stedelijk BASE, as any possibility to discern one is annulled by the self-congratulatory worshipping of the utter exchangeability and free association of artefacts. The smart but bland refusal to embrace the institution's agency to tell any story whatsoever by means of, with, and through its art collection, in the end cynically dismisses the inherent value of the heritage it entails. History, Stedelijk BASE suggests, amounts to a value-free mood board from which you can freely pick, associate, combine, and eventually like.

Many Stories to Tell

40 Mel Bochner, 'An Interview with Elayne Varian (1969),' in *Solar System & Rest Rooms: Writings and Interviews, 1965–2007* (Cambridge, MA: MIT Press, 2008), 58.

Conceptual artist Mel Bochner once beautifully phrased that the basic question in art is, 'how do you experience yourself in the world, which is to say, how do you inhabit an idea of the world.'[40] Art delivers plenty of imaginative propositions and critical depictions for the many ways in which we humans, make, think and experience our world. Architecture, we believe, is one of the most valuable companions to provide a stage for these manifold stories to be told, and retold, in all intricacy and detail.

Valuing Architecture's Entanglements

Longitudinal axis throughout the workshop spaces. Photo: Bart Decroos.

Valuing Architecture's Entanglements

The Many Faces of KANAL-Centre Pompidou

Bart Decroos and Lara Schrijver

1 'The KANAL Project', KANAL-Centre Pompidou, June 18, 2020, kanal.brussels/en/kanal-project/kanal-centre-pompidou.

In 2018, the former Citroën garage in Brussels opened its doors with a program of temporary art exhibitions, allowing the public to explore the building before its transformation by 2022 into the KANAL-Centre Pompidou (from here on simply shortened to KANAL). According to its own mission statement, this so-called 'cultural hub' will be much more than a museum of modern and contemporary art; it will also house the collections of architecture and urbanism of the Brussels-based CIVA Foundation and a variety of public spaces with different functions.[1] The early opening gives a taste of the scale and ambition of the facility to come: an exceptional project both for its intentions and its approach, which nonetheless draws on familiar strategies of using cultural facilities as catalysts for urban regeneration.

The 'Citroën garage,' as the building was commonly called, used to house a sales, service, and distribution center for the French car company in an iconic modernist building situated on a prime location along the canal, just outside the pentagonal ring road around the historical city center. The building can be reached via a busy road, by crossing one or two crossroads where traffic is continually congested. From afar, the large hippodrome-like showroom lights up in the afternoon sun, with its eleven-meters high glass facade behind which Citroën used to promote its latest car models. Walking across Sainctelette Square and past this 'cathedral of glass' toward the canal, you suddenly find yourself on a quay, where trucks and vans would deliver car parts to what used to be the largest car service center in Europe. Now an informal public space, with a few sponsored lounge chairs and tables made of wooden pallets overlooking the waterfront, the quay leads to the temporary main entrance of the vast workshop halls that lie behind the showroom of the garage building. The building is accessed through the former delivery gate on the quay, which opens onto one of two wide, central corridors that cross the building transversally.[2] The view opens up toward the upper floor and the gabled roofs of glass above, supported by rusted and dusty steel trusses, which are still as impressive as when the building opened in 1931, although perhaps appreciated for other reasons today.

    The journey throughout the temporary exhibitions in the building develops along two routes. The first is a freely accessible area, as a precursor to the ambitions of KANAL as a future public space. Walking through the entrance, you turn right beyond the interior 'street food' market, where the other central corridor leads you back to the glass showroom at the square. During this initial opening phase, the showroom has hosted mainly architecture exhibitions, most notably the architecture competition for KANAL itself. As the winning competition entry developed into a final design proposal, the showroom displayed the completed building application and future plans to the public. The second route is only accessible with a ticket, available at the counter in front of the museum shop entitled 'The New Belgian's Creator Hub'—an English

2 Longitudinal axis throughout the workshop spaces. Photo: Bart Decroos.

3 The name 'KANAL' refers to the canal along which the building is situated and is a mix of the Dutch word 'kanaal' and its French translation 'canal'. The difficult balance between Dutch and French in the capital of Belgium can be seen in the protest of Benoît Cerexhe, the faction leader of the francophone political party CDH in the Brussels parliament, who considered the name to be too Dutch and demanded the name start with a 'C.' See: 'Kanal klinkt te Nederlands voor burgemeester Cerexhe,' *Bruzz*, December 5, 2017, www.bruzz.be/videoreeks/dinsdag-5-december-2017/video-kanal-klinkt-te-nederlands-voor-burgemeester-cerexhe.

4 Upper floor workshop spaces. Photo: Bart Decroos.

phrase that indicates the project's international ambitions, but in the multilingual city of Brussels it also provides a neutral ground for the country's dominant and often conflicting languages of Dutch and French.[3] This second route provides access to the rest of the building, where the art exhibitions are held. It takes a few hours to wander through all of the spaces: the former workshops on the ground floor, where the cracked lines of parking spots, smudged skid marks, and fading traces of oil spills are reminders of the building's former life; the adjacent office rooms, which have been appropriated for site-specific art installations but where the vinyl carpet, cubicle-like rooms and yellowing tiles in the lowered ceiling still retain the memory of dusty filing rooms and office workers; and finally, the vast and sunlit spaces on the first floor underneath the greenhouse-like roofs, where the rusted steel columns and beams, the dirty glass facades, the dusty brick walls, and a continuous tangle of pipes, wiring, and chimneys form the backdrop for the occasional sculpture or installation.[4] The picturesque interior landscape plays a prominent role as the remnant of a romanticized industrial past, raising the question of what is on display here: the works of art, or the building?

The Role of a Building

KANAL is an ambitious project by the Government of the Brussels-Capital Region, originally launched under the name 'Pôle Culturel Citroën' when the government acquired the former Citroën garage in 2014 and proposed to redevelop it as a museum. Apart from this general description, little was known at the time about the specific ambitions for the project, let alone what a 'cultural pole' should be. Over the past years, the project has become more defined, with the architecture of the Citroën garage itself playing a decisive role in defining the values suggested by this generic signifier. This article examines how this empty signifier acquires meaning, on what levels its associated values are produced and for whom, and how dependent on the specific architecture of the building they are. From this perspective, one might in fact say that the Citroën garage itself was an actor in the realization of KANAL, and that its specific architecture was necessary to connect and mediate between the conflicting and contradictory agendas of the parties involved.[5] In the institutional and political landscape of Brussels, this project was complicated from the start. The messy politics of Belgium, with its six different governments for a country of not even twelve million inhabitants, comprised of three communities and three regions that are based on four language areas, is beyond the scope of this article. However, a brief background of the political and institutional context is necessary to understand the unique conditions surrounding the project.

KANAL is a direct result of the so-called 'sixth state reform of Belgium,' in which responsibilities were transferred from the federal level to the regions and communities.[6] As such, in early 2014, the bilingual government of the Brussels-Capital Region was granted autonomy in decisions on cultural matters along with greater fiscal autonomy. For various reasons discussed below, the government used this opportunity to establish a public museum for modern and contemporary art. This raised some eyebrows in relation to the WIELS Contemporary Art Center, a privately owned, non-profit organization that has been fulfilling a similar role in Brussels since 2007. As such, the relevance of the KANAL project was contested from the start and, as we will see, the eventual

[5] In this paper, we follow the general insights of actor-network theory and related 'materialist ontologies' that demonstrate how objects are never passive, but instead, that their material existence both affords and resists the agendas of other parties involved. On actor-network theory, see for example: Bruno Latour, *Reassembling the Social* (Oxford: Oxford University Press, 2005) and for more recent developments in materialist ontologies, see for example: Diana Coole and Samantha Frost, *New Materialisms: Ontology, Agency and Politics* (Durham: Duke University Press, 2010).

[6] '6 januari 2014. Bijzondere wet met betrekking tot de Zesde Staatshervorming,' *Belgisch Staatsblad*, January 31, 2014, 8654–8655.

collaboration with the Paris-based Centre Pompidou became a controversial issue that was met with a lot of disapproval in the Brussels' art scene. The fact that KANAL became a pet peeve of the francophone prime minister of the Government of the Brussels-Capital Region, Rudi Vervoort, while the WIELS is directed by the Flemish Dirk Snauwaert is perhaps not directly related. However, the apparently non-existent collaboration between both institutions does seem to be symptomatic of the underlying tensions between the francophone and Dutch-speaking communities that have since long complicated the political situation in Brussels, let alone, Belgium as a whole.

As a final note, in addition to the political and institutional background of the project, the canal area itself is the locus of some of the city's tensions. Unlike many other European cities, the waterfront was never developed into an accessible public space but today still forms a hard barrier in the fabric of the city, both spatially and socially. Since the early twentieth century, there has been a sharp contrast between the economically advantaged citizens of the city center on one side, and the disenfranchised communities on the other, where the municipality of Sint-Jans-Molenbeek lies. KANAL sits right on this border, just outside the city center, sandwiched between the canal bank and the North Quarter's business district.

Viewed within this complex context, the project of KANAL is indeed not just any museum of modern and contemporary art; the project as a whole demonstrates the entanglement of different sets of values inscribed in and perpetuated through the building itself. It embodies the complexity of the contemporary urban project, addressing the sociopolitical context of urban development as well as the global flows of cultural capital, anchored in a piece of architectural heritage rich with symbolic values of modernism and industry. The project builds on assumptions about city branding, architectural heritage and the creative class as an economic driver to instigate urban development and social transformations. While KANAL is still in full development at the time of writing, in the text below we will trace the role of the building during the genesis of the project through the various networks of value production it gets caught up in—economically, politically, and culturally.

The Architectural Heritage

The garage was built in 1933–1934 by the Citroën car company and was the largest automotive service center of Europe at the time.[7] The modernist architecture of the building was deeply intertwined with the commercial strategies of the company. In 1927, André Citroën established Citroën's own architecture office, led by the French architect Maurice-Jacques Ravazé, and developed a deliberate marketing strategy in which the values of modernity, progress, and technology were intentionally associated with the cars themselves. The combination of architectural values with corporate branding is nothing new, as it has been a common practice in advertising, marketing, and design for decades. Yet, since value is not an abstract process but relies on physical objects to become manifest, the garage itself becomes an embodiment of the entangled logics of corporate branding, technological innovation, and cultural expression.

For the design of the Citroën garage, Ravazé collaborated with the Brussels-based architects Alexis Dumont and Marcel Van Goethem. Their design fully embraced modern architecture, with a large and elongated showroom in the

[7] The following historical account draws largely from a special issue of *Erfgoed Brussel* on the occasion of the 'Open Monument Day 2015' in Belgium, see: 'De Citroëngarage te Brussel,' *Erfgoed Brussel* 15–16 (September 2015), 79–91.

8 Interior view of the original showroom in the nineteen-thirties. *Ossature Métallique*, advertising SEM, 1935. Photo: L'Epi-Devolder.

9 The viaduct in front of the Citroën garage in the nineteen-fifties. Postcard, c. 1955, SAB.

shape of a hippodrome along Sainctelette Square and expansive workshops at the back. The hippodrome was twenty-one meters high with floor-to-ceiling windows in a steel frame and a barrel vault roof of sprayed concrete, lending the showroom a sacred character.[8] Spotlights installed in the cornice just below the roof construction lit the barrel vault from below and the facades from above. The formally abstract yet luxuriously finished showroom complemented the workshops, which were designed as one large open hall with an abundance of daylight falling through the glazed facades and roofs. The workshops were intended for maintenance and repairs, with additional parking space for new cars, storage for parts, and space to prepare these parts for use. The plan was organized with functionalist efficiency: the two central passageways crossed each other orthogonally, ensuring full access to all building elements. The showroom and workshop were connected by the longest, 180-meter passageway, and the other provided easy access to the workshops from the road along the quay at the back. Glazed facades at the end of each ensured the transparency of the building, both within and from outside.

Although the building remained largely as it was, seemingly minor adaptations transformed the character of the building drastically. In the run-up to the 1958 Brussels World's Fair, the Belgian government built a large temporary viaduct over the square in front of the showroom, anticipating an increase in visitors to the city.[9] Citroën decided to entirely renovate the building and added an extra floor to the showroom for a more extended range of models. This extra level was installed at a height of six and a half meters, which allowed passers-by on the viaduct to look at the cars. Over the following years, five more floors would be added to the showroom, further diminishing its transparency. Meanwhile, an extra floor was also added to the workshops. The new levels required additional circulation, and the building became filled with various ramps. These adaptations slowly impacted the open spaces of the building over time: the showroom lost its sacred atmosphere due to the extra floors and low ceilings, and in the workshops the extra floor and additional offices and storage rooms blocked the views that had once been possible from one side to the other. Yet along the ring road, the building envelope remained identifiable as a modernist icon, reminiscent of a golden age of industrialization and progress while its architectural values would continue to define its future.

The Economic Objectives

The genesis of the KANAL project was the result of two separate events: the impending vacancy of the Citroën garage and a new ambition of the government of the Brussels-Capital Region. In June 2012, the Citroën company announced it would leave the building as a result of cutbacks.[10] The impending vacancy of the building raised public concerns about its future. Despite numerous demands by heritage organizations, the building had never been formally designated as a heritage site.[11] By the end of 2012, most of the employees were relocated to other locations, although the showroom remained in use a little longer.

This departure of Citroën coincided with the abovementioned sixth state reform of Belgium. In 2014, following these reforms, the Government of the Brussels-Capital Region decided to build a museum for modern and contemporary art by 2018, launched under the title of a 'pôle culturel.' This decision was criticized for its lack of transparency and debate, especially since it mentioned only a general function,

[10] 'Citroën-invoerder verlaat Brussel,' *Bruzz*, July 1, 2012, www.bruzz.be/samenleving/citroen-invoerder-verlaat-brussel-2012-06-01.

[11] 'Citroën gebouwen hebben geen bescherming nodig,' *Bruzz*, February 16, 2007, www.bruzz.be/politiek/citroen-gebouwen-hebben-geen-bescherming-nodig-2007-02-16.

without further specifications or budget. While there had been ideas for such a project in the years before, especially on a federal level, it was only now, with the vacancy of the Citroën garage, that it became possible to actually propose it: the potential for adaptive reuse ascribed to the building was needed to lend the project any credibility at all. Over the following months and years, the empty meaning of the signifier 'pôle culturel' would become even more apparent as other institutions were needed as stand-ins for the cultural credibility of the project: at first, the government proposed to house the federal collections of modern art, which was in dire need of a new location, but eventually it was decided that the Brussels architecture center CIVA would be relocated to the new site, while in September 2016 the government reached an agreement with the Parisian Centre Georges Pompidou to collaborate on the project. This last decision was widely criticized as a 'Parisian colonization of Brussels,'[12] both for its apparent lack of respect for the local art scene in Brussels, as well as for the payment of eleven million euros to the French art center to operate KANAL, of which two million will be used for employees in Paris.[13]

So, without an artistic agenda of its own, why then a museum? The project was first and foremost framed as part of the redevelopment plans for the canal area, explicitly following the logic of a 'Bilbao effect,' instead of a more cultural agenda focused on artistic ambitions.[14] In the Belgian financial newspaper *De Tijd*, the Brussels prime minister Rudi Vervoort said at the time: 'Brussels will have its own Guggenheim, its MoMA. The museum will help to further develop the enormous economic potential of the canal area.'[15] It was the specific location of the Citroën building next to the canal along with its iconic architecture that gave rise to the idea of a cultural spectacle as economic rejuvenation. In the

12 This critique echoed similar concerns in the nineteen-thirties when Citroën decided to build the garage in the first place. See: 'De Citroëngarage te Brussel.'

13 'KANAL betaalt bijna 2 miljoen over 10 jaar voor personeel Parijs,' *Bruzz*, March 8, 2018, www.bruzz.be/news/kanal-betaalt-bijna-2-miljoen-over-10-jaar-voor-personeel-parijs-2018-03-08.

14 Vervoort: 'Museum aan het kanaal desnoods zonder federaal niveau,' *Bruzz*, November 6, 2014, www.bruzz.be/politiek/vervoort-museum-aan-het-kanaal-desnoods-zonder-federaal-niveau-2014-11-06. See also: Witold Rybczynski, 'The Bilbao Effect,' *Atlantic Monthly* September 2002, www.theatlantic.com/magazine/archive/2002/09/the-bilbao-effect/302582/.

15 'Akkoord over museum in Citroën,' *Bruzz*, May 8, 2014, www.bruzz.be/akkoord-over-museum-citroen-2014-05-08.

end, on a policy level, the Citroën garage thus appears as an economic project, which, because of its vacancy, iconic appearance, and location in the canal area, affords the projection of an (empty) museum program as economic investment.

The Political Ambitions

The Citroën garage as a political project comes into focus when the ambitions of the KANAL project become specified as an architectural program. One of the problems that arises from the projection of a museum program onto the Citroën garage, is that the building is essentially too large for a museum. Yves Goldstein, former secretary in the cabinet of Vervoort and later project leader and director of Fondation KANAL, compares KANAL to institutions such as London's Tate Modern or the Guggenheim in Bilbao, which each have around 10,000 square meters exhibition space.[16] The Citroën garage measures 48,000 square meters, leaving the museum with an excess of open space to be filled in. In 2015, the government therefore commissioned Dutch architect Wessel de Jonge (co-founder of the International Committee for Documentation and Conservation of Buildings, Sites and Neighbourhoods of the Modern Movement, Docomomo International) and the Brussels architecture office MSA to do a study of the heritage qualities of the building and the conditions for its transformation into a museum, as well as to examine the various possibilities for 'contemporary programs opening up towards the local neighborhoods.'[17] This study would later provide the basis for an architecture competition that would be organized in 2017.

The brief for this competition opens with the 'cultural ambitions' for the project, which are summed up in five

16 Interview with Yves Goldstein by Bart Decroos on April 10, 2019.

17 'Programmatic and planning study for the CITROËN building,' MSA, www.ms-a.be/les-projets.

sentences and conclude with the statement that the project is about 'experiencing culture together.'[18] The brief instead gives more attention to the urban ambitions of the project, explicitly referring to its 'public interiors' and 'traffic routes or interior streets.' As Goldstein himself has stated: '[The Citroën garage] is structured by wide corridors that traverse the building. They will become streets, similar to the Saint-Hubertus galleries in the center.'[19] He further imagines the project as an inclusive space, 'a vision for the multicultural city of the twenty-first century.' Whereas the government addresses the strategic location of the Citroën garage as an economic potential, to Goldstein, and by extension to the curatorial program for the museum, the site can bring together the different communities of Brussels: 'The new center will not be a success, if it doesn't attract the inhabitants of both sides of the canal.'[20] An Fonteyne, one of the architects who would later on win the competition, confirms: 'The building needs to be so open, that no one who passes by wonders if they belong in that place or not.'[21] This statement expresses a different vision than the earlier one of Vervoort, and echoes the words of Brussels Government Architect Kristiaan Borret: 'This will definitely not become Bilbao, but a layered project that reflects the complexity of the city of Brussels.'[22] In other words, despite its functional program of a museum, the Citroën garage first and foremost needs to become a public, and even political, space. These statements overlook the gentrification effect the project will likely have on both sides of the canal, an effect that is explicitly aimed for on an economic level. Yet while these intentions might be laudable, they also raise the question whether the total budget of 210 million euros for the renovation and operation of KANAL until 2024 might have been used more effectively by investing directly in social programs for the neighborhoods

---

18 Interview with Yves Goldstein by Bart Decroos on April 10, 2019.

19 'KANAL wordt in de eerste plaats openbare ruimte,' *Bruzz*, March 14, 2019, www.bruzz.be/stedenbouw/kanal-wordt-de-eerste-plaats-openbare-ruimte-2019-03-14.

20 'KANAL is de nieuwe naam van Citroënmuseum,' *Bruzz*, October 10, 2017, www.bruzz.be/uit/news/kanal-nieuwe-naam-van-citroenmuseum-2017-10-10.

21 'KANAL wordt in de eerste plaats openbare ruimte,' *Bruzz*, March 14, 2019, www.bruzz.be/stedenbouw/kanal-wordt-de-eerste-plaats-openbare-ruimte-2019-03-14.

22 'KANAL wordt geen Bilbao,' *Bruzz*, March 22, 2018, www.bruzz.be/stedenbouw/kanal-wordt-geen-bilbao-2018-03-22.

that the curatorial ambitions wish to reinforce.²³ Rather than investing in the present-day 'working class,' whatever that term might mean today, the curatorial agenda fetishizes the aesthetic of a historical working class, presenting the former factory building as a contemporary democratic space, open for all.²⁴ Yet, setting aside cynical speculation, the project seems to be determined once again by the building itself: the excess of open space suggests a different and even contradictory ambition to the policy level. Here, KANAL becomes a political project, with its factory typology, transparency, and spatial organization affording the idea of a public space.

23 'Factuur KANAL bedraagt 210 miljoen,' *Bruzz*, February 6, 2019, www.bruzz.be/stedenbouw/factuur-kanal-bedraagt-210-miljoen-2019-02-06.

24 At the time of writing, the new employees of the museum even wear the blue overalls of the former mechanics, and, as a further provocation, the visitors can even buy a blue overall of their own in the museum shop, so everyone can 'experience' what it is to be a mechanic.

The Cultural Pole

From the start, KANAL was presented as a cultural project, a 'pôle culturel.' The very notion of such a cultural pole, proposed by the government as an empty signifier, was only given meaning by the architectural competition, with each of the design proposals expressing a different notion of what a cultural pole should be.

The competition was organized by the Brussels government in collaboration with the Brussels government architect. In the first phase, ninety-two teams applied to participate, among which prominent international architects such as Kengo Kuma, Peter Eisenman, Lacaton & Vassal, SANAA, Sou Fujimoto and Zaha Hadid Architects. A jury selected seven teams to make a design proposal, which consisted mostly of collaborations between a major national and an international office, such as 51N4E with Caruso St John Architects or Architecten De Vylder Vinck Taillieu with 6a architects. Renowned Swiss architect Roger Diener presided over the final jury. The competition drew international

25 Gideon Boie and Thomas Rasker, 'Please, Don't Touch the Museum: The Urban Art of the Museum Interior in the Design Competition for KANAL in Brussels,' *OASE* 101 (2018), 'Microcosms', 90–103.

26 Interior view of the industrial heritage in between the three new volumes. 'A Stage for Brussels' by Atelier Kanal.

27 Interior view of exhibition spaces. 'A Stage for Brussels' by Atelier Kanal.

attention and was widely published, thus not only contributing to the KANAL project as such, but as a form of cultural production in its own right. Whereas KANAL might have been contested on a political and economic level, the competition was widely embraced by the architectural community, fully acknowledging its cultural value. This self-referential justification was emphasized when the building was temporarily opened from May 2018 to June 2019 with an exhibition of the seven proposals inside of the museum-to-be. Here, KANAL explicitly became a cultural project in the form of models, drawings, and design proposals for its future existence inside of the Citroën garage, worthy of attention.

The seven proposals have been thoroughly analyzed by Gideon Boie and Thomas Rasker in their article 'Please, Don't Touch the Museum,'[25] so the analysis here is limited to the winning proposal of noAarchitecten, EM2N and Sergison Bates, who established the joint office Atelier Kanal specifically for this project. Residing on the fifth floor of the office tower above the garage itself, the office lends further credibility to the idea of KANAL as a 'pôle culturel' by virtue of their own presence. Titled 'A Stage for Brussels,' the winning proposal inserts three large volumes into the existing building: the museum spaces, the architecture center, and an auditorium.[26] The original axes of the building become public streets, with the slopes leading passers-by up to the sunlight and the open *piano nobile*. It is almost self-evident that the perspective drawings of the competition proposal focus mostly on the interstitial spaces and the old factory building, while the spatial qualities inside of the new volumes are mostly suggested in plan and section. Unsurprisingly, the few interior images of the exhibition spaces reveal these to be generic white boxes.[27] This is emphasized by Diener in his statement of approval: 'Interior spaces keep their former identity—workshops—while creating a soft opening to traditional exhibition spaces.' A year later, when the winning design proposal was reworked into a building application, also exhibited in the former showroom of the Citroën garage, the existing building gained further material importance, with detailed documentation of every existing column, beam and floor tile, while the actual museum spaces remained largely abstract. While this affirms the importance of the interspace as public space, it also reveals the values embedded within the architectural design: the repurposing of the Citroën garage is first and foremost a renovation of its industrial heritage, which is already a cultural project in its own right. In essence, the design affirms the building itself as the cultural ambition, which is to be restored because of its heritage value. The building's history, the atmosphere of the past, and the traces of its former glory afford this cultural value of heritage.

An Exhibition of Industrial Heritage

In the above analysis, the specific architecture of the Citroën garage appears as an actor that connects and mediates the economic, political, and cultural ambitions of the different parties involved in the genesis of KANAL. As such, the KANAL project embodies different modes of existence that produce different values.

On the policy level, KANAL exists as an *economic* project. The government is able to justify its acquisition of the building primarily through economic motives: as part of a redevelopment plan for the canal area, in which the museum functions as a lever to generate jobs and tourism revenues. On a curatorial level, KANAL exists as a *political* project. The Fondation Kanal presents the museum through political

28 As exemplified during the first opening months, when the personnel were dressed in technician overalls as if they were the same employees from the former garage.

motives: as a public space open for everyone, from the cultural elite to the disenfranchised neighborhood across the water, from the art aficionado to the passer-by, in short, as a 'vision for what a multicultural city should be.' It is, finally, on the architectural level that KANAL starts to exist as *cultural* project. The design proposal of Atelier Kanal for the repurposing of the Citroën garage is primarily aimed at the value of the existing building itself: a renovation of the industrial heritage of Brussels, which not only becomes part of the curatorial program, but of the identity of KANAL itself.[28]

From this summary, it becomes clear that KANAL exists as different kinds of projects to different kinds of parties, who rely on the material presence of the building to justify their ambitions. However, what this overview also suggests, is how each of the different parties involved rely on the other modes to justify their own. The economic project relies on the (future) existence of KANAL as a cultural one; the political project relies on the redevelopment ambitions of the economic one; and the architectural project relies on the public produced by the political one.

Epilogue

One last thing is worth noting: in the analysis of the different actors, the question of art itself is remarkably neglected. The analysis here shows that the artistic ambitions of the KANAL project are still vague, the Centre Pompidou and its collection functions as a stand-in to cover this up, and the (promised) commissions to local artists only pay lip-service to Brussels' art scene. Testimony to this apparent absence is the major exhibition that WIELS organized from April 20 to August 13, 2017 in Brussels, titled 'The Absent Museum' and subtitled

'Blueprint for a museum of contemporary art for the capital of Europe.' Although the curatorial statement of this exhibition makes no mention of the KANAL project, it is hardly coincidence this was organized shortly after the news broke that KANAL signed a partnership with Centre Pompidou. The exhibition showed existing and new work by forty-five major, contemporary, and modern artists, explicitly laying claim to its status as a museum for modern and contemporary art in Brussels. The fact that KANAL chose to collaborate with a Parisian institute instead of engaging with the local art world only affirms the circular reasoning described above, which evades the, perhaps crucial, question facing any museum: the artistic values of KANAL are still 'absent.'

While visiting the temporary opening of KANAL in 2018, a general impression of this absence seems inescapable. The vast spaces of the workshop floors, although visually marked by the traces of car tires, fading oil spills, and the footprints of heavy machinery, are nonetheless mostly defined by their contemporary soundscape: the noise of strolling visitors, the clatter of glasses of wine and beer in the food market, the occasional crying of a child in the distance—all of these sounds are multiplied in the echoes that bounce off the concrete walls and steel roofs, travelling through the empty air of the interior landscape. Exiting through the large factory gate onto the cobbles of the quay again, you mostly remember a picturesque tour of a modernist ruin, whose aesthetic values will be further cultivated in the future design of the museum, while all of its economic, political and cultural values, rely on the material endurance of the building itself.

The Protected Vista
Mapping the Value of Views
Tom Brigden

Tom Brigden

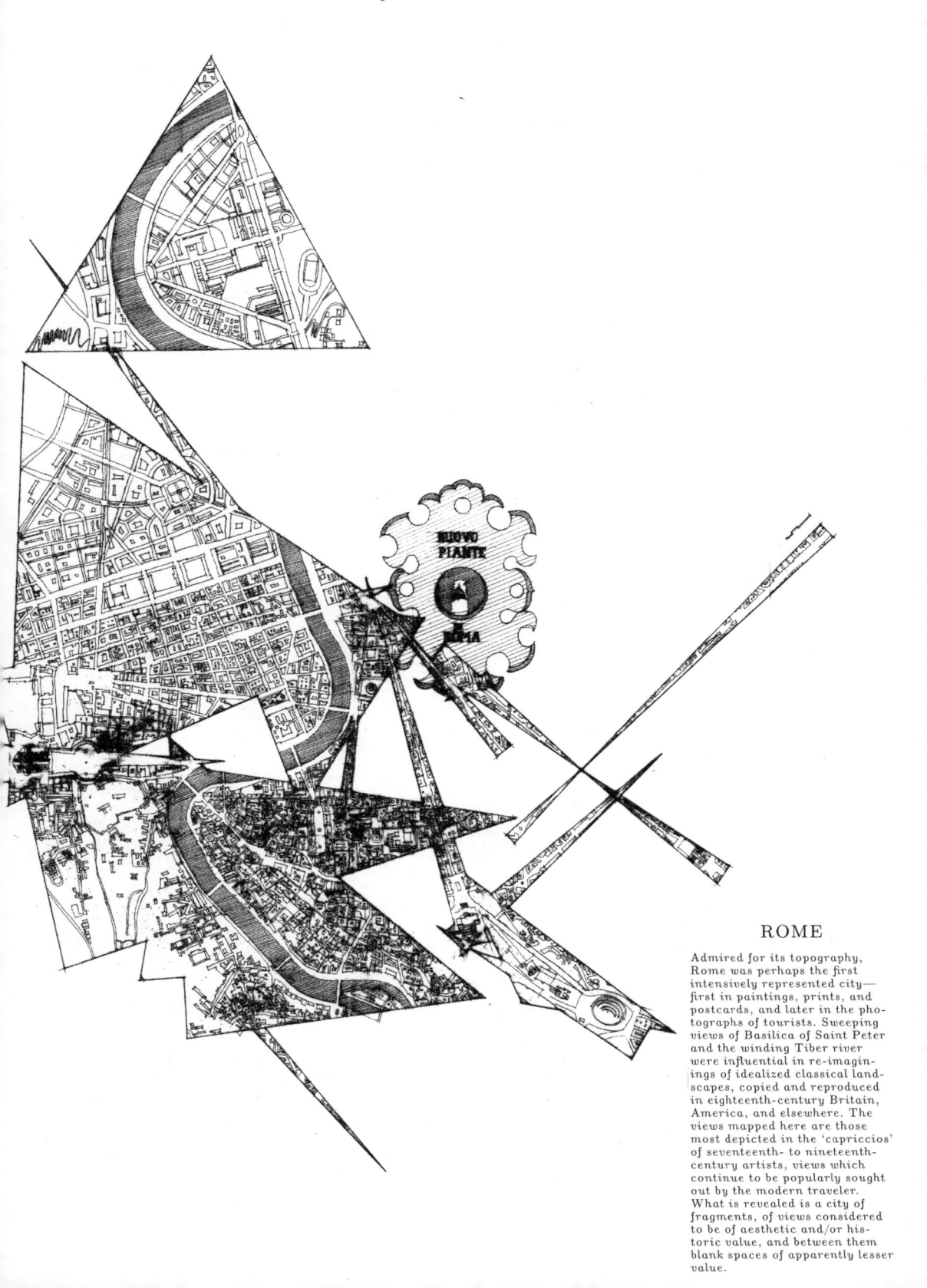

ROME

Admired for its topography, Rome was perhaps the first intensively represented city—first in paintings, prints, and postcards, and later in the photographs of tourists. Sweeping views of Basilica of Saint Peter and the winding Tiber river were influential in re-imaginings of idealized classical landscapes, copied and reproduced in eighteenth-century Britain, America, and elsewhere. The views mapped here are those most depicted in the 'capriccios' of seventeenth- to nineteenth-century artists, views which continue to be popularly sought out by the modern traveler. What is revealed is a city of fragments, of views considered to be of aesthetic and/or historic value, and between them blank spaces of apparently lesser value.

The Protected Vista

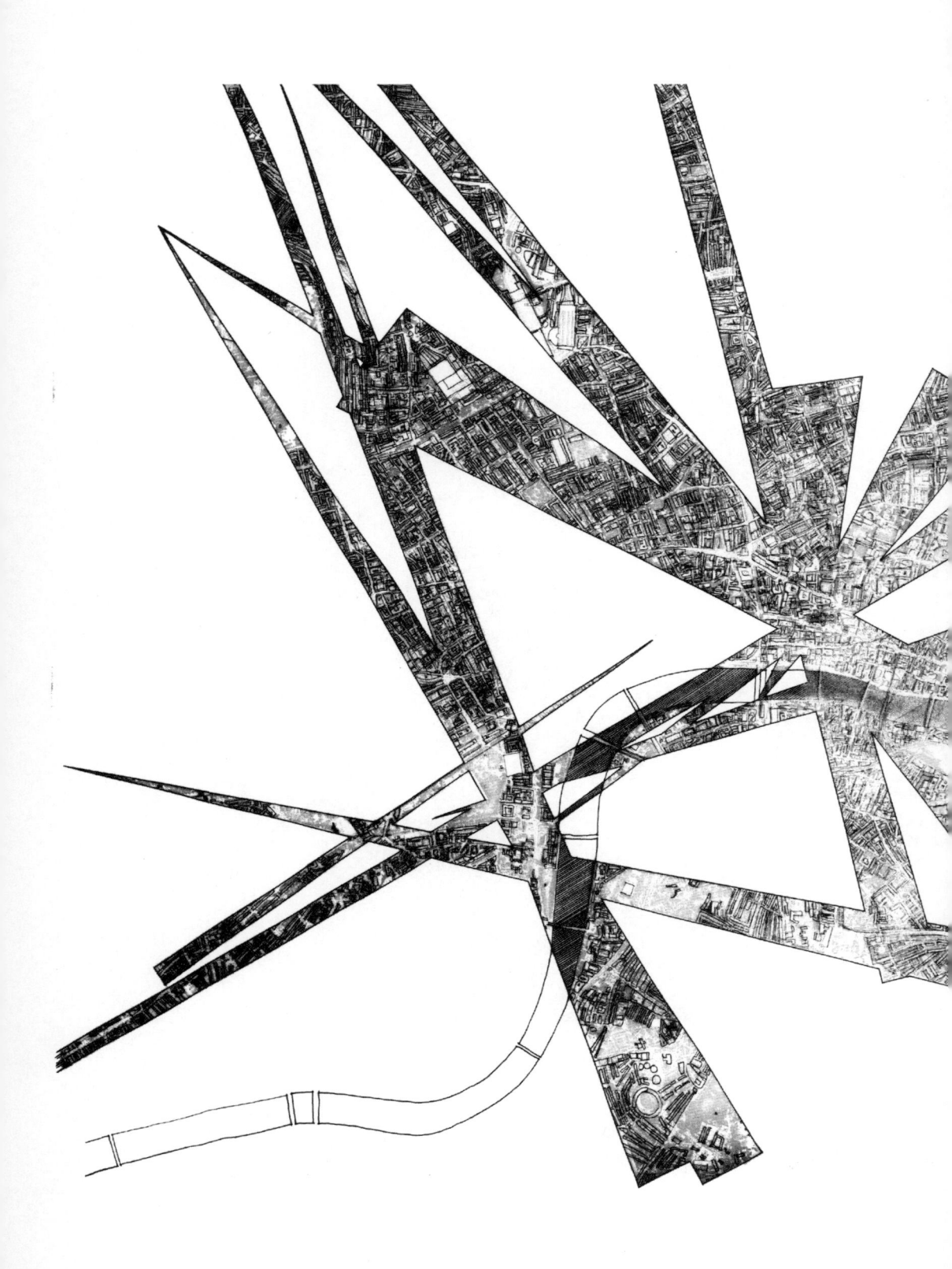

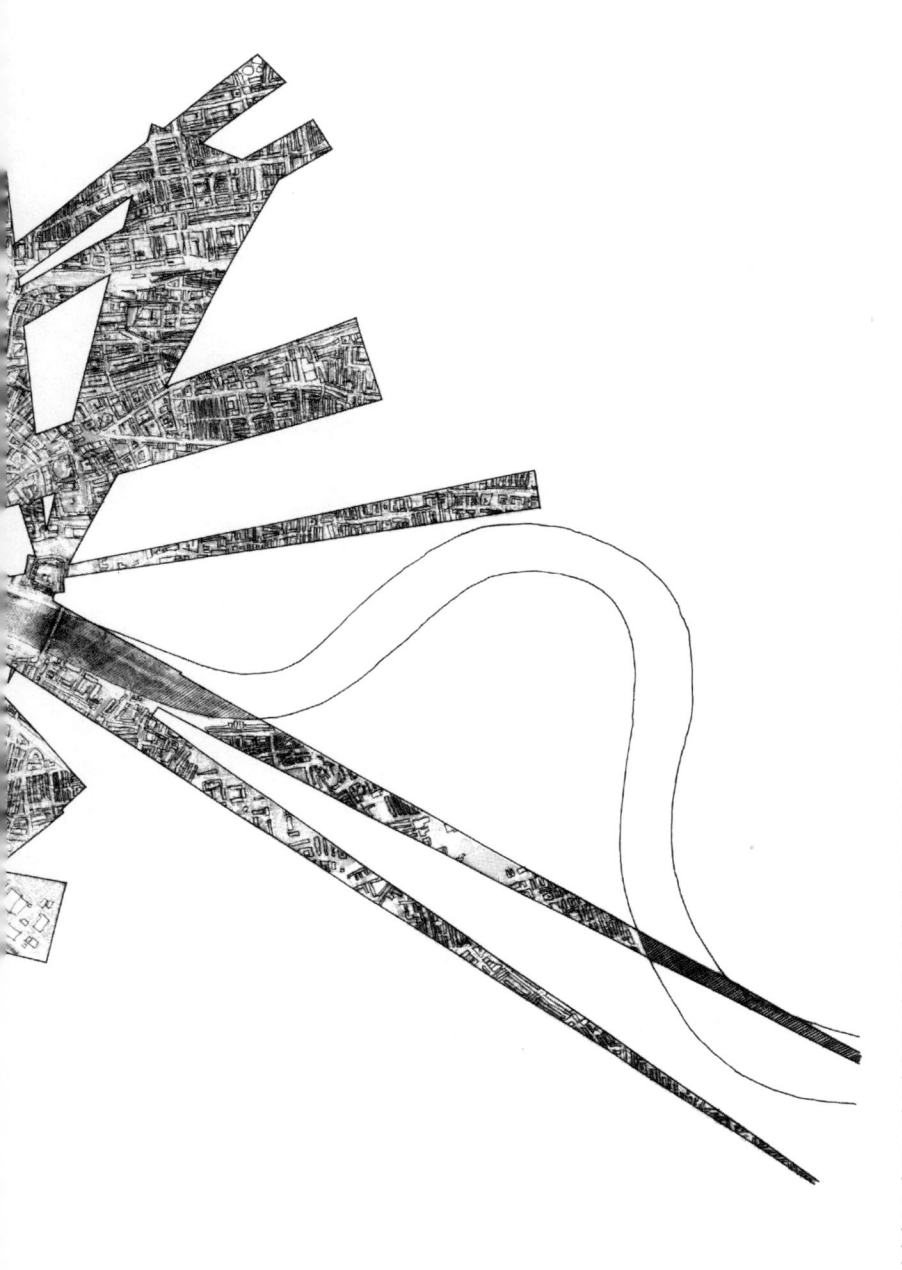

LONDON

The London Building Acts of 1888 and 1894 ruled that architects should not be allowed to build structures taller than roughly ten stories to ensure the city's finest landmarks were not obscured. At around the same time, a movement was gaining momentum in suburban Richmond, to preserve a distinctive view of the River Thames threatened by over-development. Long-admired by poets and artists, this view had been the birthplace of the eighteenth-century Picturesque movement in landscape art and architecture. Gaining protection via the Richmond, Petersham and Ham Open Spaces Act of 1902, the view from Richmond Hill was London's first officially protected vista, and remains as one of twenty-six vistas and fifty-two viewing places protected under the London 'View Management Framework', ensuring that values developed from the eighteenth-century Picturesque movement remain at work in contemporary policy. London has continued to grow upwards, particularly since the nineteen-eighties, but its strictly defined protected vistas pinwheeling around historic sites such as the Palace of Westminster, the Tower of London and St Paul's Cathedral remain etched into the cityscape. These sight lines, some spanning as far as ten miles, influence the volume and massing of new developments over vast swathes of central London, defining the edges of clusters of towers and their dividing chasms.

The Protected Vista

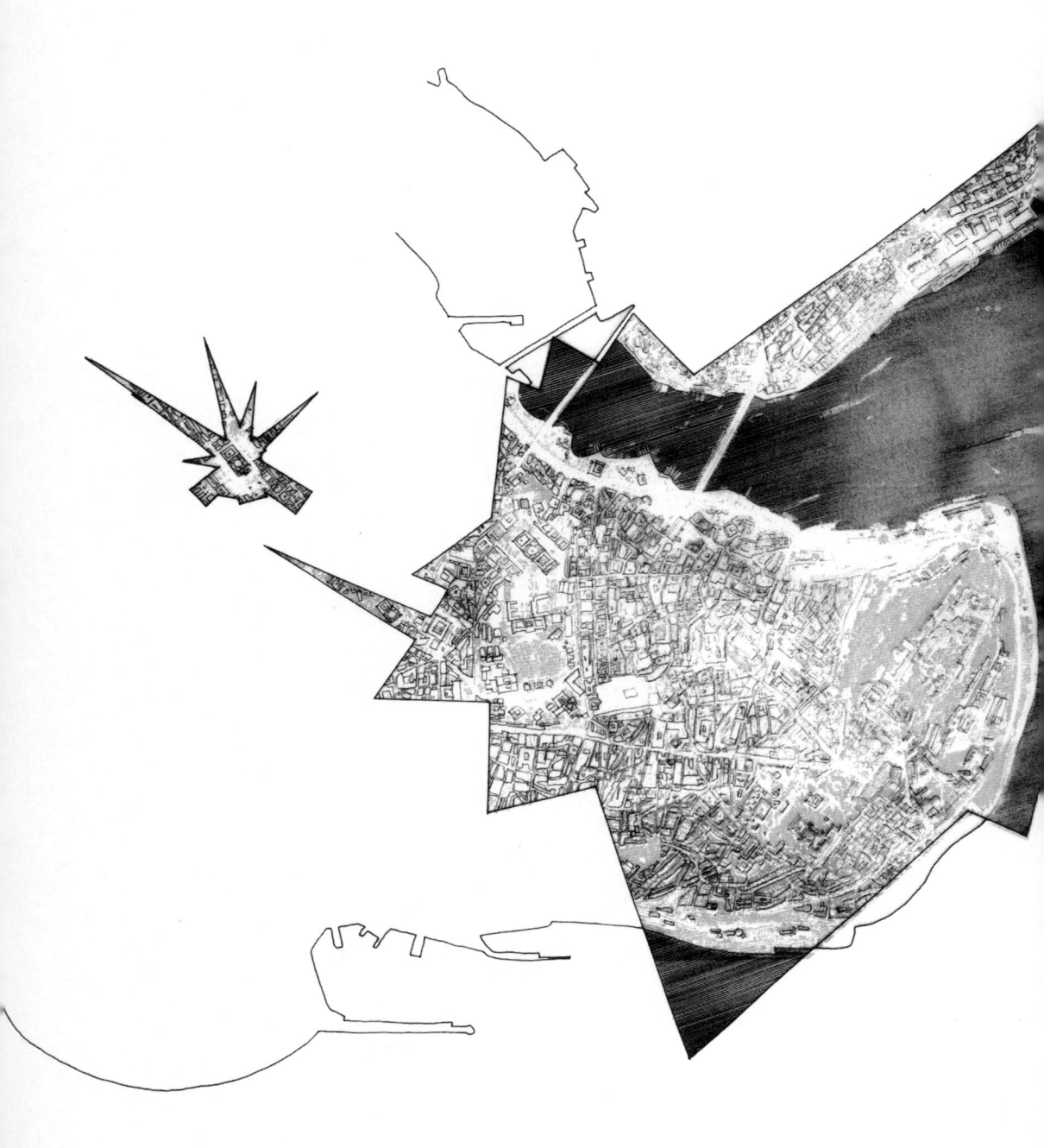

Tom Brigden

ISTANBUL

Water views were of critical importance in architecture and landscape design during the Ottoman period, particularly in the rambling wooden *yalis* [palaces] which led down to, or cantilevered out over, the Bosphorus. Open views of the Golden Horn and across the Bosphorus, with the hazy backdrop of Sultanahmet's minarets and domes, have since become instantly recognizable images of Istanbul. Views of these sites remain a key part of the city's character today, and although they lack the precise mathematical definition of London or Vancouver's protected vistas, the Turkish government is still determined to protect Sultanahmet's skyline, generally restricting tall buildings (which it has been accused of actively promoting) to the Asian and North Shores of the Bosphorus. The controversy surrounding the proposed demolition of three 'illegal' apartment towers, chastised for their impact upon the silhouette of the Blue Mosque, in many ways reflects the struggle between opposing visions for Turkey's future place in the world.

The Protected Vista

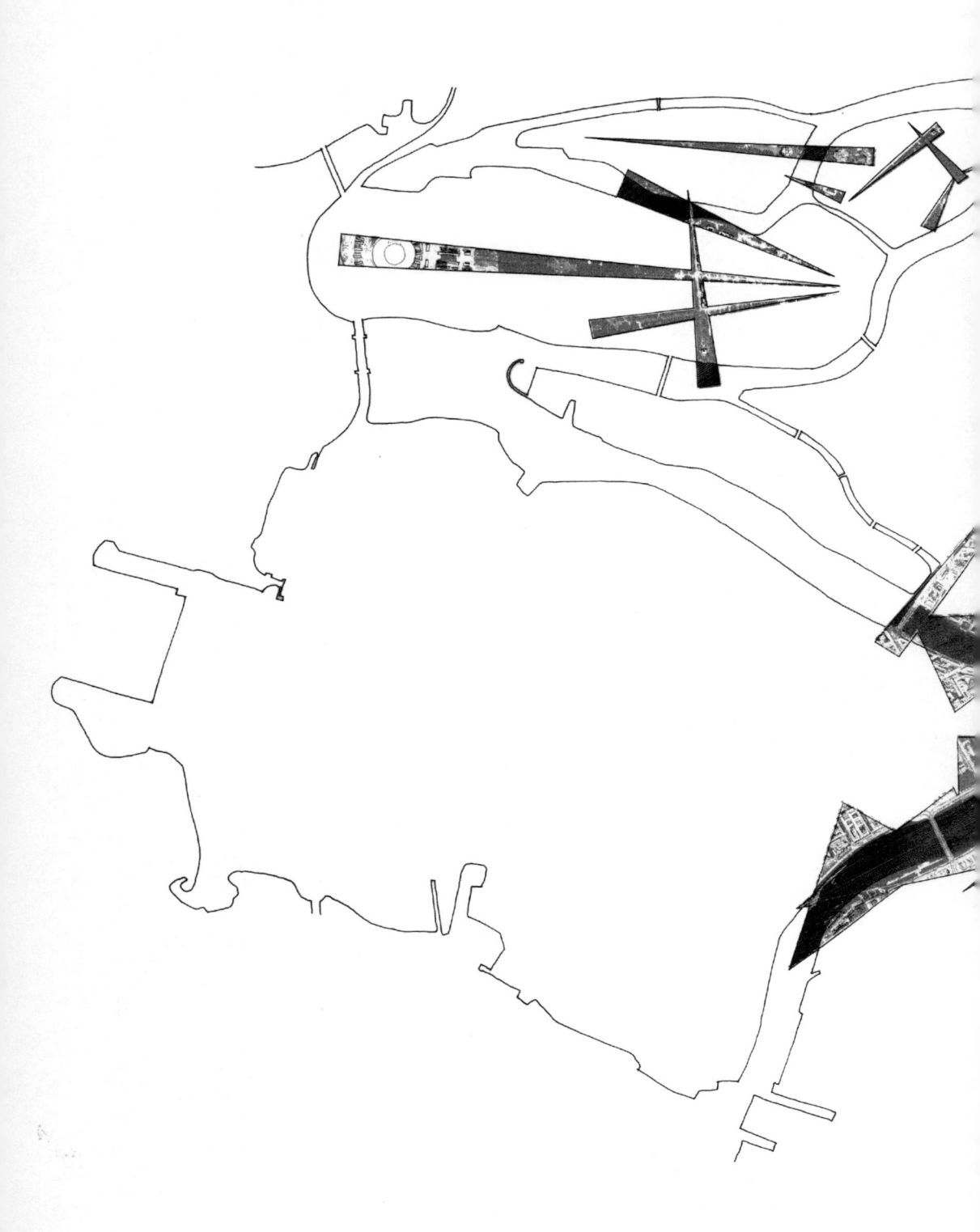

Tom Brigden

ST. PETERSBURG

St. Petersburg has long been admired for the uniform flatness of its skyline, punctuated only by the steeples of churches and the Admiralty—landmarks which set up distinctive long-views along the city's boulevards. Building heights were set by the height of the Winter Palace, and broad sweeping views across the river have become key to St Petersburg's identity. It was for these reasons that UNESCO objected strongly to the planned construction of Europe's tallest building, the Okhta Center, perceived to interrupt the uniform skyline of the city and to therefore detrimentally impact upon its outstanding universal value.

The Protected Vista

Tom Brigden

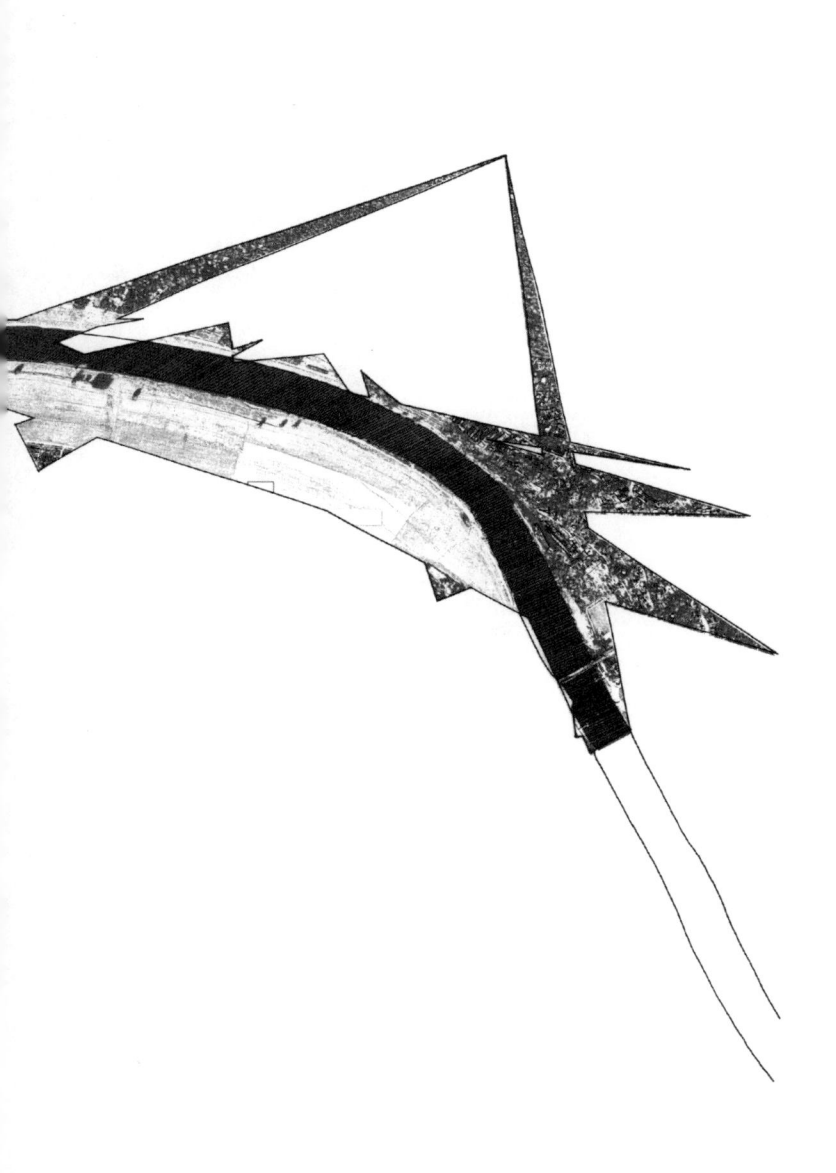

DRESDEN

The views along the green meadows by the Elbe River are Dresden's most iconic. Although the city doesn't have specifically defined protected vistas, its backdrop of medieval and Baroque buildings has defined it since the eighteenth century. Even in Dresden's post-war reconstruction, the 'resurrection' of views of the city's skyline—particularly the pinnacled Residenzschloss and domed Frauenkirche—have played a major part in acts of post-war remembrance. The construction of a new road bridge through a much-loved view of the Elbe meadows at Waldschlosschen proved to be immensely controversial among local residents who felt that Dresden's heritage was once again under threat, leading eventually to the delisting of the World Heritage Site by international cultural organization UNESCO in 2009.

The Protected Vista

Tom Brigden

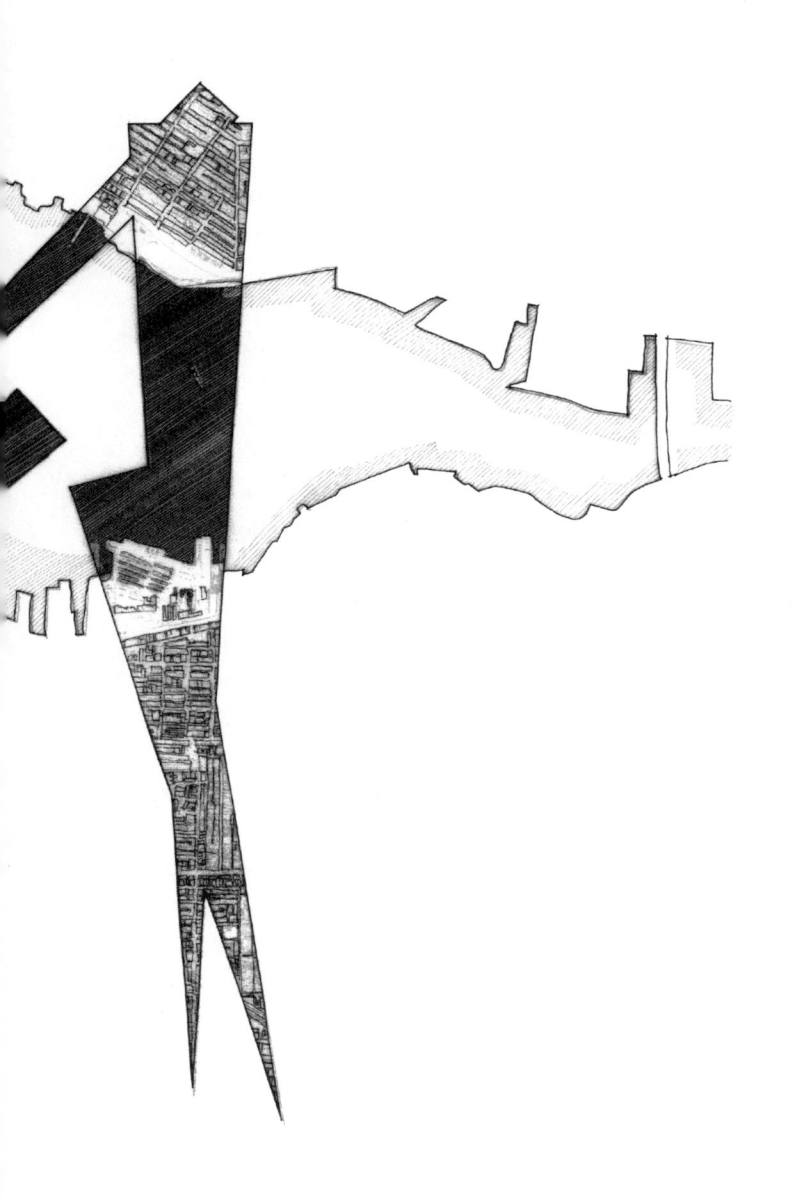

VANCOUVER

Vancouver's protected views restrict development in what is already a constrained site: a peninsula surrounded by water. Vancouver officially protects views of its natural landmarks via a system of precisely defined 'view cones.' These sightlines offer glimpses of the mountainous skyline on the northern shore of the Burrard Inlet. The careful curation of the city's views—of sea, sky, and mountains—is important to defining Vancouver's brand identity as one of the world's 'most livable cities,' and shares a connection with the branding of Vancouver's 2010 'Sea to Sky' Olympic Games. The importance of the street grid in setting up many of these views is clear from the plan, where views towards the north-east run parallel to one another indicating the importance afforded to views at eye level from principal streets. Views arranged predominantly south-north indicate the significance of setting and orientation to images of the city—the commuter's view of the city and mountainous backdrop from the bridges to the south dominate, while south-westerly views are afforded no significance at all.

The pressure to develop taller buildings on inner-city sites can put development and urban conservation in direct conflict, particularly where those buildings are in close proximity to heritage places. Such buildings are typically accused of insensitivity toward their contexts: of overwhelming the smaller scale of adjacent heritage buildings, and diminishing an appreciation of their heritage value. It follows that around the world, many urban planning policies have been developed to control the scale and massing of tall buildings within sensitive heritage contexts. At the same time, the protection of views of recognizable landmarks—and sometimes the whole skylines of cities—has become an important topic for state and metropolitan governments keen to protect a sense of identity, and to promote a 'brand,' in a globalizing world.

Although the phenomenon of view protection is now widespread, and actively encouraged by powerful international conservation bodies including the United Nations Educational, Scientific and Cultural Organization (UNESCO) and the International Council on Monuments and Sites (ICOMOS), there is a surprising diversity in the definition of such policies and the values that underpin them. In London, for example, the protection of views of historic landmarks from suburban greenspaces overlays an aesthetic understanding of the city rooted in the eighteenth-century Picturesque movement, while in Vancouver the protection of mountain and ocean views reinforces a lifestyle message. There are also differences in their practical application: from the scientific precision of coordinates, planes and angles defined in London's 'View Management Framework,' to the much broader notion that new structures should not interrupt views of Dresden's resurrected skyline from before the Second World War.

Despite the diversity in the detail and implementation of protection policies, it is clear that in each case views are afforded significant social and economic value. In some cases, it is even possible to quantify this value: for example, in 2014 the Turkish Supreme Court ruled that three newly completed thirty-story apartment towers should be demolished for interrupting the silhouette of Istanbul's Sultan Ahmed Mosque (aka the Blue Mosque). If carried through, the decision would cost the developer (not to mention the government that approved it) many millions of dollars, giving some indication of the immense economic values at stake when 'damage' is inflicted upon the city's views by developers of tall buildings.[1]

In examples such as this, the concept of view protection reveals how the creation, protection, loss, or destruction of value can occur not only as a result of the direct treatment of natural or cultural heritage assets themselves, but also in the management and control of those things that happen around them—those buildings and sites external to, and independent of, heritage places. These cases, therefore, also reveal the vulnerability of values attributed to natural and cultural heritage places, particularly in urban environments subject to immense economic development pressures. Policies of view protection are therefore increasingly held up as a seemingly logical, rational, objective, or scientific mechanism by which to negotiate between the economic value of development and the less tangible, competing values of cultural heritage and identity.

In the preceding images, I set out to map the value of views in six world cities, attempting to describe visually those views which have been raised to the status of special value. These drawings reveal the hidden structure of vistas, views, and viewpoints underlying each city, and in some cases the lines, planes, and angles that shape tall buildings and the spaces between them.

[1] Oliver Wainwright, 'Istanbuls "Illegal" Towers to Be Demolished After Landmark Court Ruling,' *The Guardian*, August 21, 2014, www.theguardian.com/artand design/architecture-design-blog/2014/aug/21/istanbuls-illegal-towers-to-be-demolished-after-landmark-court-ruling.

Antagonistic Coexistence of Values in the Machinations of a Metabolist Monument

Ari Seligmann

Kisho Kurokawa, Nakagin Capsule Tower, 1972. Photo: author, 2018.

Antagonistic Coexistence of Values in the Machinations of a Metabolist Monument

Ari Seligmann

Introduction

[1] Charles Jencks, 'Introduction,' in *Metabolism in Architecture* (London: Studio Vista, 1977), 16–17.

Kisho Kurokawa's Nakagin Capsule Tower (1972) is an iconic and canonical building, described by Charles Jencks as a combination of pasts and futures, noting that the Tower looked futuristic, capsules were equipped with latest technology, and prefabricated self-sufficient units were like space capsules, but capsules also drew on historical precedents such as small four-and-a-half mat tatami room proportions and had a round window that also featured in tea houses. Jencks aligned the oscillating temporalities (past and future) within the project with Kurokawa's notion of 'antagonistic coexistence,' which continues to be a reasonable framework for describing a host of tensions encapsulated by the Tower—between the economy and culture, decay and growth, preservation and regeneration, et cetera—as well as the divided opinions over the building's continued existence.[1] This paper uses the Tower and evolving debates over its potential demise to explore intersections of competing values, cultures, and economies that occur within and through architecture. The

Tower crystallized Metabolist ideals concerning technology and transformation. Today, its existence is at stake as varied stakeholders contest its value and wrestle over how to prioritize architectural, human, cultural, financial, and safety concerns. Despite its state of disrepair, the Tower is a fulcrum for passionate negotiation of architectural 'heritage' with assumed cultural values, a lightning rod for frictions between 'private' and 'public' interests, and a catalyst for congealing communities and conjuring collective values. This essay focuses on 'experimental preservation' efforts by the Nakagin Capsule Tower Preservation and Restoration Project (2014–) to generate audiences and support for maintaining the Tower, as well as the evolving imagery that has been used to stimulate imaginations of the building.[2] Consideration of the diverse values embedded in contentions over the building provide some context for examining efforts by the Tower Preservation Project to negotiate economic, cultural, and cultural economy frameworks and their antagonistic coexistence.

[2] Jorge Otero-Pailos, 'Experimental Preservation,' *Places Journal*, September 2016, doi.org/10.22269/160913 (accessed March 14, 2019).

Contextualizing Capsule Ambitions

Kurokawa's 'Capsule Declaration' (1969) and 'Challenge to the Capsule' (1972) articulated ambitions manifested in the Osaka Expo Takara Beautillion (1970) and encapsulated in the Nakagin Tower. Kurokawa considered capsules 'cyborg architecture' for *homo movens* that supported individuality and provided respite in a 'technetronic society,' while being mass-produced units designed for metabolic cycles.[3] From the outset, capsules had inherent tensions; they were prefabricated and unitized (with a limited range of options for customization), but also 'conceived as weapons with which man asserts his individuality and freedom in today's chaotic

[3] Kisho Kurokawa, 'Capsule Declaration,' in *Metabolism in Architecture* (London: Studio Vista, 1977), 75–83. First published in Japanese in *Space Design* March 1969.

4 Kurokawa, 'Capsule Declaration,' 84.

5 Kisho Kurokawa, 'General Outline of the Nakagin Capsule Tower Building,' *Japan Architect* 47 (October 1972), 24.

6 Kisho Kurokawa, 'General Remarks on Capsules,' *Japan Architect* 47 (October 1972), 28.

7 Kurokawa, 'General Remarks on Capsules,' 29.

8 See: Nakagin Housing Corporation, 'Nakagin Capsule Apartments Ginza: Business Capsule' (Tokyo: Nakagin Housing Corporation, 1971); Jencks, 'Introduction,' 17–19.

world.'[4] Capsules were conceived as industrial and technological components that facilitated individual existence, but were agglomerated into collectives supporting social and spatial organization. The Capsule Tower exemplified Kurokawa's ideas for Metabolism accommodating dynamism, offered alternative conceptions of architecture as facilitator, and proffered both organizational (stable cores and variable capsules) and urban models.

Kurokawa's ideas emphasized the biological, social, and technological but he was also keenly aware of economics, both that of capsule construction and of the ambitions of the developer client, Nakagin Housing Group, who were speculating on a new development model. Kurokawa was explicit about economic factors, noting that the site was selected 'because its convenience guarantees quick sales of the rooms.'[5] He also explained 'the new problem involved in designing capsules is the need to project at the outset a hypothesis—or a definition of the commercial salability [sic] of the product' and noted 'in addition to examining the functional and livability [sic] aspects of the design, sales promotion must be taken into consideration.'[6] Kurokawa unequivocally maintained that 'the capsule itself is the marketing unit.'[7] The Tower marketing brochure pitched the new accommodations as a business capsule and the speculative project attracted intended target markets with initial ownership reported as 30% companies with offices outside of Tokyo, 30% families wanting extensions (study, playroom, and so on), 20% bachelor businessmen, and 20% for miscellaneous uses (offices, storage, and so on).[8]

The prominent photographer Tomio Ohashi encoded these ambitions into the early set of Tower photos, which documented capsule production in the factory, construction on site, and suggested various forms of inhabitation of the units.⁹ Ohashi's interior photos portrayed some of the subtle variations of the capsule types—standard office, standard bed, deluxe, and super-deluxe—and their inhabitation, including several permutations of colors and equipment indicative of the different market types and the capacity for change embedded in the project. Internal capsule variation also aligned with intended expressions of individuality within the collective construction.

The critic Yasuo Uesaku connected the Tower to Metabolist ambitions, explaining that 'Kurokawa's notion of the capsule is not one of parts; the capsule is a self-sufficient component like a living cell, a functioning entity, a meaningful space unit with its own lifecycle. It lives and dies, but the *en* is always there to take on new cells. Likewise, his capsules may be moved or destroyed to make room for new capsules. The constant change in terms of time and space, is the law of the universe called metabolism.'¹⁰ Capsules provided vehicles for the transformation of space and change over time. However, the Tower was also attuned to the dynamism of real estate markets. From the outset, Kurokawa estimated the lifespan of the building to be sixty years and claimed 'the capsules themselves are individual rooms with a lifespan—social not mechanical—of from twenty-five to thirty-five years. At the end of that period they may be replaced.'¹¹ Kurokawa believed the construction system would endure, but that changes in lifestyles and technology would precipitate replacement. In 1998, after twenty-six years, Kurokawa began planning for capsule replacement, but by 2020, after forty-eight years, capsules have yet to be replaced. The building was designed to change and has not been static, frozen in either time or space. Individual capsules have been maintained, renovated and left to decay. Ongoing debates about the future of the Tower are complicated by the architectural conception of

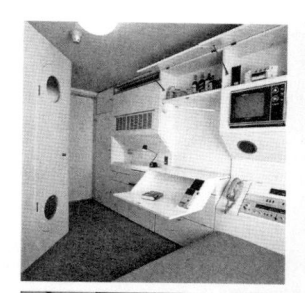

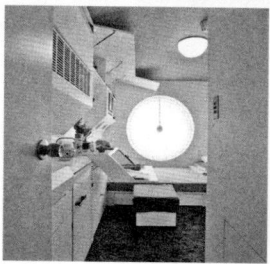

9 Nakagin Capsule Tower, iconic interiors. Photo: Tomio Ohashi, 1972.

10 Yasuo Uesaka, 'Kurokawa,' *Architecture Plus* 2, no. 1 (March 1974), 101. Reprinted in *Metabolism in Architecture*. En was described as 'media, where encountering or intercommunication takes place' and can be equated to the cores structuring the capsules and facilitating collective social interactions of the inhabitants.

11 Kisho Kurokawa, 'Challenge to the Capsule,' *Japan Architect* 47 (October 1972), 17.

the building as one that would change over time, and wrestle over whether to renovate capsules, replace the building, or replace all the capsules and reincarnate the building.

Change Management and Machinations

The negotiation of competing values has shaped the evolving private life and public reception of the Tower. The architectural press initially valued conceptual, functional, and economic aspects of the Metabolist exemplar. By 1980, water and maintenance concerns with the construction system emerged, but the first wave of public debates over the fate of the Tower began in 2005 in conjunction with the inflammatory 'Kurokawa's Asbestos Polluting Apartments' article and reports that the Nakagin Group landowner was preparing for replacement to derive more financial value from the site.[12] The 'Global Financial Crisis' curbed ambitions, which resumed with the 2018 sale of the land under the Tower and two adjacent buildings to the CTB LLC, who indicated intentions to redevelop the combined sites. The land sale stymied the Tower Preservation Project's brokering of capsule owner support to pursue Kurokawa's capsule regeneration plan and perpetuate the architectural value of the project.

The 2005 events prompted global outcry channeled through a World Architecture Network campaign and through unprecedented consensus across the Architectural Institute of Japan (AIJ), Japan Institute of Architects (JIA), The Japan Federation of Architects and Building Engineers Association, and the Japanese chapter of the International Committee for Documentation and Conservation of Buildings, Sites and Neighbourhoods of the Modern Movement (Docomomo), who all supported a petition to save

---

12 Hiroshi Watanabe, 'Evaluation and Composition of Cubes in Tokyo,' *AIA Journal* (October, 1980), 74–77. 'Kurokawa no Asbesto Osen Mansion [Kurokawa's asbestos polluting apartments],' *Shukan Shincho*, September 8, 2005, 145–147.

the building and publicly endorsed Kurokawa's capsule regeneration. The 2018 machinations, including the new CTB landowner notifying capsule owners that authorization would not be granted for transfers of leases, negating the ability to freely buy and sell capsules, precipitated a Tower Preservation Project-led global Change.org petition to Tokyo Governor Yuriko Koike to protect the building. However, the petition, like earlier institutional support, was unsuccessful in securing any heritage protection for the Tower.[13]

Documentation of the debates over the future of the building abound, from the *New York Times* to various academic journals.[14] Jason Gray's film *Nakagin Capsule Tower: Demolition & Preservation* (2007) articulated Kurokawa's final perspectives, which included marshalling economic arguments for preserving the Tower through his current regeneration plan rather than relying on claims for cultural or architectural heritage.[15] While Rima Yamazaki's documentary film *Nakagin Capsule Tower: Japanese Metabolist Landmark on the Edge of Destruction* (2010) comprehensively covered diverse positions in the debates.

Diagram 1 summarizes the varied values invoked in evolving arguments for and against perpetuation.[16] Perspectives vary from architectural historian Hiroyuki

[13] 'An Appeal for Help in Restoring a Tokyo Architectural Masterpiece,' change.org/p/東京都知事-小池百合子-東京が世界に誇る名建築-中銀カプセルタワービル-を保存してください?recruiter=895094555&utm_source=share_petition&utm_medium=twitter&utm_campaign=share_petition&utm_term=share_petition (accessed April 1, 2019).

[14] Nicolai Ouroussoff, 'Future Vision Banished to the Past,' *New York Times*, July 6, 2009; Zhongjie Lin, 'Nakagin Capsule Tower: Revisiting the Future of the Recent Past,' *Journal of Architectural Education* 65, no. 1 (October, 2011), 13–32; Aki Ishida, 'Metabolic Impermanence, The Nakagin Capsule Tower,' *Inflection* 4 (2017), 32–43.

[15] See also: 'Interview Kisho Kurokawa: Sekai no Hokoru Metabolism Kenchiku Nakagin Capsule Tower no Yukue? [Kurokawa interview: What directions for Nakagin Capsule Tower, the Global pride of Metabolist architecture?],' *Tokyojin* February 2007, 70–75.

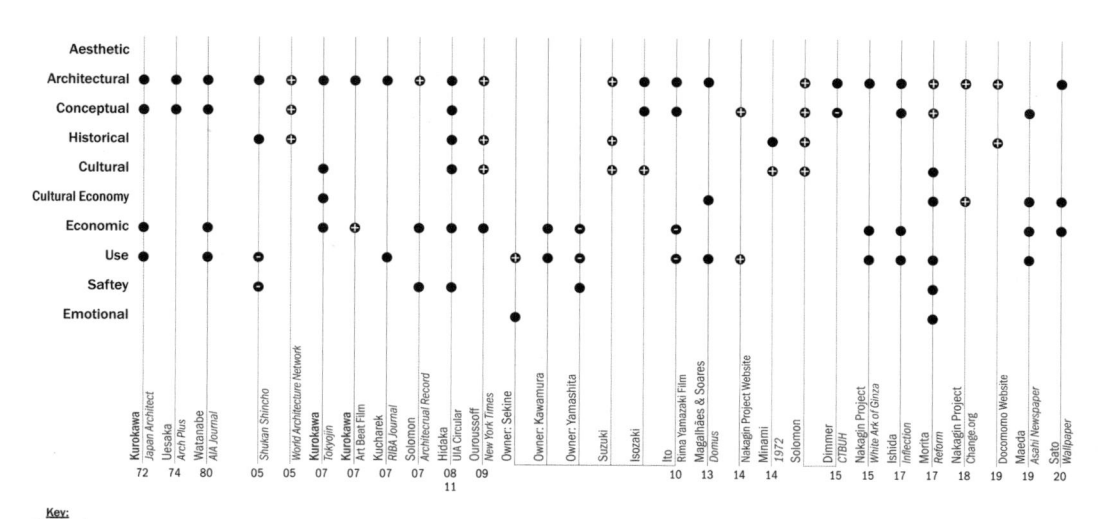

[16] Evaluating Valuations in Development and Demise Discourses. Source: author.

[17] 'Under Threat: Nakagin Capsule Tower,' *Docomomo International*, www.docomomo.com/events?sec=4&id=746 (accessed April 1, 2019).

[18] Ouroussoff, 'Future Vision Banished to the Past.'

[19] Ibid.

Suzuki's and architect Arata Isozaki's cultural advocacy, to diverse owners' positions, to Toyo Ito's pragmatism and Christian Dimmer's academic view. While Docomomo International and the new landowners oriented to predictable economic values, the leading advocates, Tower Preservation Project, changed tactics arguing for maintaining the building based on cultural economy values—international interest, media exposure, tourist attraction, and expanding uses.[17]

Reviewing the evolving discourses, different stakeholders valued the building and architecture in different ways. Kurokawa shrewdly lobbied for his capsule replacement plan, relying primarily on financial arguments to ensure his professional value. Architectural institutions predominantly promote cultural and historical values. The property owners leverage economic gains and public safety concerns with the aging and poorly maintained structure in their bids to redevelop the site. Capsule owners oscillate between property values and monetary gains, and affection for the building, while the Change.org petition coordinated by the Preservation Project relied on arguments for tourism and media contributions to the cultural economy. Competing values and value systems ensnare the building and its transformations.

In 2009, Nicolai Ouroussoff wrote in belated defense of the Tower and questioned 'how old does a building have to be before we appreciate its value? And when does its cultural importance trump practical considerations? ... why certain landmarks ... are preserved and others are not.'[18] He also fully acknowledged the challenges of public support for saving private buildings noting that 'private developments like the Capsule Tower, no matter how historically important, are regarded in terms of property rights. They are about business first, not culture. Governments don't like to interfere; the voices of preservationists are shrugged off.'[19] Beyond issues of private financial interest, in general support for saving structures has been even more difficult in Tokyo where the turnover of projects and properties occurs at an accelerated pace, with an average lifespan of buildings still around twenty-five years.[20] In Yamazaki's documentary, Isozaki noted that surviving this long has been a miracle and reaching fifty (2022)—in order to be considered 'historically significant' in the Japanese context—will be miraculous. However, Jorge Otero-Pailos, a leading advocate for 'experimental preservation' offered a compelling answer to Ouroussoff's queries, suggesting that buildings last because human connections are strong.[21]

Otero-Pailos argued that we should understand culture as a reflection of collective agreement about what is considered important, and cultural significance in terms of human attachment to buildings and objects.[22] He believes that preservation should help strengthen bonds with the built environment and not freeze objects in time and turn them into museum pieces. He strategically positioned experimental preservation as a challenge to 'governmental protection of cultural objects' and not as an 'attempt to speak for culture, but rather to solicit a cultural response.'[23] Following Reinhard Kropf and Siv Helene Stangeland, preservation is considered a negotiation of 'how people can occupy and preoccupy themselves with a building, and then forge a shared identity with others who do so too.'[24] Drawing on Pierre Bourdieu and Michel Serres, experimental preservationists can be considered 'as players in the game of cultural production whose position is to produce new quasi-heritage objects.'[25] Otero-Pailos contended that experimental preservation is guided by 'attempts to put new cultural and historic objects into our collective consciousness' and 'to verify or refute hypotheses about their capacity to become valued objects we cannot

[20] See: Botand Bognar, 'What Goes Up, Must Come Down,' *Harvard Design Magazine* 3 (Fall 1997), 33–43.

[21] Otero-Pailos, 'Experimental Preservation.' See also: Jorge Otero-Pailos, Erik Fenstad Langdalen, and Thordis Arrhenius, eds., *Experimental Preservation* (Baden: Lars Muller, 2016).

[22] Ted Shelton and Tricia Stuth 'Architecture and Human Attachment: An Interview with Jorge Otero-Pailos,' *Journal of Architectural Education* 72, no. 2 (2018), 192, 195.

[23] Otero-Pailos, 'Experimental Preservation.'

[24] Ibid.

[25] Ibid.

26 Ibid.

27 Randall Mason, 'Engaged Preservation,' *Journal of Architectural Education* 72, no. 2 (2018), 202.

imagine future generations living without.'[26] While acknowledging the contributions of experimental preservation approaches, Randall Mason argued for expanding consideration from objects to processes, and advocated for a notion of 'engaged preservation' that encompassed a broader range of practices including 'the political (advocacy in its many forms), the economic (adaptive reuse, tourism, urban regeneration), and the artistic (represented in site interpretation).'[27] Without reference to or association with preservation practices, the Tower Preservation Project represents a combination of experimental and engaged preservation efforts in a context of limited governmental protection and a Japanese collective consciousness that is conditioned for change. The Preservation Project has been exemplifying experimental preservation efforts to cultivate communities and affiliation. The organization has undertaken a multipronged strategy to broaden audiences, engagement, and support for the Tower across advocacy, promotion, tourism, adaptive reuse, renovation, and collaborations with artists.

Public Engagement, Experimental Preservation, and Capsule Restoration Project(s)

The Preservation Project organization emerged in 2014 and its members are leading the current charge to pave a future for the Tower, but without advocating for preservation following common conceptions. They do not want to designate the building as a historic monument and thereby freeze a past futurist vision. They do not want to 'preserve' the building in its current (decaying) state or faithfully return the building to an idealized past state. Rather than the form of the building, they want to preserve the spirit of Kurokawa's Metabolist ideas and support replacing the capsules to save and perpetuate concepts so that they are available to future generations.²⁸ They also do not intend to 'restore' the building to a set state, but to facilitate the regeneration and revitalization of the building both through the originally anticipated capsule replacement and through incremental renovations transforming the interiors of capsules into new configurations supporting a variety of activities. In Japanese, the term *reform* typically refers to renovation and adaptive reuse practices. More than preservation and restoration, the Project organization is reforming capsules through internal revisions and hopes to reform the external building following Kurokawa's proposed capsule replacement plan.

Even though protecting the Tower has been endorsed by key institutions and supported through international architectural media outlets, the current efforts of the Project organization operate predominantly outside of architectural circles. The chief representative, Tatsuyuki Maeda, has a marketing background and has been an enthusiastic capsule owner since 2010.²⁹ Per their website, they aim to extend the life of the historic building through three areas: negotiating collective directions for the Tower with capsule owners and the Management Association; increasing the value of the Tower and developing new ways of using the building; and conducting public relations efforts to broaden knowledge about the building.³⁰

Efforts to increase value revolve around repair, regeneration planning, and renovations. The organization works with owners and experts to address asbestos, water, plumbing, and other issues. They are concerned with safety and improving convenience to support capsule inhabitants. The organization is actively trying to marshal support to realize Kurokawa's capsule replacement. They were coordinating with

28 The cyclical rebuilding of Ise Shrine recurs in Kurokawa's explanations of Metabolism and in differentiation of Japanese conceptions of preservation. Ise changes regularly and parts are replaced maintaining the spirit of the buildings rather than their tangible persistent form. Ise Shrine and the technical knowledge required for its reproduction is perpetuated though replacement, and its parts regularly redistributed for use in other shrines across the country.

29 Maeda owns arounds fifteen capsules. Author in discussion with Maeda, December 2, 2018. See also: Akiko Ishimaru, 'Nakagin Capsule Tower Biru Nakenchiku ga Ikinobiru Hoho [Nakagin Capsule Tower Building: Ways of extending famous architecture],' *Tokyojin* January 2017, 116–121.

30 Translation by the author. See: 'Nakagin Capsule Tower,' www.nakagincapsuletower.com/project (accessed April 1, 2019).

[31] See: 中銀カプセルリノベーション [Nakagin Capsule Renovation], 2019, www.facebook.com/NakaginCapsuleRenovation (accessed April 1, 2019).

[32] See: 'Monthly Capsule,' www.nakagincapsuletower.com/monthlycapsule (accessed April 1, 2019).

Kurokawa's office, the Management Association, and local government authorities working through the legalities and logistics of enacting the plans. While negotiating towards capsule exchange they have also been supporting the renovation of capsules and expanding occupation and use. From 2015 to 2018, before the new landowners prevented further sales of capsules, the Project organization coordinated a 'Capsule Bank' to match capsule buyers and sellers and increase the number of engaged owners and useable capsules. In conjunction, the organization has facilitated information exchange amongst owner/renovators and used Facebook channels to create communities and communicate renovation outcomes.[31]

In addition to expanding the variety of capsule options, the Project organization is also trying to expand ways of using the building. Accompanying the growth of the sharing economy, both original and renovated capsules were attractive short-term options through Airbnb (launched in Japan in 2013). The capsules began as short-term business lodging and recently evolved into tourist accommodations. However, in 2015 the Management Association banned Airbnb listing of capsules and 2018 changes in national regulations further prevented capsules from participating in similar sharing platforms. In response, the Project organization launched a 'monthly capsule' program offering three unique capsules as one-month rental properties. Locals and tourists alike can choose from an original refurbished capsule, a renovated capsule with window sofa, or a Muji-themed and sponsored capsule.[32]

Further broadening audiences, engagement, and occupation the organization began a Capsule Gallery program, using capsules for display and installations. The 2017 Gallery program was partially inspired by the use of capsules in the 2016

Ginza Architecture exhibition and was an extension of the Capsule Art Projects program. Mari Takemoto's *Budou* installation was the inaugural project and was followed by the 2019 *Artists' Time Capsules* exhibition.[33]

Beyond stimulating tourism and art events, the Project organization is also actively engaging media producers who may use the building as location or backdrop. The Tower has appeared in a range of productions, from the 2016 Tokyo marathon to camera commercials, and from music videos by domestic and international artists to Hollywood productions. Originally, the Tower was a speculative development for Japan's growing business economy and it now plays various roles in supporting the expanding cultural economy.

Media exposure, whether the building is recognized or not, is part of broader efforts to increase public recognition of and build human attachments to the Tower, marshalling support for its continued existence. The Tower attracts attention across Japanese television, news, and magazines (beyond the architectural press), and the Project organization helps to broker access and exposure. The organization also maintains a website, two Facebook pages (for the Preservation and Restoration Project in general and for the Art Projects), and has published two crowdfunded books to disseminate ongoing efforts.

In conjunction with exposure, the Project organization also fosters direct engagement through tours and Art Project programs. The Tower has an international reputation as a Metabolist exemplar and attracts architecture enthusiasts from around the globe, but as it is a private residential building access to the interiors has been limited. From 2016, the Project organizers began offering regular tours to allow domestic and international audiences to witness the evolving states of the building from aging corridors to decaying infrastructure to

[33] See: 'The Nakagin Capsule Tower Building becomes a disappearing cultural heritage time capsule!' 100banch.com/projects/14702/?fbclid=IwAR1WcCAWZQjOxCSNBmaBFI7C1nAxFld0OVeoz57O n_RoG2roJQjyYxc4BWU (accessed April 13, 2019).

original capsules and exemplary renovations. They offer four to six tours in Japanese on the weekends, weekly tours in English on Thursdays, and sometimes tours in Chinese and bespoke tours for international architects.[34] The Project also supports access to the Tower via other tour providers. For example, although no longer available as accommodation on Airbnb, Capsule Tower tours were offered as Airbnb 'social impact' experiences run via AccessPoint: ARCHITECTURE-Tokyo (established 2016).[35] The tours are not simply a profit-oriented enterprise capitalizing on interest, but a mechanism for increasing architectural value through direct experience with the design ambitions and the (d)evolving state of the Tower, as well as expanding social values between the people that occupy and are preoccupied with the building.

The *Nakagin Capsule Tower Building: The White Ark of Ginza* (2015) crowdfunded publication was another experimental preservation effort that encapsulated the Project organization's endeavors and ambitions.[36] Maeda described how the photo and interview book emerged from ongoing discussions amongst owners who wanted to show the lives of Tower occupants, how terrible conditions had become, and how the Tower may be used.[37] The book presented the past, present, and future of the Tower, and was inspired by several previous photo documentations of the building.[38] The *White Ark* publication presented a comprehensive portrait of the building that combined historical accounts, interviews with ten occupants and Shigenori Ishikawa's photos of their varied use of capsules, and introduction of ongoing renovation efforts.[39]

Within the complex debates over the future of the Tower, *White Ark* validated Kurokawa's conception of the capsules by demonstrating diverse occupation, and revealing ways the capsules have changed, are changing, and can

---

34 Tatsuyuki Maeda, 'Nakagin Capsule Tower Biru no Jirei de Miru Nakenchiku wo Saisei Suru Itsutsu no Hoho [Examining the case of Nakagin Capsule Tower Building: Five ways of regenerating famous architecture],' *Reform* (October 2017), 47 and 'Central Bank Capsule Tower Tour,' www.nakagincapsuletower.com/nakagincapsuletour (accessed April 1, 2019).

35 AccessPoint tours are run by Nahoko Wada, a former Kurokawa employee. The Airbnb website described that tours 'raise awareness about the current severe situation that the Nakagin Capsule Tower finds itself in. We want to encourage support for the preservation of this culturally significant building. Your contributions also support the development of similar architectural education programs.' Airbnb (accessed April 13, 2019), www.airbnb.com.au/experiences/69229 (webpage discontinued). See also: 'About,' accesspoint.jp/en_about/ (accessed April 13, 2019).

36 Nakagin Capsule Tower Preservation and Restoration Project, *Nakagin Capsule Tower Building: The White Ark of Ginza* (Tokyo: Nakagin Capsule Tower Preservation and Restoration Project, 2015).

37 Maeda, 'Five Ways of Regenerating Famous Architecture,' 38.

38 Inspiration was drawn from Noritaka Minami's *1972* (2015) photo book on the Tower, which Maeda was involved in during shooting 2012–2013, and Filipe Magalhães and Ana Luisa Soares who documented their extended stay in 'Metabolist Routine,' *Domus*, www.domusweb.it/en/architecture/2013/05/29/the_metabolist_routine.html (accessed April 1, 2019) and 'A Year in the Metabolist Future,' failedarchitecture.com/a-year-in-the-metabolist-future-of-1972/ (accessed April 1, 2019).

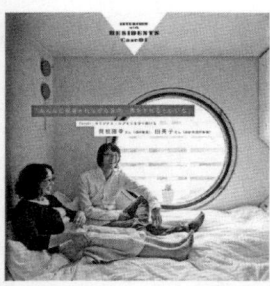

39 Nakagin Capsule Tower: *White Ark* occupation. Photo: Shigenori Ishikawa, 2015.

continue to change. *White Ark* did not valorize the Tower as an architectural achievement but celebrated the life of and lives within the building. If there was limited public sympathy for the building outside of architectural circles, then trying to generate some sympathy for the occupants and indirect support for saving the Tower was worth a try, and at the very least the publication, its crowdfunding solicitation, and its dissemination contributed to raising broader awareness of the Tower and the issues it faced.

The Preservation Project produced a subsequent crowdfunded photography book in conjunction with inaugurating the Nakagin Capsule Tower Art Projects, which began in 2016 to develop additional avenues to broaden audiences and engagement with the Tower. Maeda described intentions for the Art Projects as creating 'opportunities for architecture through art.'[40] The Tower frequently provided subject matter, inspiration or venue(s) for work and the resulting work brought additional attention to the Tower architecture. The Art Projects attracted diverse art and music audiences to the Tower and also created cultural platforms for disseminating information about the Tower, including Facebook and website channels.[41] The 2016 Art Projects included Yamamoto's *Nakagin Capsule Girl* photographs, Masahiro Yoshikawa's *Mikiritani no Kioku* film presentation and discussion in a capsule, and Naho Ishii's Tower-inspired drawings and exhibition in a capsule. 2017 projects diversified with DJ Toriena's performances in capsules and illustrations inspired by capsules, a photography event with Jun Itoi, and Inês D'Orey's Tower photos. Art projects resumed in early 2019 with a capsule concert by Alex Vincent and the *Artists' Time Capsules* project with ten artists for ten capsules.

The first Capsule Art Project by Yamamoto followed the old adage 'sex sells' using a set of capsules as backdrops for

---

[40] Tatsuyuki Maeda, 'Epilogue,' in *Nakagin Capsule Girl* (Tokyo: Nakagin Capsule Tower Preservation and Restoration Project, 2017), n.p.

[41] See: 中銀カプセルアートプロジェクト [Nakagin Capsule Art Project], www.facebook.com/NakaginCapsuleArt (accessed April 1, 2019) and 'Nakagin Capsule Tower,' Nakagin Capsule Tower Building Preservation/Regeneration Project, www.nakagincapsule-tower.com (accessed April 1, 2019).

42 Jencks, 'Introduction,' 11, 12, 20; Mie Maganuma, *Media Monster: Dare ga 'Kisho Kurokawa' wo Koroshiata ka?* [Media Monster: Who Killed Kisho Kurokawa?] (Tokyo: Shoshisha 2015); Watanabe, 'Evaluation and Composition of Cubes in Tokyo,' 74.

43 Kazan Yamamoto, 'Introduction,' in *Nakagin Capsule Girl*, n.p.

44 Nakagin Capsule Tower: Capsule Girls 'Porn.' Photo: Kazan Yamamoto, 2016.

45 Nakagin Capsule Tower: Ruin Porn.

photos of young women in various stages of undress. However, the sensuality of the resulting exhibition and photo book was not inconsistent with Kurokawa's contention that he would work for anyone (echoing associations of architecture and prostitution), with Kurokawa's unbridled attention-seeking antics (that led to his characterization as a 'media monster'), as well as the initial bachelor pad conceptualization of the capsules (Watanabe reported that Kurokawa quipped to Jencks that the capsules were 'meant to suggest Japanese bird cages for out-of-town businessmen and bachelors "with their birds"').[42] *Nakagin Capsule Girl* sought to increase recognition of the Tower across art photography circles and contemporary businessmen and bachelors who already regularly consume soft-porn pin-ups through the plethora of centerfolds in manga, newspapers, and gravure publications. While Yamamoto's photos shifted the capsules from bachelor pads to boudoirs, his expressed intention was to 'create a visual representation of the neo-futuristic world of the Nakagin Capsule Tower and women from the "real" future ... Enjoy the art created by the beauty of architecture and women.'[43] Ohashi's canonical photos suggested varied inhabitation. Ishikawa's *White Ark* photos documented capsule occupation, while Yamamoto posed speculative inhabitants and titillated broader imaginations of what might occur in the capsules.

The soft pornography of Yamamoto's art photography publication,[44] seeking to stimulate interest in and affection for the Tower, parallels an increasing proliferation of 'ruin porn,'[45] which graphically exposed decaying capsules. Exhibitionist images of dilapidated capsules created an antagonistic coexistence with images that may both stir sympathy for the sad state of the building while also providing ammunition for public safety arguments that could fuel redevelopment efforts. However, images of ruination were often strategically remediated when paired with renovation images to demonstrate the dramatic revitalization of capsules with renewed lives and potential activities.[46] Concurrently, graphic display of reformed capsules has been generating a social media driven form of 'renovation porn,' tempting further reform.

46 Nakagin Capsule Tower: Renovation Porn.

Overall, the Project organization activities sought to celebrate and stimulate the life of and lives within the Tower. Whether photo shoots, promotional videos, commercial backdrops, art venues, renovation support, or negotiating for repair and regeneration, the Project employed diverse means and media to increase cultural, social, and architectural values through (re)investment in the Tower. They followed experimental preservation in multifaceted attempts to solicit cultural responses and heighten awareness of the building within collective consciousness to increase human attachment and support. Ultimately, they value the continued existence of the Tower, some return on investment, as well as the perpetuation of Kurokawa's transformative concepts.

Machinations and Negotiations Continue

The ambitions and evolution of the Nakagin Capsule Tower and the recent efforts of the Preservation Project illuminate the antagonistic coexistence of multiple values encapsulated in architecture and the contingencies of their negotiation. Buildings are valued as artefacts, as expressions of ideas, as technical or aesthetic achievements, as facilitators of activities, as property with monetary worth, and as infrastructure for communities. From the outset, Kurokawa's capsules mediated these diverse aspects and their potentials.

The Tower was originally designed to metabolize in particular ways, to support an emerging highly mobile future society, and to evolve in dialogue with individuals and collectives. All have occurred, but none as planned. The unpredictable future transformed 'business capsules' into containers catalyzing creative industries and cultural economies while catering for even more mobility and transient forms of occupation. Capsules continue to provide refuge for individuals and congeal communities with shared interests (whether occupants, renovators, creative workers, hobbyists, or advocates for compact living). Moreover, the Tower has been simultaneously decaying and regenerating.

The Tower is nearing a critical point in its life, but is challenged by conflicting ownership structures, by tensions and machinations between private, individual, and collective interests, and by quandaries with how to preserve a building that has been designed to change. Within the unresolved debates over the future of the Tower arguments for prolonging the existence of the building rely on multiple values, spanning historical achievement, architectural and cultural significance, idealized public interests over private-capital-driven interests, cultural economy contributions, and the lives and pursuits of Tower occupants. These antagonistic values are continually negotiated and continue to metabolize.

For example, in delayed response to the new CTB landowners' machinations, in March 2019 Docomomo International sought to rally support based on historical value. In early April 2019, the *Asahi Newspaper* interviewed Maeda, who proposed that the capsules are not valuable as real estate, noting that even though capsules are inconvenient, people love the building and want to live there. He also reflected on the strong and unique character of Tower occupants. Furthermore, he suggested that people want to own capsule architecture 'as works of art' and many people from around the world regularly come to see the building. He concluded by questioning whether the value(s) of the building can be recognized enough for it to be maintained.[47] As of mid-2020, future transformation remains in question.[48]

Preservation debates bring the active negotiation of values to the forefront. Beyond governmental preservation protection sought by Docomomo, the experimental preservation approaches productively employed by the Nakagin Preservation and Restoration Project offer alternatives as 'a collective way to ask social and political questions about heritage objects; these dialogues are a way to interrogate what aspects of a cultural artefact are important to us.'[49] In the context of this publication, the Nakagin Capsule Tower provides a valuable catalyst for questioning what aspects and values of architecture (as a cultural artefact) are important to us? And in what forms—as objects, ideas, memories, images, and so on—should architecture and architectural heritage be preserved?

[47] Ayumi Ishikawa, 'Kisho Kurokawa no Nakagin Capsule Tower Biru Chiku 47 Nen no Heya ga Umidasu 'Fudosan' Igai no Katchi [Kisho Kurokawa's Nakagin Capsule Tower: 47 year old rooms creating value beyond real estate],' *Asahi Newspaper*, April 4, 2019, www.asahi.com/and_M/20190409/1450039/ (accessed April 13, 2019). In subsequent recounting of machinations laced with antagonistic coexistences, Maeda described capsule exchange as the only solution to current issues, while explaining concurrent pursuit of both foreign investors to purchase and regenerate the building and status as World Heritage site or Tangible Cultural Property. Chris Russell, 'Nakagin Capsule Tower, Saving An Urban Dream From The Ravages Of Time,' *Japan Times*, November 10, 2019, features.japantimes.co.jp/nakagin-capsule-tower/?fbclid=IwAR34NJohzFhtlwjzEH26ma-mpi-4FchZH0IUz3dbDo5nAim KT9yV2cJmZNA#part1 (accessed November 23, 2019).

[48] See also: Sanae Sato, 'Time Capsule: An Instagram Hotspot in Tokyo Is Under Threat, So Snap It Before It's Flattened,' *Wallpaper* January 2020, 33.

[49] Danielle Narae Choi, 'Juvenile Delinquents,' *Journal of Architectural Education* 72, no. 2 (2018), 283. See also: Jorge Otero-Pailos and Danielle Choi, 'The Not-Me Creation: Interview with Jorge Otero Pailos,' *Harvard Design Magazine* 44 (Fall–Winter 2017), 94–100.

Meme, Memory or Critic

Hamish Lonergan

Michael Abrahamson
(fuckyeahbrutalism),
Tumblr archive.

Meme, Memory or Critic
Revaluing Brutalism on Social Media

Hamish Lonergan

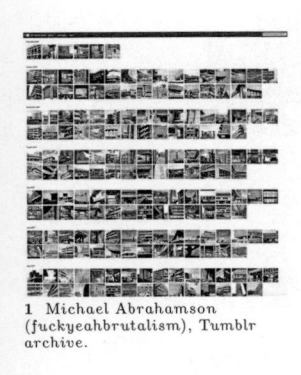

1 Michael Abrahamson (fuckyeahbrutalism), Tumblr archive.

On November 6, 2017, the Tumblr account *Fuck Yeah Brutalism* (FYB) went on indefinite hiatus. Michael Abrahamson, the page administrator, never wrote much to accompany his posts, his last post saying only that it was time to 'rethink and retool.' Since December 14, 2010—barring five days in 2016 when his account was hacked, spewing click-bait spam instead of Brutalism—Abrahamson had republished one Brutalist image each day, copied from period sources, appearing reassuringly in followers' feeds. These images accumulated over time in a vast library of the style, easily accessible in thumbnail view through Tumblr's scrollable archive function. Many images had not been published anywhere else since a buildings' completion.[1]

Over the course of these seven years, FYB had witnessed and contributed to the dramatic reversal in Brutalism's popular and academic fortunes. As recently as 2012, the International Committee for Documentation and Conservation of Buildings, Sites and Neighbourhoods of the Modern Movement (Docomomo) warned attendees of the 'Learning to Love Brutalism' conference that a key-note lecture by

Anthony Vidler, on the appreciation and preservation of Brutalist buildings, might enter an 'ambiguous territory' that some present might find 'impossible to accept.'[2] By 2017, however, the public were regularly joining with conservationists to demand heritage protection for Brutalist buildings such as Sirius in Sydney.[3] Yet, coming just two months after the demolition of Alison and Peter Smithson's Robin Hood Gardens in London, FYB's demise seemed to recognize that even as pages like this helped tip popular architectural taste toward the difficult style, key buildings continued to fall.[4]

What happens online increasingly affects our society. The Campaign to protect Philip Johnson's AT&T building in New York, for instance, originated on Instagram—a planned renovation would have removed much of the original lobby—instigated by Adam Nathaniel Furman, who posts on Postmodernism to 35,000 followers.[5] At the same time there is little serious writing to explain the appeal of Furman's and Abrahamson's pages. Part of the problem is the increasingly hermetic, self-referential world of social media itself. In April 2019, for example, Treero, an architect sharing digital drawings to 6,700 followers on Instagram, told Malapartecafé, an Instagram-only periodical with 3,900 followers, that it was 'distasteful' to theorize social media too closely. A discussion about Instagram hosted entirely on the same platform being discussed, available only to those already with an Instagram account.[6]

Treero might have a point: academic publishing inevitably lags behind the hyper speed of the internet.[7] By the time this essay goes to print, Treero's interview may be difficult to find even with academic referencing, buried under so many new posts. Yet, as architectural historian and theorist Beatriz Colomina argues, academics and designers still have an obligation to reckon with social media, as one of the most

2 Anthony Vidler, 'Learning to Love Brutalism,' lecture, 12th Docomomo International Conference, Espoo, Finland, August 2012), docomomo-us.org/news/flashback-learning-to-love-brutalism.

3 Tao Gofers, Sirius Building, 1981. Photo: Katherine Lu, 2016.

4 Alison and Peter Smithson, Robin Hood Gardens, 1972. Photo: Gunnar Klack, 2008.

5 Philip Johnson, AT&T Building, 1984. Photo: David Shankbone, 2007.

6 Malapartecafé (@Malapartecafe), 'Interview with TREES aka @treero,' Instagram, April 19, 2019.

7 As the introduction to a meme-centric issue of the Journal of Visual Culture put it '[a]cademic publishing—characterized by its long review periods and labored revision processes—habitually plays tortoise to the internet's hare.' Laine Nooney and Laura Portwood-Stacer, 'One Does Not Simply: An Introduction to the Special Issue on Internet Memes,' Journal of Visual Culture 13, no. 3 (2014), 248.

important changes to society in the twenty-first century.[8] We need to brave embarrassment and seriously consider social media and its connections to the world offline—in areas as un-cool as architectural heritage—even as social media is rapidly reorganizing what we value in buildings.

Explanations that do exist for Brutalism's revaluation tend to emphasize its nostalgic qualities—contemporary echoes of a big-government building boom not seen since—or what some perceive as a perverse sensibility similar to internet memes. Both fit neatly into a narrative of a more democratic culture online, where anyone might feel nostalgia or enjoy a meme without the approval of traditional critics. It is a comforting idea but, as internet scholar Mark Andrejevic warns, the internet was built in the image of the social and economic contexts that created it, and 'all of those potentials again find themselves enmeshed in the social systems in which they develop.'[9] It has not taken long for the loose freedom of the early web to coalesce around massively profitable publicly traded companies.

Issues of taste, freedom, and authority may have migrated to social media, but they are not new. In tracing the contemporary value of Brutalism, I turn to an understanding of taste and society informed by David Hume's empiricist philosophy, grounded in precise observation rather than generalized theory. In the eighteenth century, Hume argued that the standard of taste that allows us to compare one work of art with another can only be informed by the 'joint verdict' of trustworthy 'true critics.'[10] In doing so he placed the power and influence of the expert critic at the center of taste. To understand the value of Brutalism on social media, we must follow the critical and institutional power structures that persist online, and how they continue to contribute to public taste and heritage campaigns today.

---

[8] Beatriz Colomina, 'Broadcasting Yourself: Social Media Urbanism,' lecture, *Arkdes*, June 28, 2018.

[9] He writes that 'all of those potentials again find themselves enmeshed in the social systems in which they develop.' J. J. Sylvia and Mark Andrejevic, 'The Future of Critique: Mark Andrejevic on Power/Knowledge and the Big Data-Driven Decline of Symbolic Efficiency,' *International: Journal of Communication* 10 (2016), 32–33.

[10] David Hume, 'Of the Standard of Taste,' In *Four Dissertations* (London: A. Millar, 1757). For a longer discussion of Hume's philosophy in relation to architecture see: John Macarthur, 'Sense, Meaning and Taste in Architectural Criticism,' in *Semi-Detached: Writing, Representation and Criticism in Architecture*, ed. Naomi Stead (Melbourne: Uro Media, 2012), 230.

Social Media and Memes

It is easy to interpret the appeal of Brutalism on social media as a type of meme. These shareable units of cultural exchange are often associated with a visual sensibility that defies traditional standards of good taste, prioritizing production speed, repetition and 'in-jokes,' with invention frequently outstripping ability.[11] Tom Wilkinson, history editor for the *Architectural Review*, criticized *Fuck Yeah Brutalism* in similar language, arguing that, at best, Tumblr pages collect images without commentary and, at worst, become 'lightly "curated" composts of disconnected visual platitudes,' with an appetite for the perverse and banal.[12]

The name *Fuck Yeah Brutalism* emerged from just such a perverse and banal Tumblr trend: the *Fuck Yeah* meme. These accounts collect images strictly related to a single theme; *Fuck Yeah Sharks*,[13] the earliest, posted Great Whites beside children's toys.[14] In the context of continued accusations that Brutalist buildings are too ugly to save, this connection raises the possibility that Brutalism on social media is enjoyed in the same perverse, so-bad-it's-good manner as other memes.[15] As meme scholar Ryan Milner argues, often the joke is simply the irony of enjoying a meme that outsiders find aesthetically or ethically offensive.[16] Does this mean, then, that the visual acuity learnt to value Brutalism comes from a familiarity with memes, rather than an appreciation of the architecture itself?

Considered closely, there is something more complex at stake. Whatever irony there is in FYB is unlikely to be related to Abrahamson's followers disliking Brutalism. Simply because Brutalism is present on the same platforms as memes does not make the style itself a meme; this uncouples Brutalism online from its concrete reality. We know from

11 Nick Douglas, 'It's Supposed to Look Like Shit: The Internet Ugly Aesthetic,' *Journal of Visual Culture* 13, no. 3 (December 2014), 314–339.

12 Tom Wilkinson, 'Architectural Photography in the Age of Social Media,' *The Architectural Review* 237, no. 1415 (January 2015), 97. Elsewhere, he suggests that the taste for Brutalism is 'at worst, a perverse affectation of middle-class aesthetes who never had to live in these monstrous carbuncles.' Tom Wilkinson, *Bricks & Mortals: Ten Great Buildings and the People They Made* (London: Bloomsbury, 2014), 81.

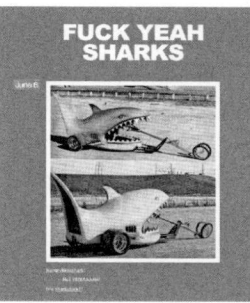

13 Rachel Dearborn (fuckyeahsharks), 2015, Tumblr post.

14 For a useful overview of *Fuck Yeah* Tumblr accounts, see: Chris Menning, 'Q&A with Ned Hepburn (Origin of F Yeah Tumblrs),' *Know Your Meme*, April 29, 2011, knowyourmeme.com/blog/interviews/qa-with-ned-hepburn-origin-of-f-yeah-tumblrs.

15 See, for example: Mirelle Harper, 'The Worst Building Decisions in the UK Ever,' *Ericmage*, July 18, 2018, ericfestival.com/155-the-worst-building-decisions; Camila Ruz and Maisie Smith-Walters; 'When concrete buildings drive people mad,' *BBC News Magazine*, November 4, 2015; Mike Ives, 'Too Ugly to Be Saved? Singapore Weighs Fate of Its Brutalist Buildings,' *The New York Times*, January 27, 2019; Fayroze Lutta, 'Sirius and the Failed Utopianism of Brutalist Architecture,' *Overland*, September 15, 2016.

16 Ryan M. Milner, *The World Made Meme: Public Conversations and Participatory Media* (Cambridge: MIT Press, 2016), 142–144.

17 Michael Abrahamson, 'Radical Nostalgia,' *Fulcrum* 63 (2013), 1.

18 Adam Nathaniel Furman (@adamnathanielfurman), #archiphorism, 2019, Instagram post.

19 Ryan Scavnicky (@sssscavvvv), who thinks this has anything to do with making you laugh, 2019, Instagram post.

20 As Douglas notes, on some internet forums such as 4chan, forum threads were deleted within a limited time frame. Douglas, 'It's Supposed to Look Like Shit,' 316. See also: Milner, *The World Made Meme*, 43–78.

21 Ugly Belgian Houses (@uglybelgianhouses), Quatro Stogi oh no, 2019, Instagram post.

Shit Gardens (@shitgardens), the postman's nightmare, 2019, Instagram Post.

Abrahamson's widely published academic interest in Brutalism that he considers the subject seriously, not with the same banal irony as other *Fuck Yeah* accounts. In an article in *Fulcrum* he appears altogether earnest, rather than ironic, writing: 'we project our desires onto the past and in the process realize what we want from the future…[i]t is this type of productive nostalgia that FYB hopes to provoke.'[17] Instead, he adopted the tongue-in-cheek title to spark future speculations grounded in Brutalism, connecting a then under-loved style to pop culture. This is consistent with other architecture social media figures, including Furman—who often shares so-called 'archiphorisms' using the bright colors and unfashionable fonts of memes[18]—and Ryan Scavnicky (@sssscavvvv, 6,6000 followers) who uses standard meme templates to offer serious critique of architectural culture.[19]

Most importantly, images of Brutalism lack the humor of memes. If their slap-dash aesthetic is due to the ephemeral nature of online images—that the joke gets stale and might be deleted—then the opposite should be true of architecture.[20] Architecture is one of our least ephemeral cultural outputs: construction, demolition, and removal means that even temporary pavilions last longer than a meme. A piece of architecture constructed in the same slap-dash way would be a failure, representing a great waste of time, energy, and money. Architectural failures can be funny: #architecturefails on Instagram and Tumblr collects images of staircases that hit walls and missing doors; the Instagram accounts @shitgardens (34,100 followers) and @uglybelgianhouses (41,900 followers) gently, even affectionately, mock suburban kitsch and absurdity.[21]

The exposed materials and utilitarian detailing of Brutalism are hardly humorous. Those who like Brutalism find its look, or politics, appealing rather than amusing. And those aspects of Brutalism that its critics regard as failures—Peter Reyner Banham's accusation that it became an aesthetic not ethic, a perceived lack of humanity and the social dysfunction of Brutalist housing estates—are failures of a much higher order than #architecturefails, not easily grasped in a single image unless the viewer knows its history.[22] Nor are they like the objective failures of a missing door. Uglybelgianhouses reflects only individual dwellings, chosen by their owners, but the perceived failure of Brutalist universities and social housing blocks would represent harm done to millions of people.

Hume writes that we take vicarious pleasure in another person's well-designed house. We place ourselves in the home, and envision how we would feel if we were its owner instead. In this way we find it beautiful even if it is not ours; our imagination allows us to visualize what sort of comforts it would afford us.[23] If a viewer thought Robin Hood Gardens, or any other Brutalist housing estate, ugly in the pejorative sense—that through empathy, the viewer imagines inhabiting the space and finds it unappealing—they would find little pleasure in it themselves, even looking at it on their phone screen. If the followers of Brutalist social media accounts were there because of a failure of this order, they would be searching for sadism not humor, which is a different type of perversity to a meme.

22 See: Reyner Banham, *The New Brutalism: Ethic or Aesthetic?* (London: The Architectural Press, 1966).

23 'So our pleasure in this beauty must come from our sympathising with the house's owner: we enter into his interests by the force of imagination, and feel the same satisfaction that the house naturally occasions in him.' David Hume, *Treatise of Human Nature Book II: The Passions* (Oxford: Clarendon Press, 1896), 364. See also: Dabney Townsend, *Hume's Aesthetic Theory: Taste and Sentiment* (London: Routledge, 2001), 110–112.

Brutalist Nostalgia

Many of Brutalism's recent commentators have offered an alternative explanation for Brutalism's revaluation, linked to memory and nostalgia. Where Abrahamson's nostalgia in *Fulcrum* was projective and productive, for Peter Chadwick—

tweeting enthusiastic amateur snaps of Brutalism as @brutalhouse (38,800 followers)—his interest stems from youthful memories in Yorkshire and Gateshead.[24] Tom Dyckhoff, on the television program *I Love Carbuncles*, spoke of a contemporary longing for the high-tech welfare state which produced Brutalism.[25] Will Self linked this nostalgia for big government to economic uncertainty in the wake of the 2008 Global Financial Crisis.[26]

Yet as Abrahamson acknowledges, many Brutalism enthusiasts are younger and, unlike Chadwick, never experienced Brutalist buildings new, or even spend much time around them today. Even in his admiring account of Brutalism, *Raw Concrete: The Beauty of Brutalism*, Barnabas Calder admits that childhood memories of the style made it harder to love, writing that he had to overcome its association with delays and cost overruns, 'perceived as an allegory for, and the source of, social evils on an unprecedented scale.'[27] Ernő Goldfinger's Balfron Tower[28] might be fashionable now—recently renovated from public housing to luxury apartments—but for years it represented the dangerous failures of Brutalist housing estates: underfunded with an inadequate understanding of human behavior.[29] This is the opposite of Self's hopeful post-GFC nostalgia; linked instead to the government's failure to provide ongoing support to the marginalized.

To value such a building now, restored for upwardly mobile young professionals, allows enthusiasts to separate Brutalism's brooding aesthetic and original public aspirations from its subsequent neglect. The same is true on social media, where poorly maintained buildings are represented in a pristine state online. There, they are depicted in carefully composed black and white images from the period, or re-shot in the same style today by photographers such as Simon

---

24 Peter Chadwick, *This Brutal World* (New York: Phaidon Press, 2016), 6–11.

25 Tom Dyckhoff, 'I Love Carbuncles,' *The Art Show*, Season 3, episode 4, directed by Chloe Thomas (London: Channel 4, September 11, 2004).

26 Will Self, 'Concrete Morality,' *Fulcrum* 63 (2013), 1; Christopher Beanland, *Concrete Concept: Brutalist Buildings around the World* (London: Frances Lincoln, 2016), 7–11. Wilkinson makes a similar, if more scathing, assessment, suggesting that 'in blogs like Fuck Yeah Brutalism [Brutalism] is easily dismissed as left-wing melancholy, a crippling nostalgia for lost battles,' Wilkinson, *Bricks & Mortals*, 81.

27 Barnabas Calder, *Raw Concrete: The Beauty of Brutalism* (London: William Heinemann, 2016), 17. See also: Liz Hoggard, 'Why We Must Learn to Love Brutalist Architecture,' *The Telegraph*, January 28, 2016.

28 Erno Goldfinger, Balfron Tower, 1967. Photo: Sebastian F, 2007.

29 Roberts notes that Goldfinger rejected the label Brutalism, though it has often been applied to his building. David Roberts, 'Make Public: Performing Public Housing in Ernő Goldfinger's Balfron Tower,' *The Journal of Architecture* 22, no. 1 (2017), 123–150.

30 Simon Phipps (@new_brutalism), Albert Sloman Library, 2019, Instagram post.

Phipps on his popular Instagram page new_brutalism (34,100 followers).[30] The appeal of these photographs is not surprising; Banham nominated 'memorability as an image' as one of the key qualities of Brutalism. In doing so, he linked the style to a way of seeing rooted in photography, characterized by a unitary, essential concept—or 'image'—easily captured on film.[31] More recently, architectural historian Claire Zimmerman argued in *Photographic Architecture in the Twentieth Century* that the Smithsons' Brutalist Hunstanton School was designed from the outset with an idea of how it would be captured and disseminated through the media.[32, 33]

This explanation of the fashion for Brutalism as welfare state nostalgia also sits uneasily with the more recent popularity of Postmodernism on Furman's Instagram account, alongside newagecocaine (42,400 followers) and bizarrecolumns (5,800 followers).[34] Postmodernism has long been associated with rampart capitalism rather than 'big government,' ever since Fredric Jameson wrote in the nineteen-eighties that we 'find the extraordinary flowering of the new postmodern architecture grounded in the patronage of multinational business.'[35] These Postmodern accounts attract an online fan base with significant overlap with that of Brutalism, undermining the narrative of an appeal rooted in memory, seemingly tied more strongly to the images than to their political content. Understood in this way, it is perhaps only those who can overcome Brutalism's history—forget it, oppose it, or never experience it—who can appreciate images of Brutalism now.

The Critic in Pop Culture

While the narrative of mass nostalgia is not wholly convincing, undoubtedly Abrahamson, Chadwick, and Dyckhoff feel

---

31 Banham traced one origin of Brutalism to the 1954 photography exhibition 'Parallel of Life and Art,' by Henderson, Paolozzi, and the Smithsons: 'Miesian or Wittkowerian geometry was only an ad hoc device for the realization of 'Images,' and when 'Parallel of Life and Art' had enabled Brutalists to define their relationship to the visual world in terms of something other than geometry, then formality was discarded.' Reyner Banham, 'The New Brutalism,' *The Architectural Review* (December 1955), 354–361.
As Macarthur notes, Banham's use of 'image' here makes a deliberate connection to Ernst Gombrich's iconography and the Warburg Institute, intended to imply a recognizable conceptual unity that transcends history and culture. John Macarthur, 'Brutalism, Ugliness and the Picturesque Object,' in *Formulation Fabrication papers from the seventeenth annual conference of the Society of Architectural Historians Australia and New Zealand*, ed. Andrew Leach (Wellington, 2000), 259–266.

32 Claire Zimmerman, *Photographic Architecture in the Twentieth Century* (Minneapolis: University of Minnesota Press, 2014). See also Claire Zimmerman, 'Photographic Images from Chicago to Hunstanton,' in *Neo-Avant-Garde and Postmodern: Postwar Architecture in Britain and Beyond*, ed. Mark Crinson and Claire Zimmerman (New Haven: Yale University Press, 2010), 203–228.

33 Alison and Peter Smithson, Hunstanton School, 1954. Photo: Xavier de Jauréguiberry, 2017.

34 Kate Sennert (@newagecocaine), Can't get out of bed this morning, 2019, Instagram post.

35 Fredric Jameson, *Postmodernism: Or, the Cultural Logic of Late Capitalism* (Durham: Duke University Press, 2012), 5.

a genuine personal or political nostalgia for Brutalism. First aired in 2004, Dyckhoff's contribution is remarkable both for its prescience and audience: broadcast to the general public on Britain's Channel 4. In 2014, Jonathan Meades' *Bunkers, Brutalism, Bloodymindedness* did the same on BBC Four. These programs communicated with a large number of people through broadcast media, on an easily accessible public channel. They attracted both a specialized audience interested in architecture and viewers who happened to tune in.[36] Meanwhile, on social media, users already familiar with Brutalism could type the term into the Tumblr search bar, or search for pages like Abrahamson's after seeing it featured in the architectural or mainstream media.[37] For others, FYB was recommended based on an algorithm 'trained' to predict a user's interests, based on interaction with similar architectural or artistic images and pages in the past.[38]

Unlike broadcast media, targeting the general public, or social media, catering to a broad stylistic niche, Zimmerman and Calder write for an architectural audience of academics and practitioners. Relatively few students and researchers will read Zimmerman's scholarly account of Brutalist photography, and only slightly more Calder's volume of essays. Yet in all these cases, from Dyckhoff to Abrahamson to Calder, the popular enthusiasm for Brutalism leads back to key critics— with their own disciplinary interest or personal nostalgia— rather than a grassroots mass nostalgia or an aesthetic enthusiasm similar to memes. We could speculate that broadcast television may have first encouraged the public to accept Brutalism, an appetite that was satisfied by Brutalist social media accounts, in turn migrating offline to glossy coffee-table books such as Chadwick's *This Brutal World*.

Although Abrahamson might not resemble a traditional critic, over seven years his regular posts built a particularly

36 Dyckhoff, 'I Love Carbuncles,' 2014.

37 See: Michael Abrahamson, '11 lesser-known Brutalist buildings that helped define the movement,' *Dezeen*, September 14, 2014, www.dezeen.com/2014/09/14/fuckyeahbrutalism-top-11-brutalist-buildings/; Duo Dickinson, 'Architectural Criticism That's Not Just For Architects,' *Common\Edge*, August 30, 2018, commonedge.org/architectural-criticism-thats-not-just-for-architects/.

38 As scholars such as Qiu and Gillespie argue, the 'feed' is not a neutral space: its recommendations are influenced by advertisers and at-times arbitrary morality standards. Jack Linchuan Qiu, 'Labor and Social Media: The Exploitation and Emancipation of (almost) Everyone Online,' in *The SAGE Handbook of Social Media*, ed. Jean Burgess et al. (London and New York: Sage Publications, 2018); Tarleton Gillespie, *Custodians of the Internet: Platforms, Content Moderation, and the Hidden Decisions That Shape Social Media* (New Haven: Yale University Press, 2018).

convincing, even eloquent, case for the value of Brutalism.[39] He always took particular care to post consistently high-quality images, capturing qualities of the architecture's materiality, muscularity, light, and even bloody-mindedness.[40] These images were scanned from journals from the nineteen-sixties and seventies, what Abrahamson called Brutalism's 'heyday,' linking Brutalism to a particular period, not just a 'look.'[41] The result was that, unlike other less discerning accounts, Abrahamson implied a precise argument of what is and is not Brutalism, contextualizing the past for the present.[42] As Alexandra Lange and Sam Jacob have argued, social media criticism is inherently serial. Lange writes that '[t]he theme that individual blogs and bloggers pursue is not always apparent in a single post, and the approach of a blog is clear only if you have been following along from the beginning.'[43]

Indeed, as Susan Sontag argued in *On Photography*, her seminal account of photography, image series have the 'authority of a document … they are taken to be pieces of reality, more authentic than extended literary narratives,' and are often simply more easily consumable than the equivalent information in text.[44] The critic's best argument may come through a feed of startling images, capturing something visual that is difficult to translate into words. Abrahamson's images of Brutalism—pristine, photographed from ideal angles and light conditions—have a rhetorical value that is arguably more persuasive than defenses in text, precisely because they confront people's expectations of dingy, dysfunctional spaces.[45] Art historian Philip Ursprung has identified a similar critical, persuasive dimension in architectural photography more specifically. These images frame the experience of a building through the individual interpretation of the photographer in a way that resembles a critic in print, while simultaneously undermining expectations of a 'true' reflection of

---

39 Tom Wilkinson argued that Abrahamson could not be considered a critic because his posts did not include any text beyond the building's name, architect, and year. As Naomi Stead notes, even when online critics do write, the light-hearted and humorous tone of internet criticism sets it apart from the solemnity we expect of architectural criticism. Wilkinson, 'Architectural Photography,' 91–97; Naomi Stead, 'On the Expert and the Amateur in Online Architectural Commentary,' in *The Routledge Companion to Criticality in Art, Architecture, and Design*, ed. by Christopher Brisbin and Myra Thiessen (Abingdon: Routledge, 2018), 389–390.

40 Abrahamson, 'Radical Nostalgia,'1.

41 Taken from an interview with Abrahamson in Davide Tommaso Ferrando and Gionvanni Benedetti, 'Beyond Blogging: Fuck Yeah Brutalism,' *Viceversa*, March 25, 2014, www.zeroundicipiu.it/2014/03/25/beyond-blogging-fuck-yeah-brutalism/.

42 Abrahamson writes that 'it's hard to say what one means when using the term Brutalism, but one knows it when one sees it.' Abrahamson, '11 Lesser-known Brutalist Buildings,' 2014.

43 Alexandra Lange, *Writing about Architecture: Mastering the Language of Buildings and Cities* (New York: Princeton Architectural Press, 2012), 176; Sam Jacob, 'How Has the Internet Changed Architecture Criticism?,' *The Architect's Newspaper*, May 22, 2018, archpaper.com/2018/05/internet-changed-architecture-criticism/.

44 Susan Sontag, *On Photography* (New York: Rosetta Books, 2005), 58.

45 Michael Abrahamson (fuckyeahbrutalism), Niigata Prefectural Gymnasium, 2017, Tumblr post.

reality.⁴⁶ Similarly, Abrahamson's selection of images represents a specific interpretation of Brutalism, whereby this selection itself draws from an array of critical positions of the photographers, layering Abrahamson's selections on the residual criticism of the original image.

It is useful here to turn again to Hume, who never nominates the medium—whether speech, writing, or form of publication—that a critic should employ to convince the public. Instead, he urged the public to avoid 'embarrassing' scuffles over who is and is not a critic. Hume arrived at the remarkable conclusion that we can identify a 'true critic' simply through the observable fact that their criticism is accepted, and sought, by society. He writes that '[t]he ascendant, which they acquire, gives a prevalence to that lively approbation, with which they receive any production of genius, and renders it generally predominant.'⁴⁷

Good critics are first recognized for their sound judgment by a small number of people, or Tumblr followers. Over time, the size of that following becomes its own kind of argument and others can recognize that their judgements are generally regarded as true, grounded in sound taste and disciplinary knowledge. Moreover, society has a vested interest in finding and following a good critic because their judgments form the basis by which we can compare one work to another, and compare our judgement against a standard that others regard highly.⁴⁸ Understood in this way, it is not so surprising that non-standard criticism, from Abrahamson and others online, has played such a significant role in the re-evaluation of Brutalism, given that the public was able to recognize the merit of his critical perspective in the quality of his content, and the size of his Tumblr following.

---

46 Philip Ursprung, 'Limits to Representation: Peter Zumthor and Hans Danuser,' *Visual Resources* 27, no. 2 (2011), 172–184. See also: Mike Christenson, 'Critical Dimensions in Architectural Photography: Contributions to Architectural Knowledge,' *Architecture_MPS* 11, no. 2 (2017), 1–17.

47 Hume, 'Of the Standard of Taste,' 241.

48 As Hume writes on government and rebellion, 'We ought always to weigh the advantages which we reap from authority against the disadvantages.' Quoted in Neil McArthur, 'Hume's Political Philosophy,' in *The Oxford Handbook of Hume*, ed. by Paul Russell (Oxford: Oxford University Press, 2016).

Brutalism in the Academy

Abrahamson's interest in Brutalism on FYB is not coincidental with his PhD studies at Taubman College, the University of Michigan. A search of the online *Avery Index of Architecture Periodicals* shows a substantial increase in publications on Brutalism between 2000–2009, and an exponential growth again in the years since.[49] Abrahamson's doctoral supervisor was Claire Zimmerman, who in 2010 co-edited a volume on Neo-Avant-Garde and Postmodern architecture in Britain that included chapters on Brutalism. The process of compiling this volume would have begun well before Abrahamson started FYB in late 2010. This critical revaluing of Brutalism can be explained a number of ways: through nostalgia, as we have seen; through the appeal of striking images; and by the urgent need to preserve Brutalist buildings before more key works were lost. But one of the factors is academic, as a new generation of researchers looked at Brutalism without the same cultural baggage as their predecessors. Or, more cynically, generated by an inevitable cycle of academic novelty where a career can be made by rediscovering something first. Abrahamson and FYB emerged from this academic context.

Abrahamson was hardly the first academic to recognize the value of Brutalism, but he was one of the first to communicate that contemporary value to the wider public. FYB sits much closer to a broadcast television program like *I Love Carbuncles* than traditional academia.[50] Tumblr users discovered pages like FYB in the same way they might have come across *Bunkers, Brutalism, Bloodymindedness* while channel surfing a decade earlier; recommended by an algorithm or promoted by a publisher wanting to sell the latest glossy Brutalist volume. As architectural sociologist Garry Stevens

[49] Nigel Whitely wrote about Banham's connection to Brutalism as early as 1990, while Calder's published an article on Lasdun's Brutalism in 2008, two years before FYB and four years before Vidler's do.co.mo.mo keynote. Nigel Whiteley, 'Banham and "Otherness": Reyner Banham (1922–1988) and His Quest for an Architecture Autre,' *Architectural History* 33 (1990), 188–221; Barnabas Calder, '"A Terrible Battle with Architecture": Denys Lasdun in the 1950s, part 2,' *Architecture Research Quarterly* 12, no. 1 (March 2008), 59–68. Other early articles include one on the connection between Brutalism and cinema and a comparison between Butterfield and Brutalism (both 1998), while a connected argument about the Picturesque and Brutalism by Macarthur followed in 2000. Katherine Shonfield, 'Glossing with Graininess: Cross Occupations in Postwar British Film and Architecture,' *Journal of Architecture* 3, no. 4 (January 1998), 355–375; Elain Hardwood, 'Butterfield and Brutalism,' *AA Files* 27 (July 1994), 39–46; Macarthur, 'Brutalism, Ugliness and the Picturesque Object,' 2000.

[50] Goncalves et al. make a similar argument for social media's consideration as broadcast media in Goncalves et al., 'Narrowcasting in Social Media: Effects and Perceptions,' *ASONAM '13 Proceedings of the 2013 IEEE/ACM International Conference on Advances in Social Networks Analysis and Mining* (New York: ACM, 2013), 502–509.

notes, the relationship between academia, the profession, and the public is complex, with universities often occupying a peripheral role in architectural discourse.[51] Traditionally, academic knowledge entered the discipline slowly through public lectures, occasional articles in the mainstream architectural media and dissemination by graduating students. What we are witnessing on social media is the speeding up of this process. Academics such as Zimmerman continue to communicate with students, academics, and engaged professionals through books. At the same time other, often younger, academics such as Abrahamson transmit similar positions to the discipline and public at large on social media. In this way—just as Andrejevic notes that offline social relationships were deeply embedded in the internet—academic structures predating social media appear to have replicated themselves in the new medium, adapting to changed conditions online while playing an even greater role in shaping architectural discourse there.

A Different Democracy?

When Hume suggested that any person recognized for their sound judgment could be a 'true critic,' in practice only wealthy men qualified. According to Hume and his contemporaries, only they possessed the required education, leisure, and correct gender. What Hume framed as unprejudicial contemplation of art reflected the prejudices of men of the dominant political class.[52] Lord Kames, Hume's patron, went so far as to write that 'those who depend for food on bodily labour, are totally devoid of taste.'[53] Instead, the 'true critic' was intended to inform a 'republic of taste' that coincided with the political 'republic' of Britain, where only landowning

---

[51] Garry Stevens, 'Angst in Academia: Universities, the Architecture Schools and the Profession,' *Journal of Architectural and Planning Research* 15, no. 2 (Summer, 1998), 152–169.

[52] See Richard Shusterman, 'The Scandal of Taste: Social Privilege as Nature in the Aesthetic Theories of Hume and Kant,' *The Philosophical Forum* 20, no. 3 (Spring 1989), 211–229; Paul Guyer, 'The Standard of Taste and the "Most Ardent Desire of Society",' in *Values of Beauty* (New York: Cambridge University Press, 2005), 37–75.

[53] Henry Home, Lord Kames, *Elements of Criticism*, ed. A. Mills (New York: Huntingdon & Savage, 1849), 471.

men could vote.⁵⁴ As we have seen here, even on social media the value of Brutalism has continued to be informed by elite academics, reflecting discussions in academia, and only fitfully making its way into society at large.

Yet, at the risk of seeming naive, I remain more optimistic. FYB was accessible to anyone with a Tumblr account, and easily consumable as part of everyday digital life. Brutalism social media accounts have continued the process begun by broadcast media on television, opening up traditional modes of architectural knowledge sharing, communicating with the general and architectural public at once. Through his postings and implicit criticism, Abrahamson gently exposed all his followers to the value of Brutalism. Over time, this exposure built the kind of visual acuity necessary for the wider public to identify, comment, and advocate for the architecture themselves, as seen in the often heated discussions over what can be included in Facebook's amateur Brutalism Appreciation Society.⁵⁵

We are even beginning to see a learnt acuity to recognize the value of Brutalism reflected back to academia and the establishment. Noisy campaigns to preserve Brutalist architecture have originated in the non-architectural community. Two recent books—*SOSBrutalism* (2017) and the *Atlas of Brutalist Architecture* (2018)—boasted that buildings and images were sourced from social media users through the #brutalism and #sosbrutalism hashtags.⁵⁶ In Australia, the campaign for heritage protection of the Sirius Building in Sydney, Save Our Sirius,⁵⁷ used hashtags to rally support and share stories.⁵⁸ Abrahamson and other key critics on social media might remain part of an academic or social elite, but they differ from Hume's aristocratic 'true critic' in their commitment to communicating the value of Brutalism to a public beyond academia or an exclusive 'republic of taste.' In turn,

54 See: John Barrel, 'Sir Joshua Reynolds and the Political Theory of Painting,' *Oxford Art Journal* 9, no. 2 (1986), 36–41; Shusterman, 'The Scandal of Taste,' 222.

55 As Hume noted 'many men, when left to themselves, have but a faint and dubious perception of beauty, who yet are capable of relishing any fine stroke, which is pointed out to them. Every convert to the admiration of the real poet or orator is the cause of some new conversion.' Hume, 'Of the Standard of Taste,' 243.

56 Catherine Hickley, 'Saving Brutalism: The Campaign to Preserve Concrete Icons,' *BBC Designed* February 8, 2018, www.bbc.com/culture/story/20180208-saving-brutalism-the-campaign-to-preserve-concrete-icons; Oliver Elser, Philipp Kurz and Peter Cachola Schmal, *SOS Brutalism: A Global Survey* (Zurich: Park Books, 2017); *Atlas of Brutalist Architecture* (London: Phaidon, 2018).

57 *Save Our Sirius*, 2016, poster.

58 Save Our Sirius, http://saveoursirius.org/.

this public has proven capable of engaging with complex issues of architectural taste—taking on the mantle of valuing and preserving this architectural heritage—on a level that remains rare in our society.

Heritage and Housing in the Post-Political City

Peter Chadwick, *Save Our Sirius*, 2017, poster. Courtesy Peter Chadwick.

Heritage and Housing in the Post-Political City

Sydney's Sirius Building

Kirsty Volz and Alex Brown

In June 2019, the New South Wales (NSW) state government sold a public housing apartment complex, known as Sirius, designed by Tao Gofers in 1979 and located in Millers Point, Sydney, to a private developer. The building's new owners plan to retain the building, albeit as part of a new, privately-owned apartment complex.

In response to the proposed sale of Sirius, residents of Sirius and Millers Point, activists, architects, planners, and academics banded together to create the Save Our Sirius campaign (now the Save Our Sirius Foundation). The campaign ran over two years and involved exhibitions, videos, rallies, petitions, online campaigns, and even a crowd-funded legal fight to stop the sale from proceeding. The case for saving Sirius transcended architectural discourse and attracted the attention of mainstream media and the broader public.

While heritage was necessarily central to the campaign to preserve Sirius, the fight to save it was also connected to larger discussions of housing affordability and the demise of egalitarian approaches to planning. This chapter does not aim to further existing debates about the aesthetic merits of postwar Brutalism. Instead, it focuses on how the case to prevent the sale of Sirius centered around questions of value—more specifically, the tension between the social value of access to affordable housing in the city and the financial value of inner-city land.

Prior to the sale of Sirius, the NSW Heritage Council, a body consisting of experts from various fields related to heritage, unanimously recommended that the building be listed on the State heritage register. In accordance with the NSW Heritage Act 1977 (Heritage Act), the ultimate decision lay with the Minister for Heritage, who refused the listing. Funded by the Save Our Sirius campaign, the Millers Point Community Association challenged the Minister's decision and, in 2017 the case was brought before the NSW Land and Environment Court.

While questions about the legitimacy of Sirius' heritage status and aesthetic value continue to dominate public discussions about the building's demolition or preservation, these concerns were largely absent from the 2017 court proceedings, which focused instead on the fair and equitable interpretation of the Heritage Act in relation to the interests of the broader community. Further, and contrary to the broader rhetoric around the future of Sirius, a heritage listing would have little to no bearing on the government's ability to sell the site or even a developer's right to demolish the building.

This chapter looks more closely at how statutory heritage instruments have been used by both sides of the Sirius debate to, respectively, activate and obscure a set of larger questions about social housing and access to the city, in a way that leaves the question of the value of architecture in flux.[1]

1 Photo: Ben Rushton, 2017. Courtesy Peter Chadwick.

Millers Point, Demolition and the Construction of Sirius

Millers Point has been described as Australia's oldest urban area.[2] Constructed on the ancestral lands of the Cadigal People of the Eora Nation, it was named Cockle Bay by early colonists, until a series of mills were erected in the nineteenth century, giving it the name Millers Point. Workers in the mills, along with wharf and maritime workers, began to call the area home throughout the nineteenth century. At the beginning of the twentieth century, the area was subject to a significant clearing out of buildings and 'clean up,' in response to health and sanitation concerns. During this period and following the purchase of many privately-owned wharves by the NSW government, the area saw a surge in residents working for maritime industries. The Maritime Services Board (formerly the Sydney Harbour Trust) managed leases for housing of waterfront workers until the Department of Housing took over the portfolio in the nineteen-eighties.[3]

The design and construction of Sirius in the nineteen-seventies was part of an agreement reached in the wake of widespread community opposition to the proposed demolition of heritage buildings in Millers Point and The Rocks. Overseen by the newly-formed Sydney Cove Redevelopment Authority, the demolition of a significant proportion of the houses in Millers Point had been approved to make way for new privately owned high-rise development. Residents opposing the planned demolition were supported by the NSW Builders Labourers Federation (BLF) who refused to undertake any building or demolition work in the Millers Point area—part of the coordinated action that Jack Mundey would refer to as 'green bans' in 1973.[4]

While not all of the properties in the area were ultimately protected from demolition, the state government agreed to

---

[2] Allen Morris, *Gentrification and Displacement: The Forced Relocation of Public Housing Tenants in Inner Sydney* (Sydney: Springer, 2019), 18.

[3] Alan Morris, '"Communicide": The Destruction of a Vibrant Public Housing Community in Inner Sydney through a Forced Displacement,' *Journal of Sociology* 55, no. 2 (2019), 275.

[4] The remit of this strike was to protect heritage buildings from demolition, and many buildings in inner city Sydney have been, and continue to be, protected because of this activism. It was also aimed at providing equal access to housing in the inner city. See Meredith Burgmann and Verity Burgmann, *Green Bans, Red Union: The Saving of a City*, (Sydney: UNSW Press, 1998); Jack Mundey, *Green Bans & Beyond* (London and Sydney: Angus & Robertson, 1981).

relocate residents of public housing into a brand-new apartment complex in the area: on Cumberland Street, The Rocks. Designed by Tao Gofers for the Housing Commission of NSW, work on this project—the Sirius Building—commenced in 1976 and was completed in 1980. The complex comprises seventy-nine one-, two-, three-, and four-bedroom apartments in varying configurations.[5] Of these, seventeen units were specially designed for the needs of ageing residents and these units share a communal room and balcony that provides a view to the Sydney Harbour Bridge and Opera House.[6]

In a continuation of Sydney's historical attempts to eradicate public housing from Millers Point, the NSW government announced plans to sell off the remaining public housing properties in the area in March 2014.[7] As journalist Peter Mac wrote at the time, 'There was no prior discussion. It was a grossly insensitive act and an insult, but it also showed that the government is worried about resistance.'[8] For many Millers Point residents, their connection to the area spanned five or six generations. There was also a high percentage of residents over sixty, for whom the prospect of moving was overwhelming.[9] What followed was a series of events, exhibitions, art installations, and peaceful protests to raise awareness about the impact on residents.[10]

Battling to 'Save' Sirius

On February 22, 2016, the NSW Heritage Council decided unanimously to put Sirius forward for heritage listing, citing the project's significance 'as a rare and fine example of the late Brutalist architectural style especially in its application to social housing.'[11] The Heritage Council's recommendation

---

5 Morris, *Gentrification and Displacement*, 18.

6 Russell Rodrigo 'Aesthetics as a Practical Ethic: Situating the Brutalist Architecture of the Sirius Apartments, 1975–80,' *Fabrications* 25, no. 2, 258.

7 Jim McIlroy, 'Residents, Unions Protest Evictions,' *Green Left Weekly* 1131 (March 28, 2017), 3, search.informit.com.au/documentSummary;dn=732684139574876;res=IELHSS.

8 Peter Mac, 'Eviction Plan for Oldest Suburbs: Massive Land Grab,' *Guardian: The Worker's Weekly*, March 26, 2014, www.cpa.org.au/guardian/2014/1632/01-eviction-plan-for-oldest-suburbs.html.

9 Mac, 'Eviction Plan for Oldest Suburbs, 1.

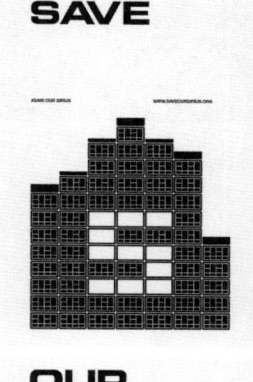

10 Peter Chadwick, *Save Our Sirius*, 2017, posters. Courtesy Peter Chadwick.

11 Heritage Council of New South Wales, 'Recommendation for State Heritage Listing Sirius Apartment Building–36-50 Cumberland Street, The Rocks,' saveoursirius.org/wp-content/uploads/2017/10/Sirius-Heritage-Council-Reccomendation-to-list.pdf.

12 Ibid.

13 Linda Cheng, "'Dangerous precedent' Averted: Court Rules Sirius Heritage Snub "Invalid,'" *ArchitectureAU*, July 26, 2017, architectureau.com/articles/dangerous-precedent-averted-court-rules-sirius-heritage-snub-invalid/.

14 Photo: Peter Chadwick, 2017. Courtesy Peter Chadwick.

for listing Sirius was framed in reference to the heritage criteria 'C' (aesthetic values) and 'F' (rarity), with Sirius being one of only a small number of publicly-commissioned Brutalist buildings in Sydney.¹²

Despite the Heritage Council's recommendation, the NSW Minister for Heritage refused the listing on the grounds of 'undue financial hardship,' indicating the NSW state government felt that the monetary value of the land that Sirius occupied far outweighed any perceived heritage value.¹³ In November of the same year, the Millers Point Community Association launched a crowd-funding campaign for legal costs associated with taking the NSW Heritage Department to court.¹⁴ The case went before the NSW Land and Environment Court in July 2017. Just over forty years on from the construction of Sirius, a new fight over access to housing in Sydney's inner city was underway with heritage 'protection' once again seemingly at the center of these debates.

Crucially, though, this more recent chapter in the history of affordable housing at The Rocks became much more about slippages between value and values. While heritage criteria were sidelined in the court's discussion of land value and financial gain, they remained firmly at the centre of broader public debates about the site. In this case, the instrumentalization of the Heritage Act on both sides of this debate has been further aided by the unavoidably nested and contentious heritage of Sirius—as a high-rise, Brutalist building that was itself constructed as part of a campaign to save the early colonial fabric of the area, and the social fabric that it supported.

The July 2017 court case of Millers Point Community Assoc. Incorporated vs. Property NSW did not involve a debate about heritage but, rather, about interpretations of the Heritage Act. As such, the court case was not to determine the heritage value of the property or whether it should be listed. Instead, the case was about deciding whether or not the Minister's decision not to list on the grounds of financial hardship could be considered valid. In fact, at no point did the Minister for Heritage, Mark Speakman, put forward any contest to the recommendation for the listing of Sirius on the NSW heritage register. Only in a post factum letter, tendered at court and never presented to the Heritage Council, did Speakman attempt to justify his intervention to listing the building. In that letter, he agreed that Sirius 'may meet the threshold of State heritage significance on aesthetic grounds,' but contended that the financial value of the building significantly outweighed its heritage value.[15]

Central to the court case was the way in which the Minister for Heritage interpreted section 32:1(d) of the Heritage Act. The purpose of the clause is specifically to address any undue financial hardship that a heritage listing would create in the maintenance and operation of its facilities. Manipulating this part of the Heritage Act, the Minister put forward that if the building was listed, the diminished value of the land that Sirius occupies would cause financial hardship for the state government—an extraordinary claim, considering the building had been used for social housing. Minister Speakman went on to speculate that a level of undue financial hardship would be triggered 'by diminishing what would otherwise be its sale value (possibly in the order of $70 million), which would potentially represent foregone funds for additional social housing.'[16] In essence, this argument was a deliberate conflation between financial *hardship* and speculative financial *loss*, as well as financial hardship and *undue* financial hardship.[17]

Perhaps unsurprisingly, Simon Molesworth, acting judge of the NSW Land and Environment Court, ruled that the Minister for Heritage had misinterpreted the Heritage Act

---

[15] Millers Point Community Assoc. Incorporated v. Property NSW, [2017] NSWLEC 92, 2016/00322494 (Land and Environment Court New South Wales, 2017).

[16] 'Why Sirius Matters,' saveoursirius.org/why-sirius-matters/ (accessed June 1, 2020).

[17] This was a key argument made by the NSW Chapter of Environmental Defenders Offices of Australia, the community legal center representing the Millers Point Community Association. *Millers Point Community Assoc. Incorporated v. Property NSW*, 2016/00322494.

when claiming that the listing of Sirius would 'cause undue financial hardship.' Molesworth reinforced the Heritage Council's decision, supported by the fact that the Heritage Council was comprised of a diverse group of experts with a wide-ranging knowledge of all aspects of the heritage listing of a building, including financial implications. In Judge Molesworth's judgment statement, he also pointed to the sentiment that the heritage listing of Sirius was about something much bigger than the preservation of a narrow framing of heritage based solely on a set of fixed criteria. Referring to the sliding scale of Australian income tax laws to make his point about the relativity of undue financial hardship, Molesworth pointed out that the basis for any act or legislation was that of fairness and equality:

> Land favoured with the most scenic attributes, which if unrestricted would offer immense opportunity to the land owner for profitable development, is frequently the very land most constrained by planning law controls. Whilst in the interests of the broader community, this legislation may concurrently fetter the financial aspirations of the wealthy landowner. With traffic regulation, the imposition of speed limits in the interest of public safety must, in a sense, be constantly frustrating for the owners of a Ferrari or a Lamborghini, who are never permitted to drive their cars at a speed at which they are designed to excel. Yet, without disrespect, this would be less of an issue for the owner of a modest Mitsubishi Colt.[18]

It is Molesworth's direct reference to the underpinning ethical attributes to the case that is most interesting in critically analyzing the case of the Sirius Building, in relation to larger issues of heritage and the value of architecture. In hearing the

[18] *Millers Point Community Assoc. Incorporated v. Property NSW*, [2017] NSWLEC 92, 2016/00322494 (Land and Environment Court New South Wales, 2017).

case, at no point was the court required to address any of the seven criteria for determining heritage listing in New South Wales. Amongst these criteria are; social, cultural, spiritual significance, individual or community historical significance, and aesthetic, or technical excellence. Nevertheless, Judge Molesworth's decision pointed to the ethical and egalitarian principles that should underpin interpretations of the Heritage Act.

Law academic Chris Butler has written about the larger ethical issues of inhabitation and access at stake in the Sirius case, noting that the strategic use of heritage by both the government and Save Our Sirius activists is symptomatic of the role that heritage protection frameworks are often called upon to play in the preservation of public housing. In this sense, an important part of the court case ruling concerned not just the economic argument made by the Minister for Heritage but also his concomitant failure to consider heritage value when making claims regarding financial hardship within the context of the Heritage Act. As Butler observed, by 'failing to take into account the mandatory relevant consideration of heritage significance and by inordinately focusing on a presumption of financial hardship, the minister had legally erred and the court ordered that the decision be remade according to law.'[19]

Shortly after the court case Mark Speakman left the Minister for Heritage role and was replaced by Gabrielle Upton, who again refused the heritage listing of Sirius despite the court's decision. Without the option to leverage the value of the land against the proposed listing, the Minister for Heritage was forced to return to the question of the architectural value of the project. This time, Upton argued that the

> While the nomination and recommendation cites the building as a 'fine' example of late brutalist architecture,

[19] Chris Butler, 'Public Housing on "The Rocks": Brutalism, Heritage and the Defence of Inhabitance,' *Acta Academica: Critical Views on Society, Culture and Politics* 51, no. 1 (2019), 4–27, journals.ufs.ac.za/index.php/aa/issue/view/416.

there are contrary expert opinions that the design of the building is not considered innovative or unique, nor did it have a lasting influence on building design or social housing either domestically or internationally.[20]

In June 2019, the Sirius Building was sold to a developer for $150 million without any heritage protection. The developer who won the tender to develop the building has proposed not to demolish, but to refurbish the building to include ten new apartments (eighty-nine in total) and add retail and commercial on the ground floor. These newly refurbished apartments will then be sold or leased privately, presumably at a cost unaffordable[21] to most. So, while the physical fabric of Sirius has been maintained and 'saved,' its principle purpose of providing affordable housing in the city has been eroded. In this sense, following the removal of its public housing residents, the retained shell of Sirius serves as a powerful reminder that forms of access to the city as a broader set of socio-political values cannot be as easily preserved as its architectural container. Moreover, despite its continued presence on the site, should we continue to think of Sirius as a Brutalist building with its social housing program no longer intact?

Brutalism—Style over Substance

Writing about the listing of postwar social housing projects in the United Kingdom, Aidan While has noted the tendency for heritage listing processes to potentially 'revalorise' these buildings and prompt wider reassessment of their cultural and social value.[22] As such, it seems important to acknowledge the significance of Sirius' enduring historical legacy as a direct product of the Green Bans and the community-led

---

20 Linda Cheng, 'Sirius Denied Heritage Protection, Again,' *Architecture Australia* (October 26, 2017), architectureau.com/articles/sirius-denied-heritage-protection-again/.

21 Photo: Peter Chadwick, 2017. Courtesy Peter Chadwick.

22 Aidan While, 'The State and the Controversial Demands of Cultural Built Heritage: Modernism, Dirty Concrete, and Postwar Listing in England,' *Environment and Planning B: Planning and Design* 34, no. 4 (August 2007), 645–663.

fight for access to the city. While ultimately being forced to make a decision on the heritage value of the building, the conservative state government were largely able to ignore broader discussions about Sirius' history. Despite being one of the criteria for heritage listing, the social history of Sirius was not included in the NSW Heritage Council's recommendation, which instead focused on aesthetic value, allowing the conservative state government to avoid engaging with this dimension of the project.

At the same time, and as Butler has pointed out, the activists of the community-led Save Our Sirius Foundation have understood the heritage-listing process as one of the few options for preventing the total destruction of the Sirius Building, while also drawing attention to the larger issues of housing affordability and access that are bound up in the history of the project as well as the recent debates concerning its future. At a rally for Save Our Sirius in January 2018, Sydney's independent Lord Mayor, Clover Moore, echoed this sentiment claiming that 'Sirius will continue to be a symbol of the state government's shocking inaction on providing affordable housing.'[23] In short, affording heritage status to Sirius would simultaneously ascribe value to the conditions of its production, while also representing the inability of the present-day government to pursue egalitarian planning processes and provide access to affordable, quality housing.

Reinier de Graaf from OMA/AMO rationalizes that the move toward private ownership of housing forces people to sync their personal economic agendas with the political right; as interest rates and inflation become the center of their political interests. Private home ownership, then, delivers more 'conservative constituents.'[24] De Graaf goes on to state that,

[23] Jim McIlroy, 'Sirius Backers' Bid to Save Iconic Building,' *Green Left Weekly*, February 6, 2018, www.greenleft.org.au/content/sirius-backers-bid-save-iconic-building.

[24] Reinier de Graaf, *Four Walls and a Roof: The Complex Nature of a Simple Profession*, (Cambridge, MA: Harvard University Press, 2017), 421.

If the egalitarian climate of the 1960s and 1970s had made top-down modern architecture generally unpopular, the neoliberal policies of the 1980s and 1990s make it obsolete. The initiative to construct the city comes to reside increasingly in the private sector.[25]

However, in the post-political city, unfettered neo-liberal governance and planning have also resulted in 'the loss of public control of the city and its processes.'[26] The disinterest by a conservative NSW state government in the fate of an inner-city public housing building is not surprising in these terms, and their dismissal of the Heritage Council recommendation and subsequent community-led campaign to heritage list the Sirius Building is symptomatic of a much bigger problem in the post-political city.

In Sydney at least, Sirius has become synonymous with Brutalist architecture and this has been a defining aspect of both complementary and disparaging public commentary about the building's significance since it was first completed. Russell Rodrigo's article, 'Aesthetics as a Practical Ethic: Situating the Brutalist Architecture of the Sirius Apartments, 1975–80' provides an excellent overview of the design for the building, underpinned by an analysis of Peter Reyner Banham's *The New Brutalism: Ethic or Aesthetic?* (1966).[27] In defining Sirius as an example of Brutalism, Rodrigo references Banham's original positioning of Brutalism as 'a powerful image of social concern, responsibility for the urban realm and an integrity of materials, structure and function.' Planning and appearances aside, it is the social history of Sirius that make it an ideal case study for discussing Brutalism. The association between Sirius and the Green Bans, the protection of Sydney's working-class history and built heritage, and equal access to quality housing in the city,

---

25 De Graaf, *Four Walls and a Roof*, 420.

26 Crystal Legacy, Nicole Cook, Dallas Rogers, and Kristian Ruming, 'Planning the Post-political City: Exploring Public Participation in the Contemporary Australian City,' *Geographical Research* 56, no. 2 (2018), 176–180.

27 Russell Rodrigo, 'Aesthetics as a Practical Ethic: Situating the Brutalist Architecture of the Sirius Apartments, 1975–80,' *Fabrications* 25, no. 2 (2015), 235–261.

are integral to situating the building within the Brutalist movement, more so than any isolated assessment of its visual aesthetic.

Brutalism—Class and Crisis, Politics and Policies

What are the consequences of understanding the anti-aesthetic ambitions of Brutalism and framing the value of Brutalist structures in broader terms? In his 2017 paper, 'Brutalism Redux: Relational Monumentality and the Urban Politics of Brutalist Architecture,' Oli Mould argues that the re-examination of the 'ethical dimension' of Brutalist architecture offers a profound critique of the politics of the neoliberal city.[28] As Mould explains, recent interest in Brutalist architecture has typically been underpinned by an aesthetically-focused, image-driven appreciation of these buildings' formal attributes. Moving beyond efforts to preserve examples of Brutalist architecture through their stylistic legitimation according to heritage norms, Mould and others[29] suggest that Brutalism's enduring value can instead be sought through re-engagement with its historically situated 'ethical ideology.'[30]

The consequences of our collective failure to recognize the 'political ethic' within the context of Sirius' demise have been devastating. The perceived ugliness and aesthetic 'aggression' of Brutalism have been effectively leveraged by both the conservative NSW state government and lobby groups representing the interests of the property developers and financiers who support the privatization of the city and concomitant reduction in social welfare programs.

It is not by accident that successive NSW Ministers for Heritage and members of the Urban Taskforce, (a non-profit

28 Oli Mould, 'Brutalism Redux: Relational Monumentality and the Urban Politics of Brutalist Architecture,' *Antipode* 49, no. 3 (2017), 701–720.

29 Peter Chadwick, *Save Our Sirius*, 2017, poster. Courtesy Peter Chadwick.

30 Mould, 'Brutalism Redux,' 702.

organization representing Australia's property developers and equity financiers) have consistently focused their arguments for the sale and demolition of Sirius around issues of style and taste, alongside anachronistic conflations of Brutalist structures with the tenets and protagonists of early-twentieth-century modern architecture.

Writing for the *Sydney Morning Herald* in 2018, former NSW Government Architect and former Executive Director, NSW Department of Planning, Chris Johnson, then CEO of the Urban Taskforce, pondered why 'these modernist brutalist buildings insult the public domain of the street?' ultimately concluding that the architects of the 'modernist brutalist' style rejected history and tradition:

> The answer, I believe, comes from the brave new world of modernist architecture that saw streets and old buildings as being depressing. The leader of this movement was Swiss architect Le Corbusier, who in 1925 proposed to demolish much of medieval Paris and replace the old buildings with tall concrete towers and green parks with streets lined by trees rather than buildings.[31]

Johnson's observation ignores a series of important and fundamental incompatibilities between Corbusier's unrealized Ville Radieuse and Brutalist projects like Sirius and more famous Brutalist buildings such as the Barbican Centre in London, executed over half a century later. Such confused comingling of Brutalism and the broader category of Modernism simultaneously exaggerates the scale of Sirius, while forcing an association with the clear-felled demolition demanded by Corbusier's much earlier speculative design. As such, it's difficult not to interpret the anachronisms and oversimplifications peppered throughout Johnson's newspaper columns as part of his broader project to deny the value of

[31] Chris Johnson, 'Brutalist is the New Black,' *Sydney Morning Herald*, February 10, 2018, 22.

Brutalist structures without having to acknowledge the more complex socio-political conditions of their production and inhabitation.

In pitting Brutalism (framed only as a kind of Corbusian modernism) against the deep heritage fabric of the city (in this case, medieval Paris), Johnson and the Urban Taskforce reveal an allegiance to notions of heritage as the physical preservation of a conservative and narrowly defined historical value. In Johnson's Sydney, architecture is reduced to convenient, apolitical window dressing for the citizen-as-passer-by.[32]

Part of a series of columns dealing with the aesthetics of Sydney's Brutalism, it's also interesting to note not only the absence of the political or ethical values of welfare-state city-making in relation to the post World War II political and socio-economic context but, with it, the lack of any mention of the buildings' programs and inhabitants. A cynical reading of the kind of discourse favored by the center-right Liberal-National NSW state government and the Urban Taskforce would be that these kinds of reductions are a useful way of editing out the more inconvenient aspects of Sirius' history and operation—namely, those that involve its residents and the public policies that support their access to the city. As a blank and 'aggressive' concrete wall that has simply become one of 'the trendiest buildings to preserve,' Sirius is pure, menacing, solid mass: a literal obstruction to progress and the development of the kind of welcoming (read: commercial) street edges made for the pedestrian as consumer.

In this sense, Johnson and the NSW state government's arguments perform what Nicholas Thoburn has recently identified as the 'class-cleansing' of Brutalist architecture in the neoliberal 'revanchist city' (using Neil Smith's term).[33] The aesthetic dimension of this position presents the Brutalist

32 Peter Chadwick, *Save Our Sirius*, 2017, poster. Courtesy Peter Chadwick.

33 Nicholas Thoburn, 'Concrete and Council Housing,' *City* 22, no. 5–6 (2018), 612–613. Thoburn refers to the 'revanchist city' as defined by Neil Smith, *The New Urban Frontier Gentrification and the Revanchist City* (London; New York: Routledge, 1996).

project as a 'concrete monstrosity' that must be removed in order to generate 'friendlier' spaces dedicated to the wealthier members of society. As Thoburn observes in relation to the Peter and Alison Smithson designed Brutalist social housing complex in London, Robin Hood Gardens, however, this tendency to revise the history of Brutalist architecture to distort or erase the reality of the working-class condition within contemporary discussions is common to its fiercest critics and most fervent admirers. Such positions form the 'two images attached to Brutalism today that have played a significant part in the demolition of the estate, where Brutalist form is either turned against itself as "concrete monstrosity" or refashioned as class-cleansed "modernist masterpiece."'[34]

Advocating a more critical exploration of the role of politics and class in discussions of Brutalist architecture, Thoburn argues against the somewhat nostalgic

> calibration of Brutalist forms to a certain image of the Welfare State, understood (whether as irrevocably past or a future at our backs) as an integrated whole comprising concrete modernism, mass housing, and class identity, a whole positively coded as a progressive, socialist, or even utopian achievement.[35]

For Thoburn, however, class in relation to Brutalist architecture can be more accurately understood in fundamentally Tafurian terms: as a 'condition not of identity but of crisis.'[36] As part of this framing of class and broadly speaking, Brutalist housing projects demand to be read as separate from the ambitions of the programs that created them. Rather than claiming to be a solution to the tensions and conflicts experienced by the building's working-class, social housing residents, such housing schemes render visible these conditions and experiences within the city. They stand as evidence of

---

[34] Thoburn, 'Concrete and Council Housing,' 613.
[35] Thoburn, 'Concrete and Council Housing,' 617.
[36] Ibid.

public housing programs and policies, rather than as solutions to the complex social conditions of their creation.[37]

Saving Space for Architecture's Ethics

In the absence of any viable way to take legal action in the protection and preservation of significant public housing sites outside of heritage listing frameworks, debates about the value of Brutalist public housing buildings remain bound to the aesthetic merits of these projects. Articulating and, ultimately, ascribing value to the ethical core of such sites in relation to their inhabitation and continued provision for affordable housing presents a significant challenge to current interpretations of heritage and conservation legislation. Ethics being integral, as Banham wrote, 'the new Brutalism is, in the brutalist phrase "an ethic, not an aesthetic".'[38] The category instead describes a program or an attitude to architecture, an interest in 'the thing itself, in its totality, and with all its overtones of human association.'[39]

At the same time that the NSW state government was challenging the heritage listing of Sirius in court, a group of people affected by access to housing established Tent City in Martin Place. Tent City occupied a very central and visible part of the Central Business District to highlight the severity of insufficient affordable housing in Sydney. This temporary inner-city settlement of people impacted by access to affordable housing forms a greater part of the Sirius story; greater than its concrete panels and physical form. The challenge now is to think of how heritage can reflect the value of program over built fabric and how ethics might be more ingrained in the value systems for heritage.

The attempts, and rejections, to have the Sirius listed as

37 Peter Chadwick, *Save Our Sirius*, 2017, poster. Courtesy Peter Chadwick.

38 Reyner Banham, 'The New Brutalism,' *Architectural Review* 118 (December 1955), 357.

39 Banham 'The New Brutalism,' 357.

a heritage building highlight limitations of both the heritage legislation and public discourse on heritage architecture. Brutalism has been awash with concerns of aesthetics and not its ethical roots.[40] It is an issue at the center of debates around the heritage listing of Brutalist buildings in Australia and internationally, as Josephine Livingstone writes:

> But this aspect of brutalism is not part of an ongoing political conversation. American culture is engaging with a postcard version of the design that found such favor with governments seeking to reimagine public space after World War II. This is the nostalgic, internet-optimized version of history, and it has become very popular.[41]

It is a problem that may not be born of laziness or lack of critical discourse, but of the paucity of frameworks for valuing architecture and their limitations. Perhaps if one of the criteria for heritage listing explicitly addressed ethics, the discussion around the merits of Sirius might have been very different. We might also see a greater diversity in what constitutes heritage value. This was especially integral to the Sirius court case where the financial focus of the case was such that the significance of the building itself could not be addressed by either party, and the judge underpinned his ruling out of fairness and equality, which he concluded that any legislation should aim to do.

Sirius and its association with the Green Bans in the nineteen-seventies has much to offer the existing discourse on Brutalist architecture and heritage, both in Australia and internationally. What is striking about this building, and its history, is that it resulted from protests that sought to protect the colonial built heritage of its surrounding site. Heritage that has enriched a section of Sydney's CBD as a tourist

---

[40] Josephine Livingstone, 'Why Brutalism and Instagram Don't Mix,' *New Republic*, August 25, 2018, newrepublic.com/article/150831/brutalism-instagram-dont-mix.

[41] Livingstone, 'Why Brutalism and Instagram Don't Mix.'

attraction, and for which Sydney's built fabric would be much poorer without. It is a sad turn of events that when the NSW state government determined, once again, to remove social housing from Sydney's inner city that the same heritage activism did not protect Sirius from privatization, nor did it bring about replacement social housing within the city. Despite its physical presence remaining, and largely intact, the day that the last tenant, Myra Demetriou, moved out of the Sirius Building on February 1, 2018, the building lost the most crucial part of its Brutalist heritage.

The Community Arts Center

Andrea Phillips

Howell Killick Partridge & Amis, New Albany Community Centre, Deptford, London, 1979-81. View of the main elevation looking west along Douglas Way. Photo: Martin Charles / RIBA Collections

The Community Arts Center

'Devaluing' Art and Architecture (The Case of the Albany Empire, London)

Andrea Phillips

Introduction

[1] See: 'Curating Architecture,' Department of Art, at Goldsmiths College, https://art.gold.ac.uk/research/archive/curating-architecture/index2.html (accessed March 18, 2020).

As an academic deeply embedded in the struggle to organize alternative epistemologies and economies of contemporary art and its antecedents, my approach to the contemporary values of architecture, as well as those produced through the inclusions and exclusions of architecture's 'heritage,' has been through the analysis of the points in the twenty and twenty-first century where art and architecture have interlinked precisely where social and aesthetic beliefs in value accrual and/or dispersal have been shared.[1] While, as will be briefly summarized, the majority of art-architecture collaborations have been highly capitalized via the forms of value accrual that remain normalized within the cultural and creative industries, there seem to have been—and continue to be—many such interlinkages that fall outside of this circuit, either by design or default. One of these can be found in the conceptualization, organization, fabrication, and sustenance of what became known in the United Kingdom and elsewhere as the community arts center.

Changing the Value Framework: Community Arts Centers

Community arts centers—which should be distinguished from the broader definition of 'community center'—have long roots in post-Enlightenment Europe through a particular infrastructural and ideological commitment to creative and cultural learning and experience as a process through which people's lives are enriched, enlivened, made social and, importantly, made *more equal*. In different locales community arts centers take different architectural form, but most are united through their broadly social-liberalist foundation within the reformist, often religiously-inflected, philanthropic and educative principles (or values) that became, in the UK at least, the basis of the creation of the Welfare State in 1946. This essay takes as its frame of reference, and principal case study, from such UK heritage, and recognizes that within such an ideological framework a tension exists between the above-named principles and the grass-roots organization of Workers' Education, forms of protest and activist organization and the historic and contemporary urgencies of women's and Black Lives rights that also took place in and around these buildings.

The community arts movement, a particular state-funded form of local social and cultural organization, was usually housed in existing but cheaply repurposed buildings, in towns and cities across the regions of the postwar UK but looking outside such confines to other histories (as an example, often housed in old buildings built as trophies of the British Empire, many sought to build critical programs around the continuity of colonialism in their own time, but many perpetuated it). A community arts center network was formalized in postwar Britain and was briefly (1965–early

2 In the context of early-twentieth-century Harlem, Saidiya Hartman recognizes the regulatory nature of the Settlement Movement, a cross-national precursor to community arts centers, when she quotes Jane Addams, co-founder of the Hull House Settlement in Chicago, on the need for urban social reform in the pursuit of 'civilizing agencies and processes.' Saidiya Hartman, *Wayward Lives, Beautiful Experiments: Intimate Histories of Riotous Black Girls, Troublesome Women, and Queer Radicals* (London: Serpents Tail, 2019), 220.

3 'They came out of hippydom, the Third Eye certainly did, a sort of psychaedelic squat where you do everything in one room and suddenly all these arts are mixed together.' Francis McKee, Director, CCA Glasgow in Angela McManus, 'CCA at 40: A Look back at the Arts Base That Ppened as the Third Eye Centre,' *Glasgow Evening Times*, April 27, 2015, www.glasgow-times.co.uk/news/13306677.cca-at-40-a-look-back-at-the-arts-base-that-opened-as-the-third-eye-centre/ (accessed March 18, 2020).

nineteen-eighties) recognized with government funding and a specific funding stream supported by Jennie Lee, the first UK Minister for the Arts in 1964. Precedents in other places such as the short-lived cultural condensation experiments in the first years of the USSR, the former-Eastern European cultural hearth and cultural house systems, and the Nordic Folkshuset provision were influential, as were the British and North American settlement movements, all of which shared—and perpetuated the aforementioned ambivalent relationship between state provision and grass-roots organizing.[2]

From the end of the Second World War, community arts centers developed as a built form from more attached or supplementary forms, located either in temporary, short-life properties or buildings owned or bought by rich liberal benefactors (depending often on historic situatedness and/or perceived need). Burgeoning as architectural form in the nineteen-sixties, such hyperbolic projects as theatre director and socialist entrepreneur Joan Littlewood and architect Cedric Price's various Fun Palace designs and programs, the Inter-Action Centre (with, again, Cedric Price's input), and the various Arts Labs in London became well known internationally, particularly in attachment to counter-cultural community and cultural movements but, in at least the vision of Price, with spectacularized flexible, participatory—though often more ad-hoc built-form. Less glamorous organizations also emerged, such as the Midland Arts Centre in Birmingham (new build, 1962), the Beaford Centre (large rural house conversion, 1966, now known as Beaford Arts), The Blackie in Liverpool (converted congregational church, 1967, now named The Black-E), and the Third Eye Centre in Glasgow (converted Victorian high street buildings, 1975, now the Centre for Contemporary Art).[3] These were often relatively rough and also flexible: the 'welfare' of welfare state was pivotal in that what was provided—often via voluntary labor in what we might now recognize as a circular economy—was semi-philanthropic, semi-therapeutic, often practical (crèches, children's food clubs, libraries, equipment loan facilities as well as music, art, theatre, and so on) and almost always politicized. Following the granting of Arts Council funding, a specific form of artist began to be defined. As Gail Fisher, writing up the published proceedings of a 1979 Community Arts conference, held in a venue no longer in use called The Warehouse, Newcastle, described,

> 1. The nature of a community artist lies in the desire to work with, and for, members of a community, on a continuing basis, to make their environment more imaginative, responsive and accessible.
> 2. A group of community artists realises, at some point, that it is capable of making their society more creatively productive, and may therefore be instrumental in effecting social-political change.
>
> The purpose of community arts' work, then, is in helping each community discover how it can best express itself. The importance of this work in a society that celebrates popular culture, with its superficial and degraded role models, cannot be overemphasised. Through providing skills and opportunities, community artists facilitate the processes whereby any community can explore its unique nature.
>
> This necessitates that the community artists maintain a low profile—encourage rather than lead—and recognise that it is a slow process. As agents, community artists are seeking nothing less than to involve an entire local population in creative expression.[4]

4 Gail Fisher, 'Editorial,' *Community Arts Conference Report 1979* (Newcastle-upon-Tyne: Tyneside Free Press, 1979), 6.

This cultural 'movement' in the UK was by no means perfect. Many internecine battles commenced, many people worked for little or no reward, scandals and divisions born of poor resources were a continual undercurrent. But, at a community arts center, you might encounter free space where the value forms of, for example, art and architecture, were irrelevant. It didn't matter how 'good' or 'successful' you were at a certain craft (although folk heroes were welcome and skill was recognized); the point was to allow space for experiment and involvement, a non-meritocratic structure run on low paid labor and practical skills exchange. In other words, a diversification of value-forms operated in close and, in the best of cases, uncontradictory proximity; from a well-thrown pot to the ability to keep children entertained; from a well-articulated argument to local government to the defense and extension of vernacular building). Community centers provided a range of services: art classes, darkrooms, crèches, theatre groups, cafes, discos, gigs, union meetings, Campaign for Nuclear Disarmament and anti-apartheid organization, scratch orchestras, sound systems, sometimes a potters' wheel and a kiln. I used to hang out at one such place in my home town in middle-England, smoking dope and learning about reggae, helping with the crèche, perfecting my amateur dramatics. No one asked about my right to be there. I encountered people unlike me and learned to negotiate my difference. I learned what a 'we' meant and how to participate in its formation. This was the nineteen-eighties—these were places to escape Thatcherism and support the Miners' Strike.

Most of these buildings have now gone, redeveloped for other purposes in processes of gentrification or expansion. Under the Blairite New Labour government of the late nineteen-nineties many were pump-primed to establish a new network of art galleries with a new breed of staff: directors, curators, and program budgets. Significantly, the architectural competitions that were established to rebuild or build anew such infrastructures became much fetishized. Art and architecture refreshed their economic relationship—affective, reputational, and fiscal. Also significantly, space use changed: gallery space became larger and predominant, social, experimental and meeting space became marginalized; here the division between curatorial and education (learning, social engagement, outreach, etc.) within arts institutions became reified. The value form of architecture reverted to more conventionally recognized aesthetic—and ideological—formats.

An Example of Trying to do Things Differently: The Albany Empire, London

There are a few places left that buck this trend, although they are under constant threat of divestment or, worse, architectural, managerial, and thus social polishing. One of these is London's Albany Empire, opened in a Victorian theatre in the nineteen-seventies, destroyed by fire in 1978, rebuilt with community funds and famously reopened by Diana, Princess of Wales. The Empire's focus is on performing arts, reflecting the diverse community of its location in Deptford, a historically marginalized area of South London's docklands where constituencies from many nations, ethnicities, and cultures settled as part of the pattern of dockworking, forming one center of London's cosmopolitical landscape. The Albany—the website has a fantastic archive of images past and present[5]—is dominated by a large community café on the ground floor, a meeting place for old people, very young people, the unemployed, the homeless. It runs many workshops, from singing and dancing to stage management and social

5 See: 'History,' The Albany, www.thealbany.org.uk/about-us/history/ (accessed March 18, 2020).

volunteering. It has lots of bookable meeting rooms. It offers extremely cheap activities for local people, and a music-hall-oriented rotation of entertainment. Outside its door is a cheap, daily local market.

The original Albany Institute was built using monies from the Deptford Fund, founded in 1894 by the Duchess of Albany (it was a settlement building that, along with its more famous cousin Toynbee Hall in nearby Whitechapel, was premised on the idea of bourgeois citizens with religious and/or humanitarian concern for the living conditions of the poor in London, 'giving back' in the form of investment and education). Following the fire in 1978 (widely presumed to be a racist arson attack),[6] the site was moved and a new building was designed by Howell Killick Partridge & Amis (1979–1981) as a 'progressive, independent community agency.'[7] They prepared for the eventual design by studying Price's Inter-Action Centre in Chalk Farm (North London) and employed Tim Ronalds as the job architect who went on to develop refurbishments of the Hackney Empire and Wilton's Music Hall, long established East London local entertainment palaces. The new Albany Empire had two foci: a large ground floor café and a theatre co-designed with resident theatre group The Combination.[8]

Granting Howell Killick Partridge & Amis the contract for the design of the new Albany sent mixed messages. Whilst the firm was certainly recognized as a glamourous adjunct to the fashionable architectural scene in London and the UK, receiving positive reviews in sector journals and magazines and now written into celebratory histories,[9] the design incorporated what might be understood as *representative* attributes of 'community' (a large café, a modular community theatre space) drawing on the 'authentic' genesis of Joan Littlewood's Theatre Workshop in Stratford as well as

---

[6] See: 'Today in London Radical History: Albany Community Centre Gutted by (Probably Fascist) Arson Attack, Deptford, 1978,' Past Tense, pasttenseblog.wordpress.com/2016/07/14/today-in-london-radical-history-albany-community-centre-gutted-by-probably-fascist-arson-attack-deptford-1978/ (accessed March 18, 2020).

[7] Geraint Franklin, *Howell Killick Partridge & Amis* (Swindon/London: Historic England/RIBA, 2017), 142.

[8] Howell Killick Partridge & Amis, New Albany Community Centre, Deptford, London, 1979–1981. View of the main elevation looking west along Douglas Way. Photo: Martin Charles/RIBA Collections.

[9] See: Alastair Fair, *Modern Playhouses: An Architectural History of Britain's New Theatres, 1945–1985* (Oxford: OUP, 2018), 240–241.

Price's work.[10] However representative in its conception and fruition, the building is nevertheless used by people in their own ways despite this cautiously patrimonial approach. This fundamental value-conglomeration should not be lost in any analysis of the use of community arts centers; architecture *does not matter* above and beyond basic necessities; its reification is side-lined through use (in a way reminiscent of the historian and ethnographer Michel de Certeau named a form of self-animating tacticality[11]).[12]

Alterity at the Level of Value

How do my examples of community arts centers, and specifically the aesthetically sanctioned but unglamorously utilized Albany Empire, relate to alternative epistemologies and economies of contemporary art and the concomitant need to rethink the values of art and architecture? In his 2018 book, *99 Theses on the Revaluation of Value*, Brian Massumi says,

> It is time to take back value. For many, value has long been dismissed as a concept so thoroughly compromised, so soaked in normative strictures and stained by complicity with capitalist power, as to be unredeemable. This has only abandoned value to purveyors of normativity and apologists of economic oppression. *Value is too valuable to be left in those hands.*[13]

While I agree with the gist of Massumi's text, my thesis is different, and concerns processes of devaluation, rather than re-assimilation (influenced by the degrowth practices of radical ecology rather than the capture politics of extraction and accelerationism). What is epistemological and what is economic, what is social and what is aesthetic is not so easy to

10 See: Eleanor Dickens, 'An Introduction to Joan Littlewood's Theatre Practice,' British Library, September 7, 2017, www.bl.uk/20th-century-literature/articles/an-introduction-to-joan-littlewoods-theatre-practice (accessed June 20, 2020).

11 'In the technocratically constructed, written, and functionalized space in which the consumers move about, their trajectories form unforeseeable sentences, partly unreadable paths across a space. Although they are composed with the vocabularies of established languages (those of television, newspapers, supermarkets, or museum sequences) and although they remain subordinated to the pre-scribed syntactical forms (temporal modes of schedules, paradigmatic orders of spaces, etc.), the trajectories trace out the ruses of other interests and desires that are neither determined nor captured by the systems in which they develop.' Michel de Certeau, *The Practice of Everyday Life* (Berkeley: UCP, 1984), 18.

12 A contemporary example of contradictory values between architecture's professional and artistic valuation and its capitalization of community value can be examined in the case of the British architectural collective Assemble, whose locally contested 'anti-gentrification' development of Granby Four Streets CIC in Liverpool went on to win the 2015 Turner Prize, awarded by Tate Britain. See: 'Granby Four Streets, 2013–,' Assemble, assemblestudio.co.uk/projects/granby-four-streets-2 (accessed June 20, 2020).

13 Brian Massumi, *99 Theses on the Revaluation of Value: A Postcapitalist Manifesto* (University of Minnesota Press, 2018), 2.

untangle, as the striving for reputational, affective, and fiscal economic growth in both art and architecture borrow methods from each other in terms of scale, selling techniques, and even, in some cases, price points.[14] Despite both art and architecture having radical histories of alterity—political, situated, organizational—that often intertwine, both are also behoven to the forms of value recognition that are suggested by their notional position within a framework of capitalist consolidation (at least those practices that are recognized as 'art' and 'architecture'; of course there are many forms of practice that escape or have successfully evaded such definition, and long may these practices lie hidden from our inquisition). Is it possible to evade value, as it is understood as an 'economy of culture' (to quote the title of the conference where this thinking was originally tried out)? Can systems and processes of *devaluation* produce an alternative logic? Can we name devaluation, rather than a process of fiscal, reputational, and perhaps personal loss, as the letting go of forms of value that are produced by capital and the loosening of the grips of property and privacy that are enmeshed within the addiction to value accrual? Devaluation might not mean 'not caring,' could involve the cutting loose of the property and possessive forms of value that are so endemic to our structural affiliations.

Contemporary art and architecture are—have always been?—mired together in a substrate of value. From the way we educate architects and artists to the way we design galleries, houses, businesses, cities, the meritocratic process of individuating ascendency is based on economic valuation. To devalue is at once a psychic and political attempt to decouple our love of things from the kind of love that demands individual possession. In a system that produces rampant inequality in the arts, destroys lives and promotes the privatization of wealth, can we uncouple forms of value from

[14] See: Andrea Phillips, 'Pavilion Politics,' *LOG* 20 (Fall 2010), 104–115.

accumulation? Devaluation can be caring less about teleology and paying more attention (but not in a libidinal-economic sense) to autochthonous knowledge and process in the sense that 'value' assumes accumulation and a telos, whilst 'devaluation' proposes not simply a different end in the future, but a concept of value/s without an 'end.' In this sense, devaluation comes close to many forms of anarchist thought and is certainly informed by feminist and ecological critiques of possession. But it is also a demand that we pay less attention to the look of things, quite literally, learning from the radical redistribution techniques of the squatting and community arts movements, as well as various indigenous understandings of matter and use. Here is the danger in Massumi's text: In contemporary art and architecture, through different processes, the style of an object or construction may bear relation to the aesthetics of redistribution in anarcho-communitarian ways, but not to the *fact* of redistribution, dispossession, radical delegation. These are/were the forms of the community arts movement both as process and content: as Gail Fisher says, being involved in community art necessitates 'that the community artists maintain a low profile—encourage rather than lead—and recognise that it is a slow process.'[15]

[15] Fisher, 'Editorial.'

Value: How It Is Produced: Homologation

The Albany Empire, and the network of community centers that it belongs to, have epitomized forms of de-homologation that struggle to exist in contemporary art and architecture collaborations (and still do where community arts centers have managed to survive with such an ethos intact despite the corporatization of public funding and its attendant demand for novel architectures). This is reflected directly in the architecture from an amateur or user's perspective: the niceties of design were less important than the function of community sustenance and provision. The ecology of relations, their careful and often difficult balance, more important than the outwards appearance of the building.

Six years ago whilst teaching at Goldsmiths I carried out an extensive research project with my colleague Suhail Malik in which we analyzed the contemporary art market in the UK.[16] This analysis was propelled by a number of factors, not least the fact that, as pedagogues on one of the world's most famous Master of Fine Art (MFA) programs, we recognized the contradiction between that which we were teaching (broadly speaking, theories of cultural value as formations of financial and affective economies influenced primarily by Marx, Bourdieu and their sociological descendants as well as emerging theories of soft power and platform capitalism) and what we were helping to produce (market-ready artists with a focus on privatized socio-cultural milieus of practice emanating through the globally dominant and historically founded studio model of practice). This research involved a detailed analysis of histories of art dealerships and developments of galleries and museums to accommodate the increasing but historically devised patronage model formulated initially during the Italian Renaissance (although even this 'starting point' has antecedents through the church and, perhaps even more substantially, within the feudal enclosure of forms of aesthetic production so brilliantly described by scholars such a Isabelle Stengers and Silvia Federici).[17]

In particular I was interested in what the art market analyst Raymonde Moulin called, in her analysis of its movement from Paris to New York in the nineteen-fifties, 'homologation.'[18] This term, drawn from the language of financial management, means the process of approval and confirmation of

[16] See: Suhail Malik and Andrea Phillips, 'Tainted Love: Art's Ethos and Capitalization,' in *Art and its Commercial Markets: A Report on Current Changes and with Scenarios for the Future*, ed. Maria Lind and Olav Velthuis (Berlin: Sternberg, 2012).

[17] See: Philippe Pignarre and Isabelle Stengers, *Capitalist Sorcery: Breaking the Spell* (London: Palgrave Macmillan, 2007) and Silvia Federici, *Caliban and the Witch: Women, the Body and Primitive Accumulation* (New York: Autonomedia, 2004).

[18] See: Raymonde Moulin, *De la valeur de l'art* (Paris: Flammarion, 1995).

value and, as such, demonstrates very clearly that value is a fiction based on the technical amassing of ratings (or taste) rather than something with any form of intrinsicality. The stock market is a method of homologation, as is the local vegetable market's settling of the rough price of a bunch of carrots, as is the demand on academics to rate the performance of their students. Today homologation works at lightning speed in flash trading and digital currency forms. In art, homologation is what dealers, gallerists, auction houses, and art consultants do: it serves to describe the coming together of value forms to produce what, in our more basic world, we might call, in the end, cost. What Suhail and I found, of course, was the impossibility of 'breaking open' the art market's process of homologation in a bid to expose distributions of power and money, which was, essentially, our aim.

With this research we were joined by an art dealer, a cultural entrepreneur, a number of gallerists, a museum director and, eventually, an art fair director, all of whom were interested in contributing significantly to our research. We learned a lot from them, of course. What we were more naïve about was the condition of their interest. In our analysis, in order to produce the forms of redistribution that were our aim, we needed to prove the ways in which individual works of art produced value through a complex matrix of primary and secondary market sales data, what we called 'artwork biographies' (how value changed as diverse artworks are made, displayed, traded, stored, re-traded, rediscovered, displayed, and so on). In other words, an unpacking of art world homologation processes, where and how value is settled. This specific methodology, if perfected, might more generally produce more accurate figures for the worth of (and thus, in our view, unequal fictions produced by) the art market (and more generally, the cultural sphere). We were, in Massumi's terms, trying to take back value. Rationally speaking, it is not surprising that people whose jobs it is to produce that value (dealers, galleries, auction houses, museums, art fairs) would both be interested in, and keen to ambiguate, such data-driven provability. On one hand, the cultural sphere is in constant search for modes through which to prove its worth, whether in order to increase public funding in a sector that is formed through privatized practices, to change tax legislation, to increase property investment as a correlate to market mechanisms in culture, or produce support structures for public-private income initiatives in the arts. On the other, the ambiguation of price is a central aspect of valuation through status. In the end, the research project failed: we were unable to collect the pivotal data on price to triangulate with other factors such as reputational and affective value produced by exhibition worth, global reach, representation, and so on.

The Context of Value: The Violence of Modernist Epistemologies and Colonial Power

All of the above needs to be contextualized within the framework of Westernly geopolitics and infrastructures of power. It goes without saying that both 'art' and 'architecture' are concepts produced by historical aesthetic frames of value operationalized by the development of physical and metaphysical structures of the occidental trade routes, epistemologies of social hierarchy, power broadcast through coloniality and colonial administration to many other parts of the world in narcissistic, violent, and engorged form. The categorizations of work forms—whether they be craft-based or organizational, or even both—has historical bearing on shifts in cartographic power at both local and trans-local levels (as it does on the process of devaluation, a method of different valuation so often deputized to the poor, the unofficial, the hippie, the indigenous). Mapping the territory involves categorization: submitting objects to order; submitting souls to the count, forcefully eradicating magical purposes and anthropophagic uses (this has bearing on and relates to forms of planetarity thought and post-anthropocenic notions of life). What shadows do the categories 'art' and 'architecture' cast across other understandings of the relation between shelter, pleasure, toil, and living? Between gender and work, sex and work, day and night?

19 See: Neil Smith, *Uneven Development: Nature, Capital, and the Production of Space* (London: Verso, 1984).

20 Giorgio Agamben, *Mean without End: Notes on Politics* (Minneapolis: University of Minnesota Press, 2000), 113.

Changing the Frame: Devaluation, Alternative Valuation

One of the critical calls we hear from the environmental movement concerns degrowth. Environmentalists warn that continued expansion not only affects the availability of resources and increases what Neil Smith called the unevenness of global development, but that we need to disentangle ourselves psychically from the concept of growth *per se*.[19] Here the non-teleological—non-ending—practice of devaluation takes on a richer meaning close to Giorgio Agamben's idea of *impotenza*:

> If there is today a social power [*potenza*], it must see its own impotence [*impotenza*] through to the end, it must decline any will to either posit or preserve right, it must break everywhere the nexus between violence and right, between the living and language that constitutes sovereignty.[20]

It is clear that contemporary art is caught up in growth addiction, and its relationship to architecture feeds this addiction through both processes of commissioning and affective and ideological intimacies. How can we counter such a frightening and destructive process? Albany Empires are one answer. The Albany Empire repurposes the cultural economy through a redistribution, or resettlement, of value. Howell Killick Partridge & Amis, though celebrated at the time within the architectural press, may not have been the most radical architectural office in their ideological commitment to building alternative paradigms for local, social, equitable life in Deptford, but in a sense, this does not matter, as has been explicated. All they had to do was build a shell for such processes. The Albany Empire is almost literally just that; a shell for use.

Devaluation is not a paradigmatic concept of loss, although forms of loss will have to be undertaken: the loss of power, de-meritocratization within the arts, the loss of 'empty' space, the loss of psychic and actual property. We need to learn to let go of value. How might this work in practice? In the UK the continued investment through public-private initiatives into new arts' buildings needs to stop. Instead the money should be spent on strategies of dissimulation, not dictated and managed by cultural quangos[21] and government agencies but by local community leaders and groups who come together through shared matters of concern. Devaluation also necessitates the real adjustment to fiscal value of art commodities on the art market: at least we need to design an economic infrastructure in the arts that is diversified at real rather than simply aesthetically organized investment level.

Devaluation in this sense means not worrying so much about the preciousness of commodities—it is a socialist call for the spread not just of fiscal amenities but also of the psychic social transfer of value within art from the few, to the

[21] An acronym meaning 'quasi non-governmental organization.'

many contexts and communities in which it exists. The community arts center is by no means a perfect model, but it is at least a model that practices caring for people over the objects of profit.

Index

6a architects   169
9 Houses   64

Abraham, Raimund   cover (r), 1, 60, 61, 64, 68
Abrahamson, Michael   209–211, 213–223
Abramson, Daniel M.   128, 135
[The] Absent Museum, Blueprint for a Museum of Contemporary Art for the Capital of Europe   172
Adams, Ruth   113
Addams, Jane   250
Adler and Sullivan Architects   50
Aedes Gallery, Berlin DE   63
Agamben, Giorgio   261
Agrest and Gandelsonas Architects   61
Agrest, Diana   67
Airbnb   200, 202
Albany Empire, The, London UK   253–255, 257, 262
Albers, Martin   139, 147
Albert, Prince   104
Albert Sloman Library, Colchester UK   216
Albertopolis, London UK   104
All This Belongs to You   116
Altamira Palace, Toledo ES   105
Ambasz, Emilio   60, 61, 64
American Folk Art Museum, New York US   118, 120

American Friends of the National Gallery of Australia   51
AMO Studio   141, 143, 148, 151
Anderson, Jay   80, 81
Andrejevic, Mark   212, 222
Apex Club Australia   89
[Les] architects du group 'De Stijl'   60, 61
Architectural Analogues   74
Architectural Institute of Japan (AIJ), Tokyo JP   194
Architectural League, New York US   74
Architecture I   59, 60, 63, 64, 66
Architecture II: Houses for Sale   60, 61, 63, 66, 68
Architecture of the École des Beaux-Arts   70, 71, 129
Architecture Without Architects   129
Arrhenius, Thordis   11, 50, 56, 116
Art + Architecture   74
Art Institute of Chicago, US   50
Artists' Time Capsules   201, 203
ARUP Engineers   96
Asia Society Hong Kong Center, CN   38
AT&T Building, New York US   211
Aulenti, Gae   61
Australian Research Council   8
Avery Coonley House, Riverside Illinois US   46, 49, 51

Bailleres House, Acapulco MX   56
Balfron Tower, London UK   216
Ballarat Historical Park Association, AU   90
Banham, Peter Reyner   29, 215, 217, 221, 238, 243
Barbican Centre, London UK   240
Barr Jr., Alfred H.   127
Bat'a, Tomás   29, 38
Batey and Mack Architects   61, 67
Batey, Andrew   67
Beaford Centre (Beaford Arts), South Molton UK   250
Becher, Hilla and Bernd   32
Bennett, Tony   105
Benthem Crouwel Architects   140, 143, 144, 146
Bergdoll, Barry   111
Betsky, Aaron   134
Bewogen Beweging   145, 146, 148
Bingham, Neil   115

Blackie, The, Liverpool UK   250
Blackwall Reach, London UK   101, 103
Bleiker, Roland   8
Block One, Fortress Louisbourg, Nova Scotia CA   87
Bochner, Mel   154
Bofill, Ricardo   61, 67
Boie, Gideon   170
Bolton, Reginald   25
Borgmann, Thomas   145
Borret, Kristiaan   168
Bourdieu, Pierre   197, 258
Breuer, Marcel   127
[The] Broad Contemporary Art Museum, Los Angeles US   104
Brody, David   122
Brown, Alex   11
Bruhn, Cameron   8
Buckminster Fuller, Richard   29
Buić, Jagoda   150
Building No.23, Zlín CZ   38
Busse   33
Butler, Chris   235, 237

Cairns, Stephen   54
Calder, Barnabas   216, 218, 221
Candilis, Georges   29
Capsule Art Projects   201, 203
Caruso St John Architects   169
Castelli, Leo, New York US   cover (r), 1, 59–61, 63, 64, 66, 67
Castelli Leone, New Jersey US   67
CBS Building, New York US   124
Center for Applied Computer Research and Development   64
Centre Canadien d'Architecture/Canadian Centre for Architecture, Montréal CA   31, 73
Centre for Architecture, Theory, History and Criticism (ATCH), Queensland University AU   8
Centre Pompidou, Paris FR   30, 121, 126, 145, 162, 166, 172, 173
Cerexhe, Benoît   160
Certeau, Michel de   255
Chadwick, Peter   215–218, 227, 229–232, 236, 239, 241, 243
Charles, Martin   247, 254
Chicago Historical Society, US   30, 53

Chicago Stock Exchange, US 50
Christie's, New York US 47
Citroën, André 163
Citroën, Brussels BE 158–161, 163–168, 170–172
CIVA Center, Brussels BE 158, 166
Clark, Roger H. 29
Clarke, Amy 16
Collaborations: Artists & Architects 74
Collin, George 63
Colomina, Beatriz 211
Colonial Williamsburg, Virginia US 80, 82–86, 89, 90, 92, 94
[The] Combination Theatre Group 254
Cook, Peter 61
Couchez, Elke 8
Crinson, Mark 101

D'Oliveira, Jaap 147
D'Orey, Inês 203
DAD (Design, Architecture and Digital Department), V&A, London UK 115
Darger, Henry 124
Dauphin demi-bastion, Fortress Louisbourg, Nova Scotia CA 87
Davidts, Wouter 8, 150, 152
De Jauréguiberry, Xavier 217
De Vylder Vinck Taillieu Architecten 169
Deckha, Nityanand 113
Decroos, Bart 157, 159, 160, 167, 168
Défense, La, Paris FR 35
Delafons, John 113
Demetriou, Myra 245
Design Society, Shenzhen CN 108
Desilvey, Caitlin 55
[The] Destruction of the Country House 1875–1975 111, 112
Deutsche Bank Building, New York US 124
Deutsches Architekturmuseum, Frankfurt DE 73
Diana, Princess of Wales 253
Diener, Roger 169, 170
Diller Scofidio + Renfro Architects 104, 133, 145
Diller, Elizabeth 104, 105, 133
Dimmer, Christian 196
DJ Toriena (Sae Shimizu) 203
Doesburg, Theo van 60

Dorset Hotel, New York US   125
Douglas, Nick   214
Drawing Center, New York US   63
Drawing Now   71
Drawing Towards a More Modern Architecture   72
Drexler, Arthur   70
DSL Studio   143
Duivenbode, Ossip van   141
Dumont, Alexis   163
Dundee Museum, Scotland   103
Dyckhoff, Tom   216–218
Dylaby   145, 146, 148

Eames, Charles & Ray   150, 152
Early Modern Architecture: Chicago 1870–1910   123
Economist Group, Westminster UK   102
Eesteren, Cornelis van   60
[L'] Effort Moderne, Paris FR   60
Egyptian Museum, Cairo EG   84
Eisenman, Peter   60, 61, 66, 67, 70, 169
Eisenman/Robertson Architects   61, 67
Elsken, Ed van der   146
English Heritage, UK   101, 102, 114
Eschauzier, Frits   146
Euston Station, London UK   32

Fallingwater, Mill Run US   52
Farrell, Yvonne   108
Federal Environment Agency, Dessau DE   33
Federici, Silvia   258
Filarski, Andrew   33
Fin d'ou T Hou S   67
Finch, Paul   114
Fior, Liza   103, 115, 116
Fisher, Gail   251, 257
Fitch, James Marston   28
Foerstner, Abigail   53
Follies: Architecture for the Late-Twentieth-Century Landscape   61, 63, 67
Fonteyne, An   168
[The] Forms of a Legend   67
Fortress Louisbourg, Nova Scotia CA   80, 82, 86, 87, 89, 90, 92, 94

Foster House and Stable, Chicago US   45
Francis W. Little House, Wayata US   47
Frauenkirche, Dresden DE   183
Frearson, Amy   102
Freespace   108
Fry, Bruce W.   87
Fujimoto, Sou   169
Furman, Adam Nathaniel   211, 214, 217
FuturePlan   103
FYB (Fuck Yeah Brutalism)   221

Gailey, Alan   81, 93
Gandelsonas, Mario   67
Gee, Emily   102
Gehry, Frank   61, 67
Ghent University, BE   8
Gillender Building, New York US   25
Gillespie, Tarleton   218
Gilman Collection of Architectural Drawings, MoMA, New York US   72, 73
Ginza Architecture   201
Goddard, Angela   8
Gofers, Tao   211, 228, 231
Golden Lane Estate, London UK   100
Goldfinger, Ernő   216
Goldsmiths College, University of London, UK   258
Goldstein, Yves   167, 168
Gombrich, Ernst   217
Goodwin, Philip   119, 122, 127
Goodwin, William A.R.   84
Goodwin-Stone Building, New York US   127–129, 131, 136
Gore House, London UK   104
Graaf, Reinier de   237
Grafton Architects   108
Grand Parc, Bordeaux FR   102
Graves, Michael   61, 67
Gray, Jason   195
Great Exhibition of the Works of Industry of All Nations   104
Greater London Council, UK   100
Gregotti, Vittorio   60
Gropius, Walter   28, 127

Gugelot, Hans   150
Guggenheim Museum, Bilbao ES   121, 126, 136, 167

Hadid, Zaha   102
Hanks, David A.   44, 52
Harrenstein, R.J.   152
Hartman, Saidiya   250
Haussmann, Georges-Eugène   28
Hémon, Sedje   150
Henderson, Nigel   217
Herzog & De Meuron Architects   145
Hine, Amelia   8
Hirshhorn Museum and Sculpture Garden, Washington D.C. US   142
Historic England, UK   101, 102
Hobsbawm, Eric   24, 27
Hoffmann, Donald   42–44, 50, 51, 57
Holabird & Roche Architects   26
Holden, Susan   8, 11, 96, 108, 109, 111
Holland Open Air Museum, Arnhem NL   80
Hollein, Hans   61
Horsfall Turner, Olivia   96, 108, 115
House El Even Odd   66, 67
House Without Walls   cover (r), 1, 64
House X Project   67
Howell Killick Partridge & Amis Architects   247, 254, 262
Hubert, Christian   61
Hull House Settlement, Chicago US   250
Hume, David   212, 215, 220, 222, 223
Hunstanton School and Gymnasium, Norfolk UK   102, 217
Hunt, Tristram   111

ICOMOS (International Council on Monuments and Sites)   186
Idea as Model   70
Instagram   211, 214, 216, 217
Institute of Architecture and Urban Studies, New York US   70
Institute of Contemporary Arts, London UK   74
Inter-Action Centre, Chalk Farm, London UK   254
International Committee for Documentation and Conservation of
    Buildings, Sites and Neighbourhoods of the Modern Movement
    (DOCOMOMO International)   167, 194–196, 206, 207, 210
Ise Shrine, JP   199

Ishii, Naho   203
Ishikawa, Shigenori   202, 204
Isozaki, Arata   60, 61, 66, 195–197
Ito, Toyo   195, 196
Itoi, Jun   203

Jack Lynn & Ivor Smith Architects   102
Jacob, Sam   111, 219
Jacobs, Jane   32, 54
Jameson, Fredric   217
Janus with His Head in the Clouds   67
Japan Federation of Architects and Building Engineers Association
    (JFABEA), Tokyo JP   194
Japan Institute of Architects (JIA), Tokyo JP   194
Jefferson, Thomas   83
Jencks, Charles   109, 190, 204
Johnson, Chris   240, 241
Johnson, Philip   128, 129, 211
Jones, Ewan   90
Jonge, Wessel de   167
Josic, Alexis   29

Kaji-O'Grady, Sandra   8
Kahn, Louis   134
Kames, Lord   222
KANAL-Centre Pompidou, Brussels BE.   158–163, 165–173
Kandinsky, Wassily   149
Kauffman, Jordan   15
Kaufman, Edward N.   93
Kaufmann, Edgar J.   105
Kelleher, Peter   109
King, Perry   150
King's Bastion, Fortress Louisbourg, Nova Scotia CA   87, 88
Klack, Gunnar   211
Koike, Yuriko   195
Koolhaas, Rem   35, 38, 126, 131, 140–146, 148–151
Koonmen, Leo   46
Kozlenko, Maksym   77, 90
Krauss, Rosalind   121
Kropf, Reinhard   197
Kuma, Kengo   103, 169

Kurokawa, Kisho   31, 189–196, 198–200, 202, 204, 205

L'Epi-Devolder   164
Lacaton & Vassal Architects   102, 169
Langdalen, Erik   11, 56, 116
Lange, Alexandra   219
Latour, Bruno   36
Lawrence Dana, Susan   41
Le Corbusier (Charles-Édouard Jeanneret-Gris)   28, 100, 240
Lee, Jennie   250
Lincoln Center, New York US   132
Linders, Jannes   144
Lindholm House, Cloquet US   49
Littlewood, Joan   250, 254
Livingstone, Josephine   244
Llewelyn-Davies, Richard   30
Lockridge Medical Clinic, Whitefish US   46
Lonergan, Hamish   11
Lousada, Sandra   cover (l), 1, 100
Lowe, Adam   56
Lowenthal, David   35
Lowry, Glenn D.   130
Lu, Katherine   211
Luckman Salas O'Brien Architects   30
Luckman, Charles   30
Lutyens, Edwin   28

Mac, Peter   231
Macarthur, John   8, 217, 221
Machado-Silvetti Architects   61
Mack, Mark   67
Maeda, Tatsuyuki   195, 199, 202, 203, 206, 207
Magalhães, Filipe   195, 202
Maison d'Artiste   60
Maison Particulière   60
Maison Tropicale   47
Malevich, Kazimir   141, 149
Malik, Suhail   258
Marlborough-Blenheim Hotel   64
Marshall Field Wholesale Store, Chicago US   26
Martelli, Federico   140, 141, 145, 146, 149, 150

Marx, Karl   258
Mason, Randall   198
Massumi, Brian   255, 257, 259
Max Protetch Gallery, New York US   61
McAlpine, Alistair   61
McCarter, Robert   44
McNamara, Shelley   108
Meades, Jonathan   218
Meier, Richard   60
Merriman, Nick   11
Metabolist Group   31
Metropolitan Museum of Art, New York US   32, 47, 51
Meyer May House, Grand Rapids US   47
Míček, Pavel   38
Midland Arts Centre, Birmingham UK   250
Mies van der Rohe, Ludwig   30, 127, 128
Mike McCurry Group   49
Miller, Arthur   57
Millers Point Community Association, Sydney AU   229, 232
Milner, Ryan   213
Minami, Noritaka   195, 202
Modern Architecture: International Exhibition   123
Molesworth, Simon   233–235
MoMA (Museum of Modern Art), New York US   32, 70, 71, 73, 120–137, 166
Monaghan, Tom   47–49
Mondrian, Piet   149
Moneo, Raphael   61
Monroe, Marilyn   57
Moore, Charles   60, 66
Moore, Clover   237
Moran, Michael   118, 120
More than One (Fragile) Thing at a Time   116
Mould, Oli   239
Moulin, Raymonde   258
MSA Architects, Brussels BE   167
Mudřík, Pavel   38
muf architecture/art   96, 103, 109, 110, 116
Muschamp, Herbert   124
Museum of Manufactures, London UK   104
Museum of the City of New York, US   119, 127

Nakagin Capsule Tower, Shimbashi Tokyo JP   31, 189–191, 193, 202–205, 207
Nakagin Housing Group, Shimbashi Tokyo JP   192
National Association of Building Owners and Managers, Chicago US   26
National Center for the Study of Frank Lloyd Wright, Chicago US   48
National Institute of Demolition Contractors, UK   31
Nederlands Fotomuseum, Rotterdam NL   147
New Albany Community Centre, Deptford London UK   247
New National Gallery, Berlin DE   30, 128
Newman, Barnett   150, 152
Niigata Prefectural Gymnasium, JP   219
noAarchitecten   170
Nordstrom, Eric J.   41
Northwick Park Hospital, Harrow London UK   30
Norwegian Folk Museum, Oslo NO   80
Nouvel, Jean   132
NSW Builders Labourers Federation (BLF), AU   230
NSW Heritage Council, AU   229, 231–234, 237, 238

O'Donnell + Toumey Architects   104
O'Regan, Tom   8
Oak Park, Illinois US   45, 57
Ohashi, Tomio   31, 192, 193, 204
Okhta Center, St. Petersburg RU   181
Old Millfun, Shanghai CN   23, 36
OMA Architects   144, 140
OMA/AMO Architects, Rotterdam NL   140, 237
Otero-Pailos, Jorge   11, 47, 56, 116, 133, 197
OTTO/Raven & Snow   118, 120
Oud, J.J.P.   127
Ouroussoff, Nicolai   195–197

Packard, Vance   32
Paine, Ashley   8, 15
Paolozzi, Eduardo   217
Parallel of Life and Art   217
Pardo, Jorge   108
Park Hill, Sheffield UK   102
Pelli, Cesar   60, 129
Pennsylvania Station, New York US   32
Phillips, Andrea   8

Phipps, Simon   216, 217
Piano, Renzo   30
Picasso, Pablo   134, 150
Pichler, Walter   60
Platforms, Pavilions, Pylons and Plants   66
Pôle Culturel Citroën   160
Pommer, Richard   72, 73
Potteries Thinkbelt Projects   31
Prada Foundation, Milan IT   35, 38
Price, Cedric   31, 60, 66, 250, 254, 255
[The] Prison   67
Public Hospital, Colonial Williamsburg, Virginia US   85

Qiu, Jack Linchuan   218
Quinlan Terry, John   61

R. Charlton's Coffeehouse, Colonial Williamsburg, Virginia US   85
Rams, Dieter   150
Rasker, Thomas   170
Rauch, John   60, 64
Rauschenberg, Robert   146
Ravazé, Maurice-Jacques   163
Raysse, Martial   146
Rentzhog, Sten   85
Residenzschloss, Dresden DE   183
RIBA Collections   247
Richter, Gerhard   134
Riegl, Alois   44
Rietveld, Gerrit   152
Robert W. Roloson Houses, Chicago US   50
Robertson, Jacquelin   67
Robie House, Chicago US   43, 47, 48
Robin Hood Gardens, London UK   cover (l), 1, 96, 98–103, 106–109, 111, 113–117, 211, 215, 242
Robin Hood Gardens: A Ruin in Reverse   96, 108–111, 107, 114
Roche Dinkeloo Architects   124
Rockefeller Center, New York US   127
Rockefeller Jr., John D.   84, 122, 129
Rockefeller, Nelson   122, 127, 129
Rodrigo, Russell   238
Rogers, Sir Richard   30, 102, 109

Ronalds, Tim   254
Rooij, Gert Jan van   152
Rosenberg, Léonce   60
Rossi, Aldo   33, 60
Rudolph, Paul   33, 61, 134
Ruf, Beatrix   141, 142, 144, 145, 148, 151, 153
Rushton, Ben   229
Rykwert, Joseph   61, 67

Saarinen, Eero   124
Saint Peter Basilica, Rome IT   175
Saint Phalle, Niki de   146
Samuel Freeman House, Los Angeles US   53
San Cataldo Cemetery, Modena IT   33
SANAA Architects   169
Sandberg, Willem   140, 146–148
Sant'Elia, Antonio   28
Sargentini, Johannes   146
Sauerbruch Hutton Architects   33
Save Our Sirius Foundation, Sydney AU   223, 228, 229, 235, 237
Scanlab Projects   108
Scarpa, Carlo   134
Scavnicky, Ryan   214
Schröder-Schräder, Truus   152
Scott-Brown, Denise   126
Self, Will   216
Sergison Bates Architects   170
Serres, Michel   197
Seuphor, Michel   147
Shankbone, David   211
Sheffield City Architects' Department, UK   102
Silver, Joel   48
Sirius Building, Sydney AU   211, 223, 228–241, 243–245
Skansen Open-Air Museum, Stockholm SE   80, 94
Smith, Laurajane   107
Smith, Neil   241, 261
Smithson, Alison and Peter   cover (l), 1, 98, 100–102, 108–110, 211, 217, 242
Smithsonian Institution, Washington D.C. US   59, 64, 66, 67, 142
Smout Allen Studio   108
Snauwaert, Dirk   162

Soane, Sir John   124
Soares, Ana Luisa   195, 202
Sontag, Susan   219
Sorkin, Michael   134, 135
Sotheby's, New York US   49
Sottsass, Ettore   150
Sovereign Hill Museums Association, AU   90
Sovereign Hill, Ballarat AU   77, 80, 82, 89–94
Speakman, Mark   233
Spoerri, Daniel   146
St Paul's Cathedral, London UK   177
Stadsarchief, Amsterdam NL   139, 147
Stangeland, Siv Helene   197
Stead, Naomi   219
Stedelijk Museum Amsterdam, NL   139–142, 144, 145, 147, 150–152
Stengers, Isabelle   258
Stevens, Garry   221
Stewart, Susan   52
Sticks and Stones   108
Stirling, James   60, 64, 65
Stone, Edward Durell   119, 122, 127
Storrer House, Los Angeles US   48
Strong, Roy   111–113
Suh, Do Ho   107, 109, 110
Sultan Ahmed Mosque (aka Blue Mosque), Istanbul TR   179, 187
Suzuki, Hiroyuki   195, 196

Tacoma Building, Chicago US   26
Takara Beautilion, Osaka JP   31, 191
Taliesin West, Scottsdale US   42, 53
Taniguchi, Yoshio   123, 130, 131, 133
Tate Modern, London UK   145, 167
Taubman College, University of Michigan, US   221
Team X Architects   100
Temple-House   67
Temple Street Garage, New Haven US   33
Tent City, Sydney AU   243
[The] Tent   67
Theatre Workshop, Stratford UK   254
Third Eye Centre (Centre for Contemporary Art), Glasgow Scotland   250
Thoburn, Nicholas   102, 241, 242

Throsby, David   16, 105, 106
Tinguely, Jean   146
Tod Williams Billie Tsien Architects   38, 118, 120
Tower Hamlets Council, London UK   101
Tower Preservation and Restoration Project, Tokyo JP   191, 194–196, 198
TREES aka @treero   211
Tronzo, William   54
Trump, Donald   135
Tschumi, Bernard   61
Tsien, Billie   120, 123–125, 133, 134, 136
Tumblr   209, 210, 213, 214, 218–221, 223
Turner, Christopher   96, 108

Uesaku, Yasuo   193, 195
Ultvedt, Per Olof   146
UNESCO (United Nations Educational, Scientific and Cultural Organization)   34, 44, 181, 183, 186
Ungers, Oswald Mattias   60
Unity Temple, Oak Park US   52
University of Cambridge History Building, UK   64, 65
University of London, UK   29
University of Queensland AU   8
Upton, Gabrielle   235
Urban Taskforce Australia   239–241
Ursprung, Philip   219

Valentine, Nina   90
Values of Design   108
Van Gerrewey, Christophe   150, 151
Van Goethem, Marcel   163
Vega de León, Macarena de la   8
Venice Architecture Biennale   96, 99, 100, 107, 108, 114, 115
Venturi and Rauch Architects   64
Venturi Scott Brown Architects   144
Venturi, Robert   60, 64, 126
Vervoort, Rudi   162, 166–168
Victoria and Albert Museum (V&A), London UK   96, 98, 99, 100, 104–107, 111–117
Vidler, Anthony   211, 221
Ville Radieuse   240
Vincent, Alex   203

Volz, Kirsty 11

Wada, Nahoko 202
Wade, Robin 112
Wallach, Alan 129
Warburg Institute, London UK 217
Ward Willits House, Highland Park US 47, 53
Washington, George 83
Watanabe, Hiroshi 195, 204
Waterton, Emma 93
Watkins, Charles Alan 85
Weeks, John 30
Weil, Stephen E. 142
Weissman, A.W. 140
West Green House, Hampshire UK 61
Westminster Palace, London UK 177
While, Aidan 236
Whiteley, Nigel 221
Whitney Museum of American Art, New York US 74
WIELS Contemporay Art Center, Brussels BE 161, 162, 172
Wilkinson, Tom 213, 216, 219
Williams, Tod 120, 123–125, 133, 134, 136
Willink, Rosemary 11
Wilson, Harold 112
Windfohr, Robert F. 56
Windows Legacy Fund, US 52
Winter Palace, St. Petersburg RU 181
Woods, Shadrach 29
World Architecture Network 194, 195
World Trade Center, New York US 132
Wright, Eric Lloyd 53
Wright, Frank Lloyd 41–57, 105, 134
Wright, Olgivanna 42

Yamamoto, Kazan 203, 204
Yamazaki, Rima 195, 197
Yoshikawa, Masahiro 203

Zaha Hadid Architecs 169
Zimmerman, Claire 217, 218, 221, 222
Zuk, William 29

Contributors

Daniel M. Abramson
Daniel M. Abramson is Professor of Architectural History and Director of Architectural Studies at Boston University. His research focuses on matters of economics, society, and architecture from the eighteenth through twentieth centuries. He is the author of three monographs, most recently *Obsolescence: An Architectural History* (2016), as well as being co-editor of *Governing by Design: Architecture, Economy, and Politics in the Twentieth Century* (2012) with the Aggregate Architectural History Collaborative, of which he is also a founding director. Current work includes projects on the American welfare state, and on evidence and narrative in architectural history. Abramson lives and works in Massachusetts.

Tom Brigden
Tom Brigden is an AABC registered architect and heritage consultant at specialist conservation architects Purcell. Brigden's work in both academia and practice is informed by the same fascination with processes of change within historic environments, particularly the visual impact of new construction within sensitive settings. Recent publications include: *The Protected Vista: An Intellectual and Cultural History, As Seen from Richmond Hill* (2019) and *Value in the View: Conserving Historic Urban Views* (2018). Brigden lives in rural West Yorkshire and works in Manchester, United Kingdom.

Alex Brown
Alex Brown is an architect and Senior Lecturer within the Department of Architecture at Monash University. Her research explores twentieth-century

and contemporary art-architecture relationships, as well as architecture and radicality from the 1960s onwards. Recent papers have been published in, *Architectural Theory Review* (with Léa-Catherine Szacka) and *The Journal of Architecture*. Brown has also contributed chapters to a number of edited volumes, including *Spaces of Justice: Peripheries, Passages, Appropriations* (eds. Chris Butler and Edward Mussawir, 2017) and *On Discomfort: Moments in a Modern History of Architectural Culture* (ed. David Ellison and Andrew Leach, 2017). Brown lives and works in Melbourne, Australia.

Amy Clarke

Amy Clarke is an architectural historian and heritage practitioner, and Senior Lecturer in History at the University of the Sunshine Coast. Her research ranges across matters relating to identity, authenticity, regionalism/nationalism and the politicization of history and heritage; she is an expert on 'Big Things' (large roadside attractions) and key contributor to discourses on 'heritage diplomacy.' Recent publications include: 'Should Old Acquaintance Be Forgot? The Uses of History in Scottish Nationalist Politics, 2007–Present' (2020, in print); 'Can't Touch This' (with Stuart King, Andrew Leach and Wouter Van Acker, 2019); and 'Heritage Diplomacy' in the *Handbook of Cultural Security* (ed. Yasushi Watanabe, 2018). Clarke lives and works in Brisbane, Australia.

Wouter Davidts

Wouter Davidts is Partner Investigator of the Australia Research Council funded project 'Is Architecture Art?' and teaches at the Department of Architecture & Urban Planning and the Department of Art History, Musicology and Theatre Studies, Ghent University. He has published widely on the museum, contemporary art, and architecture, including *Triple Bond* (2017), *Luc Deleu – T.O.P. office: Orban Space* (co-edited with Stefaan Vervoort and Guy Châtel, 2012) and *The Fall of the Studio* (2009). With Mihnea Mircan and Philip Metten, he curated *The Corner Show*, Extra City Antwerp, 2015. Davidts lives and works in Antwerp, Belgium.

Bart Decroos

Bart Decroos is a PhD candidate at the University of Antwerp Faculty of Design Sciences with a fellowship from the Research Foundation Flanders (FWO). He graduated as an architect at Sint-Lucas Brussels and previously worked as an editor at the Flanders Architecture Institute and de vylder vinck taillieu architects. He is a member of the editorial board of *OASE Journal for Architecture* and has published in various architecture magazines. Decroos lives and works in Antwerp, Belgium.

Susan Holden

Susan Holden is an architect and Senior Lecturer at the University of Queensland. Recent research focuses on historical and theoretic aspects of architecture as a subject of culture, and its institutional and governance contexts. She has published in a range of journals, including *The Journal of Architecture*, *Leonardo* and *AA Files*, and contributes to the professional journal *Architecture Australia*. Susan is a Fellow of the Australian Institute of Architects (AIA) and has been a jury member for their annual awards program. She lives and works in Brisbane, Australia.

Jordan Kauffman

Jordan Kauffman is Research Fellow in the history, theory, and criticism of architecture at Monash University. Kauffman's present work focuses on architectural representations from the Renaissance to the late twentieth century. His book, *Drawing on Architecture, The Object of Lines, 1970–1990*, was published by the MIT Press in 2018. Kauffman has taught architectural history at the Massachusetts Institute of Technology, Brandeis University, Tufts University, and Boston University. He sits on the editorial board of the Society of Architectural Historians Australia and New Zealand. Kauffman lives and works in Melbourne, Australia.

Hamish Lonergan

Hamish Lonergan is a doctoral candidate at the gta Institute at ETH Zurich, as part of the EU-funded project 'TACK/Communities of Tacit Knowledge.' His research—on issues of taste, authority, and tacit knowledge in architectural culture off- and online—has appeared in international conferences and journals including *Inflection* and *Footprint*. Previously, he worked at COX architecture in Brisbane and curated the exhibition 'Bathroom Gossip,' Boxcopy ARI, Brisbane, 2019. Lonergan lives and works in Zurich, Switzerland.

John Macarthur

John Macarthur is Professor of Architecture at the University of Queensland where he teaches history, theory and design. His research focuses on the intellectual history of architecture and its relation to the visual arts from the picturesque to the present. He has also published on the history of Queensland architecture, and consulted on cultural heritage assessments. He is a Fellow of the Australian Academy of the Humanities, and a Life Member of the Society of Architectural Historians, Australia and New Zealand. Macarthur lives and works in Brisbane, Australia.

Joanna Merwood-Salisbury

Joanna Merwood-Salisbury has taught at Parsons School of Design, the University of Illinois Chicago, Bard and Barnard Colleges, and the Pratt Institute. She is currently Professor of Architecture at Victoria University of Wellington. Her research focuses on modern American architecture and urbanism, with special emphasis on issues of race and labor. Her publications include: *Design for the Crowd: Patriotism and Protest in Union Square* (2019); *After Taste: Expanded Practice in Interior Design* (co-edited with Kent Kleinman and Lois Weinthal, 2012); and *Chicago 1890: The Skyscraper and the Modern City* (2009). Merwood-Salisbury lives and works in Wellington, New Zealand.

Ashley Paine

Ashley Paine is a Senior Lecturer in the School of Architecture at the University of Queensland. His research spans a range of subjects including the history of striped façades, the collection and reconstruction of architecture by museums, contemporary pavilions, and the preservation of Frank Lloyd Wright's built works. He has contributed to journals including AA *Files*, *Future Anterior*, and *Interstices*, and is co-author of the book, *Pavilion Propositions* (with John Macarthur, Susan Holden, and Wouter Davidts, 2018), and co-editor of *Trading between Architecture and Art* (with Wouter Davidts and Susan Holden, 2019). Paine is also a practicing architect, and co-founder of Brisbane-based practice, PHAB Architects. Paine lives and works in Brisbane, Australia.

Anton Pereira Rodriguez

Anton Pereira Rodriguez is a PhD candidate at the Department of Art History, Musicology and Theatre Studies at Ghent University and the Department of Cultures and Civilizations at the University of Verona. His research focuses on the artistic and institutional exchange between the Italian and the Belgian art scene during the 1980s and the 1990s, with a strong emphasis on Jan Vercruysse as key protagonist. Recent publications include: *Jan Vercruysse 1990, a film by Jef Cornelis* (co-edited with Kristien Daem, 2020) and 'George Maciunas and the Flux-Labyrinth (1974/1976): Staging a SoHo way of Life' (co-authored with Wouter Davidts, 2018). Pereira Rodriguez lives and works in Brussels, Belgium.

Andrea Phillips

Andrea Phillips is BALTIC Professor and Director of BxNU Research Institute, Northumbria University & BALTIC Centre for Contemporary Art. Andrea lectures and writes about the economic and social construction of public value within contemporary art, the manipulation of forms of participation and the potential of forms of political, architectural, and social reorganization within artistic and curatorial culture. Her current research project, conducted with artist Jason E Bowman, involves a social and aesthetic re-reading of the British community arts movement from the mid-1970s to the present. Phillips lives in London and works in Newcastle, United Kingdom.

Lara Schrijver

Lara Schrijver is Professor in Architecture Theory at the University of Antwerp Faculty of Design Sciences. Earlier, she taught at Delft University of Technology (2005–2014) and the Rotterdam Academy of Architecture (2007–2013). She is editor for the KNOB *Bulletin* and has served as editor for the journals *Footprint* and OASE. Her work has been published in various academic and professional journals. She is author of *Radical Games* (2009) and co-editor of *Autonomous Architecture in Flanders* (2016). She was co-editor for three editions of the annual review *Architecture in the Netherlands* (2016–2019). Schrijver lives in Rotterdam, the Netherlands, and works in Antwerp, Belgium.

Ari Seligmann

Associate Professor Ari Seligmann is currently the Deputy Head of Monash University's Architecture Department and a Critical Practices Research Lab contributor. He is a critic, historian, and designer examining contemporary Japanese architecture, and relations between architecture and media. He regularly lectures and publishes on the historiography and representations of Japanese architecture, including *Japanese Modern Architecture 1920–2015: Developments and Dialogues* (2016). Current research examines the multifaceted roles of post-war Japanese architectural photographers in shaping our understanding of the built environment. Seligmann lives and works in Melbourne, Australia.

Kirsty Volz

Kirsty Volz is an architect and Lecturer at the Queensland University of Technology. Her work is focused on the important role that architects play in providing good-quality, affordable housing. Her creative works, in collaboration with David Toussaint, include the Two Pavilion House in Brisbane, Australia (2014). Recent articles have been published in the IDEA *Journal*, TEXT *Journal*, *Lilith: A Feminist History Journal*, and the *International Journal of Interior Architecture and Spatial Design*. Volz lives and works in Brisbane, Australia.

Rosemary Willink

Rosemary Willink is a PhD candidate in the School of Architecture at the University of Queensland and part of the Australia Research Council Discovery Project 'Is Architecture Art? A History of Categories, Concepts and Recent Practices.' With prior experience working in cultural institutions in Australia, Europe, and the United Kingdom, Willink's research focuses on how museums and galleries collect, curate, and commission architecture. Willink's qualifications include a Master of Contemporary Art from Sotheby's Institute in London and a Bachelor of Music Performance from the Victorian College of the Arts in Melbourne. Willink lives and works in Washington DC, USA.

Editors: Ashley Paine, Susan Holden, John Macarthur
Contributors: Daniel M. Abramson, Tom Brigden, Alex Brown, Amy Clarke, Wouter Davidts, Bart Decroos, Susan Holden, Jordan Kauffman, Hamish Lonergan, John Macarthur, Joanna Merwood-Salisbury, Ashley Paine, Anton Pereira Rodriguez, Andrea Phillips, Lara Schrijver, Ari Seligmann, Kirsty Volz, Rosemary Willink
Editorial assistant: Charles Rowe
Conference conveners: John Macarthur, Susan Holden, Ashley Paine, Elke Couchez
Copy-editing: Leo Reijnen
Proofreading: Els Brinkman
Index: Elke Stevens
Design: Sam de Groot
Layout assistance: Laura Opsomer
Typefaces: Eldorado (William Addison Dwiggins, 1953),
    Computer Modern (Donald Knuth, 1984),
    SKI D—ATA (Tariq Heijboer, 2014)
Printing and binding: Wilco Art Books, Amersfoort
Publisher: Valiz, Amsterdam, Astrid Vorstermans & Pia Pol, ‹www.valiz.nl›

The editors wish to thank Charles Rowe for his careful review of the chapter manuscripts prior to publication.

Publishing Partners
The University of Queensland
The Australian Research Council
Ghent University

Project's financial support
Discovery Grant (DP160101569) of the Australian Research Council (ARC), and The University of Queensland's School of Architecture and Centre for Architecture Theory Criticism History (ATCH).

Creative Commons CC–BY–NC–ND
© For all images: all rights reserved.

Distribution
USA: D.A.P., ‹www.artbook.com›
GB/IE: Anagram Books, ‹www.anagrambooks.com›
NL/BE/LU: Centraal Boekhuis, ‹www.cb.nl›
Europe/Asia: Idea Books, ‹www.ideabooks.nl›
Australia: Perimeter, ‹www.perimeterdistribution.com›
Individual orders: ‹www.valiz.nl›

This book has been produced on FSC-certified paper.

ISBN 978-94-92095-93-0
Printed and bound in the EU, 2020

The text essays in this book are licensed under a Creative Commons Attribution-Non-Commercial-NoDerivativeWorks license.

The user is free to share – to copy, distribute and transmit the work under the following conditions:
○ Attribution – You must attribute the work in the manner specified by the author or licensor (but not in any way that suggests that they endorse you or your use of the work).
○ Noncommercial – You may not use this work for commercial purposes.
○ No Derivative Works – You may not alter, transform, or build upon this work.

With the understanding that:
○ Waiver – Any of the above conditions can be waived if you get permission from the copyright holder.
○ Other Rights – In no way are any of the following rights affected by the license:
  ○ Your fair dealing or fair use rights;
  ○ The author's moral rights;
  ○ Rights other persons may have either in the work itself or in how the work is used, such as publicity or privacy rights.

Notice – For any reuse or distribution, you must make clear to others the license terms of this work. The best way to do this is with a link to the web page mentioned below.
    The full license text can be found at ‹http://creativecommons.org/licenses/by-nc-nd/3.0/nl/deed.en_GB›.

vis-à-vis

The vis-à-vis series provides a platform to stimulating and relevant subjects in recent and emerging visual arts, architecture and design. The authors relate to history and art history, to other authors, to recent topics and to the reader. Most are academic researchers. What binds them is a visual way of thinking, an undaunted treatment of the subject matter and a skilful, creative style of writing.

Series design by Sam de Groot, ‹www.samdegroot.nl›.

2015

Sophie Berrebi, *The Shape of Evidence: Contemporary Art and the Document*, ISBN 978-90-78088-98-1

Janneke Wesseling, *De volmaakte beschouwer: De ervaring van het kunstwerk en receptie-esthetica*, ISBN 978-94-92095-09-1 (e-book)

2016

Janneke Wesseling, *Of Sponge, Stone and the Intertwinement with the Here and Now: A Methodology of Artistic Research*, ISBN 78-94-92095-21-3

2017

Janneke Wesseling, *The Perfect Spectator: The Experience of the Art Work and Reception Aesthetics*, ISBN 978-90-80818-50-7

Wouter Davidts, *Triple Bond: Essays on Art, Architecture, and Museums*, ISBN 978-90-78088-49-3

Sandra Kisters, *The Lure of the Biographical: On the (Self-)Representation of Artists*, ISBN 978-94-92095-25-1

Christa-Maria Lerm Hayes (ed.), *Brian O'Doherty/Patrick Ireland: Word, Image and Institutional Critique*, ISBN 978-94-92095-24-4

2018

John Macarthur, Susan Holden, Ashley Paine, Wouter Davidts, *Pavilion Propositions: Nine Points on an Architectural Phenomenon*, ISBN 978-94-92095-50-3

Jeroen Lutters, *The Trade of the Teacher: Visual Thinking with Mieke Bal*, ISBN 978-94-92095-56-5

Ernst van Alphen, *Failed Images: Photography and its Counter-Practices*, ISBN 978-94-92095-45-9

Paul Kempers, *'Het gaat om heel eenvoudige dingen': Jean Leering en de kunst*, ISBN 978-94-92095-07-7

Eva Wittocx, Ann Demeester, Melanie Bühler, *The Transhistorical Museum: Mapping the Field*, ISBN 978-94-92095-52-7

2019

Nathalie Zonnenberg, *Conceptual Art in a Curatorial Perspective: Between Dematerialization and Documentation*, ISBN 978-90-78088-76-9

Wouter Davidts, Susan Holden, Ashley Paine (eds.), *Trading between Architecture and Art: Strategies and Practices of Exchange*, ISBN 978-94-92095-67-1

Jeroen Lutters, *In the Shadow of the Art Work: Art-Based Learning in Practice*, ISBN 978-94-92095-66-4

2020

Jeroen Lutters, *Creative Theories of (Just About) Everything: A Journey into Origins and Imaginations*, ISBN 978-94-92095-74-9